SERVICE DESK ANALYST BOOTCAMP

MAINTAINING, CONFIGURING AND INSTALLING HARDWARE AND SOFTWARE

4 BOOKS IN 1

BOOK 1
SERVICE DESK ESSENTIALS: A BEGINNER'S GUIDE TO HARDWARE AND SOFTWARE BASICS

BOOK 2
MASTERING SERVICE DESK TROUBLESHOOTING: CONFIGURING SOFTWARE FOR EFFICIENCY

BOOK 3
ADVANCED SERVICE DESK TECHNIQUES: HARDWARE MAINTENANCE AND OPTIMIZATION

BOOK 4
EXPERT SERVICE DESK STRATEGIES: INSTALLING AND MANAGING COMPLEX SOFTWARE SYSTEMS

ROB BOTWRIGHT

Published by Rob Botwright
Library of Congress Cataloging-in-Publication Data
ISBN 978-1-83938-743-2
Cover design by Rizzo

Disclaimer

The contents of this book are based on extensive research and the best available historical sources. However, the author and publisher make no claims, promises, or guarantees about the accuracy, completeness, or adequacy of the information contained herein. The information in this book is provided on an "as is" basis, and the author and publisher disclaim any and all liability for any errors, omissions, or inaccuracies in the information or for any actions taken in reliance on such information. The opinions and views expressed in this book are those of the author and do not necessarily reflect the official policy or position of any organization or individual mentioned in this book. Any reference to specific people, places, or events is intended only to provide historical context and is not intended to defame or malign any group, individual, or entity. The information in this book is intended for educational and entertainment purposes only. It is not intended to be a substitute for professional advice or judgment. Readers are encouraged to conduct their own research and to seek professional advice where appropriate. Every effort has been made to obtain necessary permissions and acknowledgments for all images and other copyrighted material used in this book. Any errors or omissions in this regard are unintentional, and the author and publisher will correct them in future editions.

BOOK 1 - SERVICE DESK ESSENTIALS: A BEGINNER'S GUIDE TO HARDWARE AND SOFTWARE BASICS

BOOK 2 - MASTERING SERVICE DESK TROUBLESHOOTING: CONFIGURING SOFTWARE FOR EFFICIENCY

BOOK 3 - ADVANCED SERVICE DESK TECHNIQUES: HARDWARE MAINTENANCE AND OPTIMIZATION

BOOK 4 - EXPERT SERVICE DESK STRATEGIES: INSTALLING AND MANAGING COMPLEX SOFTWARE SYSTEMS

Introduction

Introducing the "Service Desk Analyst Bootcamp: Maintaining, Configuring, and Installing Hardware and Software" bundle – a comprehensive collection of books designed to equip service desk analysts with the essential skills and knowledge needed to excel in their roles. In today's fast-paced and technology-driven world, service desk analysts play a critical role in ensuring the smooth operation of hardware and software systems, providing technical support to end-users, and resolving IT-related issues efficiently and effectively.

Book 1, "Service Desk Essentials: A Beginner's Guide to Hardware and Software Basics," serves as the starting point for beginners, providing a solid foundation in hardware and software fundamentals. From understanding hardware components to navigating operating systems and performing basic troubleshooting, this book lays the groundwork for success in the service desk environment.

Building upon the foundational knowledge gained in Book 1, Book 2, "Mastering Service Desk Troubleshooting: Configuring Software for Efficiency," delves deeper into troubleshooting techniques specific to software configuration. Readers learn how to identify and resolve common software issues, optimize software performance, and troubleshoot application compatibility problems, enabling them to provide efficient support to end-users.

In Book 3, "Advanced Service Desk Techniques: Hardware Maintenance and Optimization," readers explore advanced strategies for hardware maintenance and optimization. From hardware diagnostics and troubleshooting to preventive maintenance and performance optimization, this book equips service desk analysts with the expertise needed to ensure the reliability and performance of hardware systems.

Finally, Book 4, "Expert Service Desk Strategies: Installing and Managing Complex Software Systems," addresses the complexities of installing and managing complex software systems. Readers learn advanced techniques for deploying, configuring, and managing enterprise-level software applications, including strategies for software deployment automation, configuration management, and patch management.

Together, these four books provide a comprehensive and structured approach to service desk management, covering everything from hardware and software basics to advanced troubleshooting techniques and complex software system management. Whether you are a beginner looking to establish a strong foundation or an experienced professional seeking to expand your expertise, the "Service Desk Analyst Bootcamp" bundle offers valuable insights and practical guidance to help you succeed in your role as a service desk analyst.

BOOK 1
SERVICE DESK ESSENTIALS
A BEGINNER'S GUIDE TO HARDWARE AND SOFTWARE
BASICS

ROB BOTWRIGHT

Chapter 1: Introduction to Service Desk Operations

Service Desk Roles and Responsibilities encompass a wide array of tasks and duties crucial for the efficient functioning of IT support operations. At the forefront of these roles is the Service Desk Analyst, who serves as the primary point of contact between end-users and the IT department. Service Desk Analysts play a pivotal role in resolving technical issues, providing assistance, and ensuring seamless communication between users and technical teams. They are adept at troubleshooting a variety of hardware and software issues, guiding users through technical processes, and escalating complex problems to specialized teams when necessary. Additionally, Service Desk Analysts are responsible for accurately documenting all incidents, requests, and resolutions in a ticketing system, maintaining comprehensive records for future reference and analysis.

Beyond the frontline role of Service Desk Analysts, there are often hierarchical structures within the service desk team. Service Desk Supervisors or Team Leads oversee the daily operations of the service desk, providing guidance and support to analysts, ensuring service level agreements (SLAs) are met, and coordinating resources to address high-priority incidents. They also play a key role in training new analysts, conducting performance evaluations, and implementing process improvements to enhance efficiency and customer satisfaction.

In larger organizations or those with more complex IT infrastructures, there may be specialized roles within the service desk team. For example, some service desks have dedicated Desktop Support Technicians who focus on resolving hardware and software issues specific to end-user devices such as laptops, desktops, and mobile devices. These technicians may perform tasks such as hardware diagnostics, software installations, and hardware replacements to ensure users have fully functional equipment to perform their tasks. Furthermore, Service Desk Managers are responsible for overseeing the entire service desk operation, including setting strategic objectives, managing budgets, and liaising with other departments to ensure alignment with organizational goals. They play a crucial role in defining service desk policies, procedures, and performance metrics, as well as identifying areas for improvement and implementing initiatives to enhance service quality and efficiency.

One common responsibility across all service desk roles is effective communication. Service Desk Analysts must possess strong verbal and written communication skills to effectively convey technical information to users with varying levels of technical expertise. They must also demonstrate patience, empathy, and professionalism when interacting with users who may be frustrated or stressed due to technical issues.

To streamline communication and incident management processes, service desks often utilize ticketing systems such as ServiceNow, Jira Service Desk, or Zendesk. These systems allow analysts to log, track, and prioritize incidents and requests, assign tasks to appropriate teams or individuals, and provide updates and resolutions to users in a centralized and organized manner. CLI commands such as "ticket create" or "ticket update" are often used to interact with these ticketing systems, enabling analysts to efficiently manage their workload and ensure timely resolution of issues.

In addition to incident management, service desk teams are also responsible for proactive maintenance and monitoring of IT systems to prevent potential issues before they escalate into problems. This may involve tasks such as applying software updates and patches, conducting routine hardware checks, and monitoring system performance metrics. Service Desk Analysts may use CLI commands such as "apt update" or "yum update" to update software packages on Linux systems, or "sfc /scannow" to scan and repair system files on Windows systems.

Overall, Service Desk Roles and Responsibilities are essential for providing timely, efficient, and high-quality support to end-users, maintaining productivity and minimizing disruptions to business operations. By effectively fulfilling their roles and responsibilities, service desk teams contribute significantly to the overall success and effectiveness of the IT organization.

Importance of Service Desk in IT Operations cannot be overstated, as it serves as the central hub for handling technical issues, providing support to end-users, and ensuring the smooth functioning of IT systems within an organization. The service desk acts as the first point of contact for users seeking assistance with various IT-related matters, ranging from simple password resets to complex software configurations. By serving as a single point of contact, the service desk streamlines communication channels and facilitates efficient resolution of issues, minimizing downtime and disruptions to business operations.

One of the primary roles of the service desk is incident management, which involves logging, prioritizing, and resolving incidents reported by users. This includes troubleshooting hardware and software issues, identifying root causes, and implementing solutions to restore service functionality. CLI commands such as "ticket create" or "incident log" are commonly used to document incidents in a ticketing system, enabling service desk analysts to track the status of each incident and ensure timely resolution.

Furthermore, the service desk plays a crucial role in providing support during IT emergencies and critical incidents. In such situations, service desk analysts must quickly assess the severity of the issue, prioritize response efforts, and coordinate with relevant technical teams to address the problem. CLI commands such as "emergency alert" or "incident escalation" may be used to notify key stakeholders and escalate critical incidents to specialized teams for immediate attention.

In addition to incident management, the service desk is responsible for fulfilling service requests from users, such as software installations, hardware replacements, or access permissions. These requests are typically logged in the ticketing system and assigned to the appropriate team or individual for fulfillment. CLI commands such as "request create" or "permission grant" may be used to initiate and track service requests, ensuring prompt delivery of requested services to users.

Moreover, the service desk serves as a valuable resource for providing technical guidance and assistance to users, especially those with limited technical knowledge or experience. Service desk analysts must possess strong communication skills to effectively communicate technical information to users in a clear and understandable manner. By offering guidance and support, the service desk empowers users to resolve simple issues independently and enhances overall user satisfaction with IT services.

Another critical function of the service desk is proactive monitoring and management of IT systems to prevent potential issues before they escalate into problems. This may involve monitoring system performance metrics, conducting routine health checks, and applying software updates and patches to mitigate security vulnerabilities. CLI commands such as "system monitor" or "update apply" are used to perform these tasks, ensuring the stability and security of IT systems.

Additionally, the service desk plays a key role in maintaining accurate documentation of IT assets, configurations, and service agreements. This information is essential for inventory management, license compliance, and auditing purposes. CLI commands such as "asset register" or "configuration document" may be used to record and update information in a centralized database, enabling service desk analysts to track IT assets and configurations effectively.

Furthermore, the service desk serves as a focal point for communicating IT-related announcements, updates, and maintenance schedules to users. This helps keep users informed about upcoming changes or disruptions to IT services and facilitates smooth transitions during system upgrades or maintenance activities.

Overall, the service desk is a critical component of IT operations, providing essential support, guidance, and assistance to users and ensuring the efficient functioning of IT systems within an organization. By effectively fulfilling its roles and responsibilities, the service desk helps enhance productivity, minimize disruptions, and drive overall business success.

Chapter 2: Understanding Hardware Components

CPU, RAM, and Storage Devices are foundational components of computer systems, each playing a crucial role in the overall performance and functionality of the system. The CPU (Central Processing Unit) acts as the brain of the computer, executing instructions and performing calculations necessary for running software applications. Commonly referred to as the processor, the CPU processes data by fetching instructions from memory, decoding them, executing them, and then storing the results. CLI commands such as "lscpu" on Linux or "wmic cpu get name, maxclockspeed, numberofcores" on Windows can be used to retrieve detailed information about the CPU, including its model, clock speed, and number of cores, providing insights into its capabilities and performance.

In addition to the CPU, RAM (Random Access Memory) plays a vital role in computer systems by providing temporary storage for data and instructions that are actively being used by the CPU. Unlike storage devices such as hard drives or SSDs (Solid State Drives), which store data persistently even when the computer is powered off, RAM is volatile memory that loses its contents when the power is turned off. CLI commands such as "free -h" on Linux or "wmic memorychip get capacity" on Windows can be used to check the amount of installed RAM and monitor its usage, allowing users to optimize system performance by ensuring adequate memory resources are available for running applications.

Furthermore, storage devices, such as hard drives, SSDs, and hybrid drives, are essential for storing and retrieving data on computer systems. Hard disk drives (HDDs) use spinning magnetic disks to store data, while SSDs utilize flash memory chips for faster access times and improved durability. CLI commands such as "lsblk" on Linux or "wmic diskdrive get size" on Windows can be used to list available storage devices and their capacities, facilitating storage management tasks such as partitioning, formatting, and mounting.

Moreover, understanding the specifications and capabilities of CPU, RAM, and storage devices is essential for optimizing system performance and selecting hardware components that meet the requirements of specific computing tasks. For example, CPUs with higher clock speeds and more cores are better suited for multitasking and demanding applications, while larger amounts of RAM allow for smoother multitasking and better performance with memory-intensive applications. Similarly, storage devices with higher read and write speeds offer faster data access and improved system responsiveness, making them ideal for tasks such as video editing, gaming, and running virtual machines.

Additionally, upgrading CPU, RAM, or storage devices can be a cost-effective way to enhance the performance and capabilities of an existing computer system. For example, replacing an older CPU with a newer model with higher clock speeds and more cores can significantly improve processing power and overall system responsiveness. Similarly, adding more RAM allows the system to handle larger workloads and run more applications simultaneously without experiencing slowdowns or performance bottlenecks. Upgrading storage devices to faster SSDs can also result in noticeable improvements in system boot times, application loading times, and overall responsiveness.

Furthermore, proper maintenance and management of CPU, RAM, and storage devices are essential for ensuring the long-term reliability and performance of computer systems. This includes regular monitoring of system resources, performing routine maintenance tasks such as disk cleanup and defragmentation, and implementing backup and disaster recovery strategies to protect valuable data stored on storage devices. CLI commands such as "df -h" on Linux or "wmic logicaldisk get size,freespace" on Windows can be used to check disk space usage and identify potential issues such as low disk space or disk fragmentation.

Moreover, optimizing CPU, RAM, and storage device configurations can help maximize system performance and efficiency. This includes adjusting system settings such as power management options, CPU frequency scaling, and memory allocation to ensure optimal resource utilization and minimize energy consumption. CLI commands such as "cpufreq-set" on Linux or "powercfg" on Windows can be used to adjust CPU frequency scaling settings and power management options, allowing users to optimize system performance based on their specific requirements and usage patterns.

In summary, CPU, RAM, and storage devices are essential components of computer systems, each playing a critical role in determining overall system performance and functionality. By understanding the specifications and capabilities of these components, users can make informed decisions when selecting hardware, optimizing system configurations, and troubleshooting performance issues. Additionally, regular maintenance and management of CPU, RAM, and storage devices are necessary for ensuring the long-term reliability and performance of computer systems.

Peripheral Devices: Input and Output Components are integral parts of computer systems, facilitating interaction between users and the digital environment. Input devices enable users to input data and commands into the computer system, while output devices present processed information to users in a human-readable format. Common input devices include keyboards, mice, touchpads, and scanners, which allow users to enter text, move the cursor, and capture images or documents. CLI commands such as "lsusb" on Linux or "wmic path Win32_PnPEntity" on Windows can be used to list connected USB devices and identify input devices connected to the computer system, providing insights into device types and configurations.

Moreover, keyboards are primary input devices that enable users to enter text, issue commands, and interact with software applications. Modern keyboards come in various layouts and designs, including standard QWERTY keyboards, ergonomic keyboards, and gaming keyboards with customizable keys and backlighting. CLI commands such as "xev" on Linux or "Get-WmiObject -Class Win32_Keyboard" on Windows can be used to test keyboard functionality and detect key presses, allowing users to troubleshoot issues such as stuck or malfunctioning keys.

Additionally, mice and touchpads are input devices used for controlling the cursor and interacting with graphical user interfaces (GUIs). Mice typically feature buttons and scroll wheels for performing various actions such as clicking, dragging, and scrolling, while touchpads utilize touch-sensitive surfaces for cursor movement and gesture-based interactions. CLI commands such as "xinput list" on Linux or "Get-WmiObject -Class Win32_PointingDevice" on Windows can be used to list connected pointing devices and configure settings such as sensitivity and button assignments.

Furthermore, scanners and digital cameras are input devices used for capturing images, documents, and other physical objects and converting them into digital format. Scanners are commonly used for digitizing printed documents, photographs, and artwork, while digital cameras are used for capturing still images and recording videos. CLI commands such as "scanimage" on Linux or "Import-Module -Name Dism -Verbose" on Windows can be used to initiate scanning operations and import images from connected scanners or digital cameras.

In addition to input devices, output devices play a crucial role in presenting processed information to users in a readable format. Common output devices include monitors, printers, speakers, and projectors, which enable users to view visual content, print documents, listen to audio, and display presentations or multimedia content. CLI commands such as "xrandr" on Linux or "Get-WmiObject -Class Win32_VideoController" on Windows can be used to detect connected displays and configure display settings such as resolution, refresh rate, and orientation.

Moreover, monitors are primary output devices used for displaying graphical user interfaces, multimedia content, and other visual information generated by the computer system. Monitors come in various types and sizes, including LCD (Liquid Crystal Display), LED (Light-Emitting Diode), and OLED (Organic Light-Emitting Diode) displays, with features such as high resolutions, fast refresh rates, and wide color gamuts. CLI commands such as "xrandr --output" on Linux or "Set-WmiInstance -InputObject $p -Arguments @{Brightness = $value}" on Windows can be used to adjust display settings and calibrate colors for optimal viewing experience.

Additionally, printers are output devices used for producing physical copies of digital documents, images, and other electronic content. Printers come in various types, including inkjet, laser, and thermal printers, with features such as color printing, duplex printing, and wireless connectivity. CLI commands such as "lp" on Linux or "Get-Printer | Format-Table Name, PrinterStatus" on Windows can be used to manage printing operations, check printer status, and troubleshoot printing issues.

Furthermore, speakers and headphones are output devices used for reproducing audio content such as music, sound effects, and voice recordings. Speakers come in various configurations, including stereo, surround sound, and Bluetooth speakers, while headphones offer features such as noise cancellation, wireless connectivity, and customizable sound profiles. CLI commands such as "aplay" on Linux or "Add-Type -TypeDefinition $code -Language CSharp" on Windows can be used to play audio files and test speaker functionality.

In summary, Peripheral Devices: Input and Output Components are essential components of computer systems, enabling users to interact with digital content and access information in various formats. By understanding the functions and capabilities of input and output devices, users can effectively utilize these components to perform tasks, enhance productivity, and experience immersive computing experiences. Moreover, proper configuration, maintenance, and troubleshooting of input and output devices are necessary for ensuring optimal performance and reliability of computer systems.

Chapter 3: Introduction to Software Systems

Types of Software: System Software vs. Application Software play distinct roles in the functioning of computer systems, each serving specific purposes and catering to different user needs. System software comprises essential programs and utilities that facilitate the operation of computer hardware and provide a platform for running application software. Examples of system software include operating systems, device drivers, and utility programs, which work behind the scenes to manage hardware resources, coordinate software interactions, and ensure smooth operation of the computer system. CLI commands such as "lsb_release -a" on Linux or "systeminfo" on Windows can be used to display information about the installed operating system, including its version, build number, and system architecture.

Operating systems (OS) are a core component of system software, serving as the interface between users and computer hardware. Operating systems manage hardware resources such as CPU, memory, storage, and input/output devices, providing a platform for executing application software and coordinating system operations. Popular operating systems include Microsoft Windows, macOS, Linux distributions such as Ubuntu and Fedora, and mobile operating systems like Android and iOS. CLI commands such as "uname -a" on Linux or "ver" on Windows can be used to display information about the installed operating system, including its kernel version and build date.

Moreover, device drivers are specialized software components that enable communication between the operating system and hardware devices such as printers, graphics cards, and network adapters. Device drivers facilitate the transfer of data between the hardware device and the operating system, allowing users to interact with peripheral devices and utilize their functionalities. CLI commands such as "lsmod" on Linux or "Get-WmiObject -Class Win32_PnPSignedDriver" on Windows can be used to list installed device drivers and check their status, ensuring that all hardware devices are properly recognized and functioning correctly.

Furthermore, utility programs are software tools designed to perform specific tasks or provide additional functionalities that enhance system performance and user productivity. Utility programs include disk cleanup tools, antivirus software, backup and recovery programs, and system optimization utilities, which help users manage system resources, protect against malware threats, and maintain system stability. CLI commands such as "du -sh" on Linux or "Get-WmiObject -Class Win32_OperatingSystem" on Windows can be used to check disk usage and system information, allowing users to identify and resolve issues such as disk space shortages or system errors.

In contrast to system software, application software refers to programs and tools designed to perform specific tasks or serve particular user needs. Application software encompasses a wide range of programs, including productivity suites, multimedia applications, web browsers, games, and communication tools, each tailored to fulfill distinct user requirements. Examples of application software include Microsoft Office, Adobe Photoshop, Google Chrome, and Minecraft, which provide users with tools for creating documents, editing images, browsing the web, and playing games. CLI commands such as "ps" on Linux or "tasklist" on Windows can be used to list running processes and check resource utilization, helping users monitor system performance and identify resource-intensive applications.

Moreover, application software can be further categorized into productivity software, entertainment software, educational software, and specialized industry-specific software, each serving specific user needs and purposes. Productivity software includes word processors, spreadsheets, presentation software, and email clients, which help users create, edit, and manage documents, spreadsheets, and presentations for personal and professional use. Entertainment software encompasses video games, multimedia players, and streaming services, providing users with entertainment and leisure activities such as gaming, watching movies, and listening to music. Educational software includes e-learning platforms, interactive tutorials, and educational games, offering users opportunities for learning and skill development in various subjects and disciplines. Specialized industry-specific software caters to specific professions or industries such as engineering, healthcare, finance, and design, providing tools and functionalities tailored to meet the unique requirements and challenges of each sector.

Furthermore, application software can be distributed as standalone programs, web-based applications, or mobile apps, each offering different deployment and usage models. Standalone programs are installed locally on the user's computer system and run independently of web browsers or internet connectivity, providing users with offline access to application functionalities and data. Web-based applications are accessed through web browsers and run on remote servers, allowing users to access and use application functionalities over the internet without the need for installation or local storage. Mobile apps are designed for smartphones and tablets, offering users access to application functionalities and services on portable devices with touchscreen interfaces and mobile operating systems such as iOS and Android.

In summary, Types of Software: System Software vs. Application Software serve distinct purposes and play complementary roles in the operation and functionality of computer systems. System software provides the foundation for running application software, managing hardware resources, and ensuring the smooth operation of the computer system. Application software, on the other hand, offers users tools and functionalities tailored to specific tasks, needs, and industries, enhancing productivity, creativity, and entertainment. By understanding the differences between system software and application software, users can effectively utilize both types of software to meet their computing needs and achieve their goals.

Operating Systems: Windows, macOS, Linux are the three most widely used operating systems, each offering unique features, functionalities, and user experiences tailored to different computing environments and user preferences. Windows, developed by Microsoft, is a dominant operating system known for its widespread adoption in personal computers, laptops, and enterprise environments. Windows provides users with a familiar graphical user interface (GUI), extensive software compatibility, and robust system security features, making it a popular choice for both home and business users. CLI commands such as "ver" can be used on Windows to display the operating system version and build number, providing users with information about the installed Windows version.

Moreover, Windows offers a wide range of built-in utilities and tools for managing system resources, configuring settings, and troubleshooting issues. For example, the Task Manager allows users to monitor and manage running processes, view system performance metrics, and identify resource-intensive applications. CLI commands such as "tasklist" can be used to list running processes and their details, enabling users to identify and terminate problematic processes that may be affecting system performance.

Additionally, Windows includes a comprehensive set of administrative tools and control panel utilities for managing user accounts, network settings, and system preferences. For example, the Control Panel provides users with access to a wide range of system settings and configuration options, allowing them to customize the appearance, behavior, and functionality of their Windows environment. CLI commands such as "net user" can be used to manage user accounts and permissions from the command line, providing administrators with additional flexibility and control over user management tasks.

In contrast to Windows, macOS is the operating system developed by Apple Inc. exclusively for Macintosh computers and MacBooks. macOS is known for its sleek design, intuitive user interface, and seamless integration with other Apple products and services. macOS offers a range of productivity features and built-in applications, including Safari web browser, Mail email client, and iMessage messaging app, designed to enhance user productivity and creativity. CLI commands such as "sw_vers" can be used on macOS to display the operating system version and build number, providing users with information about the installed macOS version.

Furthermore, macOS provides users with a powerful command-line interface (CLI) called Terminal, which allows advanced users and developers to perform system administration tasks, run scripts, and execute commands directly from the command line. The Terminal provides access to a wide range of command-line utilities and tools, enabling users to perform tasks such as file management, network troubleshooting, and software installation. CLI commands such as "ls" can be used to list files and directories in a specified directory, while commands such as "sudo" allow users to execute commands with administrative privileges.

Moreover, macOS offers a range of accessibility features and assistive technologies designed to support users with disabilities and special needs. For example, VoiceOver provides spoken feedback to users with visual impairments, enabling them to navigate and interact with the macOS interface using voice commands and gestures. Similarly, macOS includes built-in support for Braille displays and screen magnification tools, allowing users to customize the user interface to suit their individual needs.

On the other hand, Linux is an open-source operating system kernel that serves as the foundation for a wide range of Linux distributions, or "distros," each offering a unique combination of software packages, desktop environments, and system configurations. Linux is known for its flexibility, customization options, and robust security features, making it a popular choice for developers, system administrators, and enthusiasts. CLI commands such as "uname -a" can be used on Linux to display information about the operating system kernel version and system architecture, providing users with details about their Linux environment.

Furthermore, Linux distributions come with a variety of desktop environments, including GNOME, KDE, XFCE, and LXDE, each offering a different look and feel and catering to different user preferences. Desktop environments provide users with graphical interfaces for interacting with the operating system, managing files, and launching applications. CLI commands such as "lsb_release -a" can be used to display information about the installed Linux distribution and its version, helping users identify their Linux environment.

Moreover, Linux offers a rich ecosystem of software packages and repositories, providing users with access to thousands of free and open-source applications for productivity, multimedia, gaming, development, and more. Package managers such as apt, yum, and pacman allow users to search for, install, and manage software packages from official repositories or third-party sources. CLI commands such as "apt-get install" can be used to install software packages on Debian-based distributions like Ubuntu, while commands such as "yum install" can be used on Red Hat-based distributions like Fedora.

In summary, Operating Systems: Windows, macOS, Linux are three distinct operating systems, each offering its own set of features, functionalities, and user experiences. Windows is known for its widespread adoption, extensive software compatibility, and user-friendly interface, making it a popular choice for home and business users alike. macOS offers a sleek design, seamless integration with Apple products, and a range of built-in productivity tools, catering to the needs of creative professionals and Mac enthusiasts. Linux provides flexibility, customization options, and robust security features, appealing to developers, system administrators, and users who value open-source software and community-driven development.

Chapter 4: Basic Troubleshooting Techniques

Problem Identification Methods are essential techniques used in various fields to identify, analyze, and resolve issues or challenges encountered during projects, operations, or processes. One common method is Root Cause Analysis (RCA), which aims to identify the underlying cause or causes of a problem by tracing its origins back to their source. CLI commands such as "traceroute" on Linux or "tracert" on Windows can be used to trace the route that packets take from the source to the destination, helping identify network issues or bottlenecks. Additionally, the 5 Whys technique involves asking "why" multiple times to drill down to the root cause of a problem. For example, if a software application crashes, asking "why did it crash?" may lead to identifying insufficient memory as the root cause, prompting further investigation into memory usage and allocation. Another problem identification method is Fishbone Diagrams, also known as Ishikawa or Cause-and-Effect diagrams, which visually represent the potential causes of a problem across different categories such as people, processes, equipment, and environment. CLI commands such as "ps" on Linux or "tasklist" on Windows can be used to list running processes and identify potential software-related issues or resource conflicts. Furthermore, Failure Mode and Effects Analysis (FMEA) is a systematic approach used to identify potential failure modes of a product or process and assess their potential impact on system performance or safety. FMEA involves analyzing each potential failure mode, determining its likelihood and severity, and prioritizing mitigation measures accordingly. CLI commands such as "smartctl" on Linux or "wmic diskdrive get status" on Windows can be used to check the status of hard disk drives and identify potential hardware failures or imminent disk failures. Moreover, Brainstorming is a creative problem-solving technique that involves generating a large number of ideas or solutions to a problem in a short amount of time. During brainstorming sessions, participants are encouraged to express their ideas freely, without criticism or judgment, to stimulate creativity and innovation. CLI commands such as "ping" on Linux or "ping" on Windows can be used to test network connectivity and identify potential network issues such as packet loss or high latency. Additionally, SWOT Analysis is a strategic planning tool used to identify Strengths, Weaknesses, Opportunities, and Threats related to a project, organization, or situation. SWOT Analysis involves assessing internal strengths and weaknesses, such as technical expertise or resource constraints, as well as external opportunities and threats, such as market trends or competitive pressures. CLI commands such as "netstat" on Linux or "netstat" on Windows can be used to display network connections, routing tables, and interface statistics, helping identify network-related issues such as unauthorized access or unusual network traffic patterns. Furthermore, Pareto Analysis, also known as the 80/20 rule, is a problem-solving technique that involves identifying and prioritizing the most significant or frequent causes of a problem based on their relative contribution to the overall issue. Pareto Analysis helps focus resources and efforts on addressing the "vital few" root causes that account for the majority of problems, rather than the "trivial many" minor causes. CLI commands such as "top" on Linux or "task manager" on Windows can be used to monitor system resource usage and identify potential performance bottlenecks or resource constraints. Lastly, Benchmarking is a problem identification method that involves comparing the performance or characteristics of a system, process, or product against those of competitors or industry standards to identify areas for improvement or optimization. Benchmarking helps organizations identify best practices, innovative approaches, and opportunities for performance enhancement, leading to improved efficiency and competitiveness. CLI commands such as "iperf" on Linux or "iperf" on Windows can be used to measure network bandwidth and identify network performance issues such as congestion or packet loss. In summary, Problem Identification Methods encompass a variety of techniques and approaches used to identify, analyze, and resolve problems encountered in various domains. By employing these methods effectively, organizations can diagnose issues accurately, prioritize solutions appropriately, and implement targeted interventions to improve performance, efficiency, and quality.

Step-by-Step Troubleshooting Process is a structured approach used to diagnose and resolve technical issues encountered in computer systems, software applications, and electronic devices. This methodical process involves several sequential steps aimed at identifying the root cause of a problem and implementing appropriate solutions to restore functionality and performance. The first step in the troubleshooting process is to Define the Problem, which involves gathering information about the symptoms, error messages, and any recent changes or events that may have contributed to the issue. For example, if a computer fails to boot, the user may observe error messages on the screen or hear unusual sounds coming from the system. CLI commands such as "dmesg" on Linux or "eventvwr" on Windows can be used to view system logs and error messages, providing insights into the nature and severity of the problem.

Once the problem is clearly defined, the next step is to Identify Possible Causes by systematically analyzing the factors that may have contributed to the issue. This may involve considering hardware failures, software conflicts, configuration errors, user errors, or environmental factors such as power outages or physical damage. For example, if a printer fails to print, possible causes may include printer hardware issues, driver compatibility issues, connectivity problems, or paper jams. CLI commands such as "lsusb" on Linux or "Get-WmiObject -Class Win32_Printer" on Windows can be used to list connected USB devices and identify potential printer connectivity issues.

After identifying possible causes, the next step is to Isolate the Problem by narrowing down the list of potential causes through a process of elimination or testing. This may involve disconnecting peripheral devices, uninstalling recently installed software, or booting into safe mode to determine if the issue persists under different conditions. For example, if a computer crashes randomly, isolating the problem may involve disconnecting external devices such as printers, scanners, or USB drives to rule out hardware compatibility issues. CLI commands such as "lsmod" on Linux or "msconfig" on Windows can be used to list loaded kernel modules and disable unnecessary startup programs, helping isolate software-related issues.

Once the problem is isolated, the next step is to Develop a Plan of Action by formulating a strategy for resolving the issue based on the identified root cause and available resources. This may involve researching solutions online, consulting technical documentation or manuals, or seeking assistance from colleagues or online communities. For example, if a software application crashes frequently, developing a plan of action may involve updating the application to the latest version, reinstalling the application, or troubleshooting compatibility issues with the operating system. CLI commands such as "apt-get update" on Linux or "sfc /scannow" on Windows can be used to update package repositories and scan system files for integrity violations, respectively.

After developing a plan of action, the next step is to Implement Solutions by applying the chosen troubleshooting techniques or corrective measures to address the root cause of the problem. This may involve configuring system settings, updating device drivers, applying software patches or updates, or replacing faulty hardware components. For example, if a computer overheats and shuts down unexpectedly, implementing solutions may involve cleaning dust from the internal components, improving airflow within the system case, or replacing a malfunctioning cooling fan. CLI commands such as "apt-get upgrade" on Linux or "chkdsk /f" on Windows can be used to upgrade installed packages and check disk integrity, respectively.

Once solutions are implemented, the next step is to Test the System to verify that the problem has been resolved and that the system is functioning as expected. This may involve performing diagnostic tests, running software applications, or simulating user scenarios to ensure that the issue no longer occurs. For example, if a network connection is intermittent, testing the system may involve pinging network devices, browsing websites, or transferring files to verify network stability. CLI commands such as "ping" on Linux or "ipconfig /all" on Windows can be used to test network connectivity and display network configuration details, respectively.

After testing the system, the final step is to Document the Solution by recording the steps taken, the solutions implemented, and any relevant information about the problem and its resolution. This documentation serves as a reference for future troubleshooting efforts, helps other users facing similar issues, and enables knowledge sharing within the organization. For example, documenting the solution to a printer connectivity issue may involve recording the steps taken to reinstall printer drivers, adjust network settings, or replace defective cables. CLI commands such as "history" on Linux or "Get-History" on Windows can be used to display a list of previously executed commands and their results, facilitating documentation of troubleshooting steps.

In summary, the Step-by-Step Troubleshooting Process is a systematic approach used to diagnose and resolve technical issues encountered in computer systems, software applications, and electronic devices. By following this structured process, users can effectively define problems, identify root causes, isolate issues, develop action plans, implement solutions, test systems, and document resolutions, leading to efficient problem resolution and improved system reliability.

Chapter 5: Communication Skills for Service Desk Analysts

Effective Listening Techniques are essential skills that contribute to successful communication, collaboration, and problem-solving in various personal and professional contexts. Active Listening is a fundamental technique that involves fully concentrating on what is being said, understanding the message, and providing appropriate feedback to demonstrate understanding. To practice active listening, individuals should maintain eye contact, nod occasionally to show attentiveness, and refrain from interrupting the speaker. Additionally, paraphrasing or summarizing the speaker's message in one's own words can help clarify understanding and confirm comprehension. Another effective listening technique is Reflective Listening, which involves mirroring the speaker's feelings and emotions to convey empathy and understanding. For example, if a colleague expresses frustration about a project deadline, acknowledging their feelings by saying, "It sounds like you're feeling stressed about the upcoming deadline," can help validate their emotions and build rapport. CLI commands such as "netstat" on Linux or "netstat" on Windows can be used to display network connections and statistics, helping identify potential network issues or security threats.

Moreover, Nonverbal Communication plays a significant role in effective listening, as body language, facial expressions, and gestures can convey important cues and signals that enhance understanding and interpretation. Maintaining an open posture, facing the speaker, and nodding in agreement can signal attentiveness and encourage the speaker to continue sharing their thoughts and feelings. Similarly, providing appropriate nonverbal feedback such as smiling, nodding, or leaning forward can convey interest and engagement in the conversation. Additionally, Active Engagement involves asking clarifying questions, seeking additional information, and actively participating in the conversation to demonstrate interest and encourage dialogue. For example, asking open-ended questions such as "Can you tell me more about that?" or "How do you feel about the situation?" can prompt the speaker to elaborate on their thoughts and feelings, leading to deeper understanding and connection. CLI commands such as "ps" on Linux or "tasklist" on Windows can be used to list running processes and identify potential software-related issues or resource conflicts.

Furthermore, Empathetic Listening is a powerful technique that involves understanding and validating the speaker's emotions, perspectives, and experiences without judgment or criticism. Empathetic listeners strive to put themselves in the speaker's shoes, acknowledge their feelings, and offer support and encouragement. For example, if a friend shares their concerns about a difficult situation at work, responding with empathy by saying, "I can imagine how challenging that must be for you," can help validate their emotions and provide comfort. Additionally, maintaining a nonjudgmental attitude and refraining from offering unsolicited advice or solutions can create a safe and supportive environment for the speaker to express themselves freely. Furthermore, Mindful Listening involves being fully present and focused on the speaker, without allowing distractions or preconceptions to interfere with the listening process. To practice mindful listening, individuals should minimize distractions, such as turning off electronic devices or finding a quiet space, and actively engage their senses to tune into the speaker's words, tone of voice, and body language. CLI commands such as "ls" on Linux or "dir" on Windows can be used to list files and directories in a specified directory, helping identify potential file management issues or storage constraints.

Additionally, Critical Listening is a technique that involves analyzing and evaluating the speaker's message, reasoning, and evidence to make informed judgments or decisions. Critical listeners assess the credibility of the information presented, consider alternative perspectives, and ask probing questions to clarify ambiguities or inconsistencies. For example, when listening to a persuasive argument or presentation, critical listeners may evaluate the validity of the evidence presented, assess the logic of the reasoning, and identify any logical fallacies or biases. Furthermore, Reflective Listening involves actively reflecting on the speaker's message, thoughts, and emotions to gain insight into their perspective and deepen understanding. To practice reflective listening, individuals should pause periodically to reflect on the speaker's words, consider their own reactions and responses, and explore the underlying meanings and implications of the conversation. CLI commands such as "ping" on Linux or "ping" on Windows can be used to test network connectivity and identify potential network issues such as packet loss or high latency.

Moreover, Feedback is an essential component of effective listening, as it provides an opportunity for the listener to validate understanding, clarify information, and express agreement or disagreement with the speaker's message. Constructive feedback should be specific, objective, and focused on behaviors or observations rather than personal judgments or assumptions. For example, when providing feedback on a colleague's presentation, focusing on specific strengths such as clear organization or engaging visuals can reinforce positive behaviors and encourage continued improvement. Additionally, Active Listening involves demonstrating genuine interest and engagement in the conversation, which can be conveyed through verbal and nonverbal cues such as maintaining eye contact, nodding in agreement, and providing verbal affirmations such as "I see" or "That makes sense." CLI commands such as "history" on Linux or "Get-History" on Windows can be used to display a list of previously executed commands and their results, facilitating documentation of troubleshooting steps.

In summary, Effective Listening Techniques are essential skills that contribute to successful communication, collaboration, and relationship-building in personal and professional settings. By practicing active listening, reflective listening, empathetic listening, and critical listening, individuals can enhance their communication skills, deepen their understanding of others, and foster positive connections and relationships. Additionally, providing constructive feedback, actively engaging in conversations, and maintaining mindfulness and presence can further improve listening effectiveness and contribute to meaningful and productive interactions.

Professional Email and Phone Etiquette are essential skills in today's workplace, as they contribute to effective communication, professionalism, and positive relationships with colleagues, clients, and stakeholders. When composing professional emails, it's important to use clear, concise language and adhere to standard formatting conventions, such as using a professional email address, including a clear subject line, and using proper salutations and sign-offs. Additionally, it's crucial to proofread emails carefully for spelling, grammar, and punctuation errors before sending them, as typos or mistakes can detract from professionalism and credibility. CLI commands such as "mail" on Linux or "Send-MailMessage" on Windows can be used to send emails from the command line, providing a convenient way to automate email communications or integrate email functionality into scripts or applications.

Moreover, when addressing recipients in professional emails, it's important to use appropriate titles and names, especially when communicating with superiors, clients, or individuals outside the organization. For example, addressing a client as "Mr. Smith" or "Ms. Johnson" demonstrates respect and professionalism, while using generic or informal greetings such as "Hey" or "Hi there" may be perceived as unprofessional or disrespectful. Additionally, when replying to emails, it's important to respond promptly and courteously, even if the response is brief or requires further follow-up. CLI commands such as "mutt" on Linux or "Outlook" on Windows can be used to access email clients from the command line, providing users with additional flexibility and control over their email communications.

Furthermore, when composing professional emails, it's important to be mindful of tone and language to ensure that messages are polite, respectful, and appropriate for the context and recipient. Avoid using slang, jargon, or emoticons in professional emails, as these can detract from professionalism and may be misunderstood or misinterpreted by recipients. Additionally, it's important to use neutral or positive language, especially when delivering feedback or addressing sensitive topics, to avoid causing offense or conflict. For example, instead of saying "You made a mistake," consider saying "There appears to be an error that needs to be addressed," which is more constructive and less accusatory. CLI commands such as "grep" on Linux or "Select-String" on Windows can be used to search for specific keywords or phrases in email messages, helping users filter and analyze email communications more effectively.

Moreover, when using email for professional communication, it's important to respect recipients' time and privacy by keeping emails concise and focused on the main message or purpose. Avoid including unnecessary or irrelevant information in emails, as this can clutter the message and make it difficult for recipients to discern the key points or actions required. Additionally, when sending attachments, it's important to ensure that files are properly formatted, labeled, and relevant to the content of the email. For example, when attaching documents or presentations, provide a brief description or context in the body of the email to help recipients understand the purpose or significance of the attachment. CLI commands such as "zip" on Linux or "Compress-Archive" on Windows can be used to compress files or folders before attaching them to email messages, reducing file size and facilitating faster transmission.

Furthermore, when communicating via phone, it's important to follow proper phone etiquette to convey professionalism and respect for the caller or recipient. Answering calls promptly and courteously, using a clear and professional tone of voice, and identifying oneself and the organization or department are important aspects of phone etiquette. Additionally, when leaving voicemail messages, it's important to speak clearly and concisely, state the purpose of the call, and provide relevant contact information for follow-up. CLI commands such as "dial" on Linux or "New-CsCall" on Windows can be used to initiate phone calls from the command line, providing users with additional flexibility and control over their phone communications.

Moreover, when engaging in phone conversations, it's important to listen actively and attentively to the caller, asking clarifying questions and providing appropriate responses to demonstrate understanding and empathy.

Avoid interrupting the caller or engaging in side conversations while on the phone, as this can be perceived as rude or disrespectful. Additionally, when placing callers on hold or transferring calls, it's important to do so courteously and with the caller's consent, providing clear instructions and alternatives if necessary. For example, if placing a caller on hold, inform them of the reason for the hold and offer to return to the call as soon as possible. CLI commands such as "call" on Linux or "New-CsAudioSession" on Windows can be used to initiate audio calls or conference calls from the command line, providing users with additional flexibility and control over their phone communications.

In summary, Professional Email and Phone Etiquette are essential skills that contribute to effective communication, professionalism, and positive relationships in the workplace. By following best practices for composing professional emails, addressing recipients respectfully, using appropriate tone and language, and respecting recipients' time and privacy, individuals can enhance their credibility, build trust, and foster productive communication and collaboration with colleagues, clients, and stakeholders. Similarly, by following proper phone etiquette, including answering calls promptly and courteously, listening actively and attentively, and providing clear and concise information, individuals can convey professionalism and respect in phone communications, contributing to positive interactions and outcomes.

Chapter 6: Customer Service Fundamentals

Understanding Customer Needs and Expectations is crucial for businesses to deliver products and services that meet or exceed customer satisfaction levels, foster loyalty, and drive long-term success. It involves gathering insights into customers' preferences, desires, and pain points through various channels such as surveys, feedback forms, social media, and direct interactions. By understanding customer needs and expectations, businesses can tailor their offerings, marketing strategies, and customer service efforts to better align with customer preferences and deliver value-added experiences. Additionally, conducting market research and analysis can provide valuable insights into customer demographics, behaviors, and trends, helping businesses anticipate evolving customer needs and stay ahead of the competition. CLI commands such as "curl" on Linux or "Invoke-RestMethod" on Windows can be used to retrieve data from web APIs or endpoints, facilitating the collection of customer feedback or sentiment analysis from online sources.

Moreover, listening to customer feedback and complaints is essential for gaining insights into areas where products or services may fall short of customer expectations. By actively soliciting and responding to customer feedback, businesses can identify areas for improvement, address customer concerns, and enhance overall satisfaction levels. Additionally, businesses can leverage customer relationship management (CRM) systems to track and analyze customer interactions, preferences, and purchase histories, enabling personalized marketing campaigns, targeted promotions, and proactive customer service initiatives. CLI commands such as "grep" on Linux or "Select-String" on Windows can be used to search for specific keywords or phrases in customer feedback or support tickets, helping businesses identify common issues or recurring themes.

Furthermore, developing customer personas or profiles can help businesses better understand their target audience and tailor their marketing messages, product features, and service offerings to meet specific customer needs and preferences. Customer personas are fictional representations of ideal customers based on demographic, psychographic, and behavioral characteristics, providing insights into their motivations, goals, and pain points. By creating detailed customer personas, businesses can segment their target audience more effectively, identify niche markets or customer segments, and tailor their marketing strategies and product offerings to better meet the needs of different customer groups. Additionally, businesses can conduct customer surveys or interviews to gather feedback directly from customers and gain insights into their preferences, experiences, and expectations. CLI commands such as "awk" on Linux or "Select-Object" on Windows can be used to filter and extract specific fields or attributes from customer survey data, enabling deeper analysis and segmentation.

Moreover, monitoring customer sentiment and brand reputation on social media platforms and online review sites can provide valuable insights into customer perceptions, opinions, and experiences with a brand or product. By monitoring social media mentions, hashtags, and reviews, businesses can identify trends, detect emerging issues or concerns, and engage with customers in real-time to address their needs and concerns. Additionally, businesses can leverage sentiment analysis tools or sentiment analysis APIs to automatically analyze customer feedback and sentiment from social media and online sources, providing actionable insights into customer attitudes, opinions, and preferences. CLI commands such as "jq" on Linux or "ConvertFrom-Json" on Windows can be used to parse and extract specific data fields or attributes from JSON-formatted social media or review data, facilitating sentiment analysis and trend identification.

Furthermore, creating a seamless and personalized customer experience across all touchpoints and channels is essential for meeting and exceeding customer expectations. By integrating customer data and insights across marketing, sales, and customer service platforms, businesses can deliver consistent and personalized experiences that resonate with customers and drive engagement and loyalty. Additionally, investing in employee training and development programs can help frontline staff understand customer needs and expectations better, improve communication and interpersonal skills, and enhance the overall customer experience. CLI commands such as "sed" on Linux or "ForEach-Object" on Windows can be used to manipulate and transform customer data or feedback collected from various sources, enabling businesses to derive actionable insights and inform decision-making.

Moreover, leveraging technology and automation tools such as chatbots, artificial intelligence (AI), and predictive analytics can help businesses anticipate customer needs, streamline processes, and deliver proactive and personalized customer service. By analyzing historical customer data and behaviors, businesses can predict future needs and preferences, identify upsell or cross-sell opportunities, and tailor marketing messages and product recommendations to individual customers. Additionally, implementing self-service options such as knowledge bases, FAQs, and online support forums can empower customers to find answers to their questions or solutions to their problems quickly and efficiently, reducing the need for direct customer support interactions. CLI commands such as "grep" on Linux or "Select-String" on Windows can be used to search for specific keywords or phrases in customer support tickets or chat transcripts, enabling businesses to identify common issues or trends and develop targeted solutions or resources. In summary, Understanding Customer Needs and Expectations is essential for businesses to succeed in today's competitive marketplace. By actively listening to customer feedback, gathering insights from various channels, and leveraging technology and data analytics, businesses can gain a deeper understanding of their target audience, anticipate evolving customer needs, and deliver personalized and value-added experiences that drive customer satisfaction, loyalty, and advocacy. By prioritizing customer-centricity and continuously striving to exceed customer expectations, businesses can differentiate themselves from competitors and build lasting relationships with customers that drive long-term growth and success.

Building Rapport with Customers is a fundamental aspect of customer service and relationship management, as it involves establishing a connection, fostering trust, and creating positive interactions that enhance customer satisfaction and loyalty. One effective way to build rapport with customers is by demonstrating empathy and active listening skills, which involves paying attention to customers' concerns, acknowledging their feelings, and responding with compassion and understanding. By listening attentively to customers' needs and concerns, and responding thoughtfully and empathetically, businesses can show customers that their opinions and feelings are valued, and build a foundation of trust and mutual respect. CLI commands such as "grep" on Linux or "Select-String" on Windows can be used to search for specific keywords or phrases in customer interactions or feedback, enabling businesses to identify common issues or concerns and respond accordingly.

Moreover, demonstrating genuine interest and enthusiasm in helping customers can go a long way in building rapport and fostering positive relationships. By approaching customer interactions with a positive attitude and a willingness to help, businesses can create a welcoming and supportive environment that puts customers at ease and encourages open communication. Additionally, taking the time to get to know customers on a personal level, such as remembering their names, preferences, and past interactions, can help strengthen the bond and create a sense of familiarity and connection. CLI commands such as "awk" on Linux or "Select-Object" on Windows can be used to filter and extract specific fields or attributes from customer data or CRM systems, enabling businesses to personalize interactions and tailor their approach to individual customers.

Furthermore, demonstrating professionalism and competence in handling customer inquiries and resolving issues is essential for building rapport and instilling confidence in customers. By providing accurate information, offering timely solutions, and following through on commitments, businesses can demonstrate their reliability and commitment to customer satisfaction. Additionally, effectively managing customer expectations and communicating transparently about products, services, and policies can help prevent misunderstandings and build trust and credibility with customers. CLI commands such as "sed" on Linux or "ForEach-Object" on Windows can be used to manipulate and transform customer data or feedback collected from various sources, enabling businesses to derive actionable insights and inform decision-making.

Moreover, going above and beyond to exceed customer expectations can leave a lasting impression and strengthen the bond between businesses and their customers. By anticipating customer needs, offering personalized recommendations, and providing exceptional service, businesses can create memorable experiences that differentiate them from competitors and inspire customer loyalty and advocacy. Additionally, soliciting feedback from customers and incorporating their suggestions and ideas into products, services, and processes can help businesses demonstrate their commitment to continuous improvement and customer satisfaction. CLI commands such as "awk" on Linux or "Select-Object" on Windows can be used to filter and extract specific fields or attributes from customer feedback or survey data, enabling businesses to identify trends and opportunities for improvement.

Furthermore, leveraging technology and data analytics can help businesses personalize interactions, streamline processes, and deliver proactive and predictive customer service. By analyzing customer data and behavior, businesses can identify patterns, preferences, and trends that enable them to anticipate customer needs and tailor their approach accordingly. Additionally, implementing self-service options such as knowledge bases, FAQs, and online support forums can empower customers to find answers to their questions or solutions to their problems independently, reducing the need for direct customer support interactions. CLI commands such as "grep" on Linux or "Select-String" on Windows can be used to search for specific keywords or phrases in customer support tickets or chat transcripts, enabling businesses to identify common issues or trends and develop targeted solutions or resources.

Moreover, building rapport with customers is an ongoing process that requires consistent effort and attention to detail. By fostering positive relationships, demonstrating empathy and active listening, and providing exceptional service, businesses can create a customer-centric culture that drives customer satisfaction, loyalty, and advocacy. Additionally, investing in employee training and development programs can help frontline staff develop the skills and confidence needed to effectively engage with customers, handle difficult situations, and deliver memorable experiences. CLI commands such as "sort" on Linux or "Sort-Object" on Windows can be used to organize and prioritize customer data or feedback, enabling businesses to identify high-priority issues or opportunities for improvement.

In summary, Building Rapport with Customers is essential for businesses to succeed in today's competitive marketplace. By demonstrating empathy and active listening, showing genuine interest and enthusiasm, providing professional and competent service, and exceeding customer expectations, businesses can create positive interactions that enhance customer satisfaction, loyalty, and advocacy. By prioritizing customer-centricity and continuously striving to build trust and strengthen relationships with customers, businesses can differentiate themselves from competitors and position themselves for long-term success and growth.

Chapter 7: Incident Management Basics

Incident Classification and Prioritization are critical components of effective incident management processes, as they help organizations efficiently allocate resources, prioritize responses, and minimize the impact of disruptions on business operations. Incident classification involves categorizing incidents based on their nature, severity, and potential impact on the organization, while prioritization involves assigning priority levels to incidents based on their urgency, impact, and business criticality. By classifying and prioritizing incidents systematically, organizations can ensure that resources are allocated appropriately, and the most critical issues are addressed promptly. CLI commands such as "grep" on Linux or "Select-String" on Windows can be used to search for specific keywords or phrases in incident reports or logs, enabling organizations to identify patterns and trends and classify incidents accurately.

Incident classification typically involves categorizing incidents into different types or categories based on their characteristics and attributes. Common incident categories may include hardware failures, software glitches, security breaches, network outages, or user errors. Additionally, incidents may be classified based on their impact on business operations, such as minor disruptions, major outages, or critical failures. By classifying incidents systematically, organizations can establish clear and consistent criteria for incident handling and ensure that appropriate response procedures are followed for each incident type. CLI commands such as "awk" on Linux or "Select-Object" on Windows can be used to filter and extract specific fields or attributes from incident data or logs,

46

enabling organizations to categorize incidents accurately and efficiently.

Once incidents are classified, prioritization is essential for determining the order in which incidents should be addressed based on their urgency and impact on the organization. Incident prioritization typically involves assigning priority levels or severity levels to incidents, such as low, medium, high, or critical. Priority levels are determined based on factors such as the severity of the incident, the number of users affected, the potential impact on business operations, and any regulatory or compliance considerations. By prioritizing incidents effectively, organizations can ensure that critical issues are addressed promptly, and resources are allocated efficiently to minimize the impact on business operations. CLI commands such as "sort" on Linux or "Sort-Object" on Windows can be used to organize and prioritize incident data or tickets based on priority levels or severity levels.

Moreover, incident prioritization may also consider service level agreements (SLAs) or service level objectives (SLOs) established between the organization and its customers or stakeholders. SLAs define the expected response times and resolution times for different types of incidents, while SLOs specify the performance targets or service quality metrics that must be met. By aligning incident prioritization with SLAs and SLOs, organizations can ensure that response times and resolution times meet customer expectations and contractual obligations. Additionally, incident prioritization may consider the potential business impact or financial implications of incidents, such as lost revenue, productivity losses, or reputational damage. CLI commands such as "cut" on Linux or "Select-Object" on Windows can be used to extract specific fields or attributes from incident data or logs, enabling organizations to calculate the potential impact or financial cost of incidents and prioritize them accordingly.

Furthermore, organizations may use incident prioritization matrices or frameworks to assess the urgency and impact of incidents systematically and assign priority levels accordingly. These matrices typically categorize incidents based on their urgency (e.g., immediate, high, medium, low) and impact (e.g., critical, major, minor) and provide guidelines or criteria for prioritizing incidents within each category. By using incident prioritization matrices, organizations can standardize the prioritization process, facilitate decision-making, and ensure that response efforts are aligned with business objectives and priorities. Additionally, incident prioritization may involve collaboration and consultation with stakeholders from different departments or functional areas to gather input, assess the business impact, and make informed decisions about incident response priorities. CLI commands such as "uniq" on Linux or "Group-Object" on Windows can be used to identify and aggregate similar incidents or patterns, enabling organizations to prioritize response efforts and allocate resources effectively.

Moreover, incident prioritization may be dynamic and evolve over time based on changing circumstances, emerging threats, or evolving business priorities. Organizations should regularly review and reassess their incident prioritization criteria, processes, and frameworks to ensure that they remain relevant and effective in addressing current and emerging challenges. Additionally, organizations may use incident management tools or software platforms to automate incident classification and prioritization processes, streamline workflow management, and facilitate collaboration and communication among incident response teams. By leveraging technology and automation, organizations can improve the efficiency and effectiveness of incident management processes and enhance their ability to respond to incidents promptly and effectively. CLI commands such as "uniq -c" on Linux or "Group-Object" on Windows can be used to count and aggregate similar incidents or patterns, enabling organizations to identify trends and prioritize response efforts accordingly.

In summary, Incident Classification and Prioritization are essential aspects of effective incident management processes, enabling organizations to allocate resources efficiently, prioritize response efforts, and minimize the impact of disruptions on business operations. By systematically classifying incidents based on their characteristics and assigning priority levels based on urgency and impact, organizations can ensure that critical issues are addressed promptly, and response efforts are aligned with business objectives and priorities. Additionally, by considering factors such as SLAs, SLOs, business impact, and stakeholder input, organizations can make informed decisions about incident response priorities and allocate resources effectively to mitigate risks and safeguard business continuity. Escalation Procedures for Critical Incidents are essential for ensuring timely and effective resolution of high-priority incidents that pose significant risks to business operations, customer satisfaction, or regulatory compliance. When a critical incident occurs, it's crucial to have clear escalation paths and procedures in place to escalate the issue to the appropriate stakeholders, teams, or management levels for immediate attention and action. By following predefined escalation procedures, organizations can minimize the impact of critical incidents, expedite resolution efforts, and prevent escalation into larger-scale crises. CLI commands such as "grep" on Linux or "Select-String" on Windows can be used to search for specific keywords or phrases in incident reports or logs, enabling organizations to identify critical incidents and initiate escalation procedures promptly.

The first step in escalation procedures for critical incidents is typically to identify and classify the incident based on its severity, impact, and urgency. Incidents that pose significant risks to business operations, customer safety, or regulatory compliance are classified as critical and require immediate attention and escalation. Once a critical incident is identified, the next step is to notify the appropriate stakeholders or teams responsible for incident response and resolution. This may involve contacting an incident response team, a designated incident manager, or senior management personnel who have the authority and expertise to address critical incidents effectively. CLI commands such as "awk" on Linux or "Select-Object" on Windows can be used to filter and extract specific fields or attributes from incident data or logs, enabling organizations to classify incidents accurately and initiate escalation procedures promptly.

Moreover, escalation procedures for critical incidents typically involve predefined escalation paths and communication channels to ensure that critical issues are escalated to the appropriate stakeholders or teams in a timely manner. This may include escalation matrices or contact lists that specify who to notify, when to escalate, and how to communicate during different stages of the incident response process. By establishing clear escalation paths and communication channels, organizations can streamline the escalation process, minimize delays, and ensure that critical incidents are addressed promptly and effectively. CLI commands such as "sort" on Linux or "Sort-Object" on Windows can be used to organize and prioritize escalation contacts or lists based on their roles or responsibilities.

Furthermore, escalation procedures for critical incidents may involve setting escalation thresholds or criteria that trigger automatic escalations when certain conditions are met. For example, organizations may define thresholds based on incident severity, impact, or response times, and configure automated alerts or notifications to escalate incidents when these thresholds are exceeded. By automating escalation procedures, organizations can ensure that critical incidents are escalated promptly and consistently, even during non-business hours or when key personnel are unavailable. Additionally, organizations may use incident management tools or software platforms to automate escalation workflows, track escalation statuses, and provide real-time visibility into incident response efforts. CLI commands such as "cut" on Linux or "Select-Object" on Windows can be used to extract specific fields or attributes from incident data or logs, enabling organizations to configure automated escalation rules and notifications.

Moreover, escalation procedures for critical incidents may include predefined escalation paths for different types of incidents, such as technical failures, security breaches, or service disruptions. Each escalation path may specify the roles, responsibilities, and escalation criteria for different stakeholders or teams involved in incident response and resolution. By defining specific escalation paths for different types of incidents, organizations can ensure that critical issues are escalated to the appropriate teams or specialists with the necessary expertise and authority to address them effectively. Additionally, organizations may conduct regular training and drills to familiarize stakeholders with escalation procedures, test communication channels, and validate response capabilities. CLI commands such as "uniq" on Linux or "Group-Object" on Windows can be used to identify and aggregate similar incidents or patterns, enabling organizations to refine escalation procedures and improve response effectiveness.

Furthermore, escalation procedures for critical incidents should include mechanisms for monitoring and tracking escalation statuses, providing regular updates and notifications to stakeholders, and documenting escalation activities for post-incident analysis and review. This may involve using incident management tools or dashboards to track the status of escalated incidents, communicate updates and resolutions to stakeholders, and capture feedback or lessons learned for continuous improvement. By maintaining transparency and accountability throughout the escalation process, organizations can ensure that critical incidents are managed effectively, stakeholders are kept informed, and incidents are resolved in a timely manner. CLI commands such as "uniq -c" on Linux or "Group-Object" on Windows can be used to count and aggregate similar incidents or patterns, enabling organizations to identify trends and patterns in escalation activities and prioritize improvements accordingly.

In summary, Escalation Procedures for Critical Incidents are essential for ensuring timely and effective resolution of high-priority incidents that pose significant risks to business operations, customer satisfaction, or regulatory compliance. By establishing clear escalation paths, communication channels, and criteria for escalating incidents, organizations can expedite response efforts, minimize the impact of critical incidents, and maintain business continuity. Additionally, by automating escalation workflows, tracking escalation statuses, and conducting regular training and drills, organizations can enhance their incident response capabilities and improve their ability to manage critical incidents effectively.

Chapter 8: Introduction to Ticketing Systems

The Ticket Lifecycle, encompassing the phases of Creation, Assignment, and Resolution, serves as the backbone of incident management processes, facilitating the efficient handling and resolution of customer inquiries, service requests, and technical issues. The lifecycle begins with the Creation phase, where users or customers report incidents or request services through various channels such as email, phone, or self-service portals. During this phase, it's crucial to capture all relevant information accurately, including the nature of the issue, contact details, and any supporting documentation. This information forms the basis for further analysis and action by support teams. CLI commands such as "grep" on Linux or "Select-String" on Windows can be used to search for specific keywords or phrases in ticketing system logs or databases, enabling organizations to identify incoming tickets and initiate the creation process promptly.

Moreover, once a ticket is created, it enters the Assignment phase, where it is assigned to the appropriate support team or individual responsible for resolving the issue. Assignments may be based on various factors such as the type of issue, the skillset of the support team, or predefined routing rules within the ticketing system. Assignments should be made promptly to ensure timely response and resolution, with clear communication to all stakeholders regarding assignment details and expectations. Additionally, organizations may use ticketing system features such as automatic assignment rules or round-robin assignment algorithms to streamline the assignment process and distribute workload evenly among support teams. CLI commands such as "awk" on Linux or "Select-Object" on

Windows can be used to filter and extract specific fields or attributes from ticket data, enabling organizations to route tickets to the appropriate teams or individuals based on predefined criteria.

Furthermore, the Resolution phase marks the culmination of the ticket lifecycle, where support teams work to resolve the reported issue or fulfill the service request. Depending on the nature and complexity of the issue, resolution may involve troubleshooting technical problems, providing instructions or guidance to users, or coordinating with other teams or vendors for assistance. It's essential to track progress and updates throughout the resolution process, ensuring that stakeholders are kept informed of any developments or delays. Additionally, organizations may use ticketing system features such as status updates, timestamps, and notifications to monitor resolution progress, escalate overdue tickets, and communicate status updates to stakeholders proactively. CLI commands such as "sort" on Linux or "Sort-Object" on Windows can be used to organize and prioritize tickets based on resolution status or priority levels, enabling organizations to focus resources on high-priority tickets and expedite resolution efforts.

Moreover, effective collaboration and communication are critical during the Resolution phase to ensure that tickets are resolved promptly and accurately. Support teams may need to collaborate with other departments, vendors, or third-party providers to address complex issues or fulfill specific service requests. Clear communication channels should be established to facilitate information sharing, updates, and coordination among stakeholders, with regular checkpoints or status meetings to review progress and address any roadblocks or challenges. Additionally, organizations may use collaboration tools or integrations within the ticketing system to streamline communication and collaboration, such as chat features, file attachments, or integration with project management platforms. CLI commands such as "cut" on Linux or "Select-Object" on Windows can be used to extract specific fields or attributes from ticket data or communication logs, enabling organizations to track collaboration efforts and document resolution activities.

Furthermore, proactive monitoring and analysis of ticket data can provide valuable insights into support team performance, ticket trends, and areas for improvement. Organizations may use ticketing system reports or analytics dashboards to track key metrics such as ticket volume, response times, resolution times, and customer satisfaction scores. By analyzing ticket data, organizations can identify recurring issues, root causes of problems, or opportunities to optimize support processes and enhance the overall customer experience. Additionally, organizations may use machine learning algorithms or predictive analytics to forecast ticket volumes, identify patterns or anomalies, and anticipate future support needs proactively. CLI commands such as "uniq" on Linux or "Group-Object" on Windows can be used to identify and aggregate similar tickets or patterns, enabling organizations to analyze ticket data and derive actionable insights.

Moreover, continuous improvement is essential for optimizing the ticket lifecycle and enhancing support operations over time. Organizations should regularly review and refine ticketing system workflows, processes, and procedures to address pain points, streamline operations, and adapt to evolving business needs or customer expectations. This may involve soliciting feedback from stakeholders, conducting post-incident reviews or retrospectives, or implementing service improvement initiatives based on lessons learned from previous tickets. Additionally, organizations may invest in training and development programs to enhance support team skills, knowledge, and capabilities, enabling them to handle tickets more effectively and deliver exceptional customer service. CLI commands such as "uniq -c" on Linux or "Group-Object" on Windows can be used to count and aggregate similar tickets or patterns, enabling organizations to identify trends and prioritize improvement efforts accordingly.

In summary, the Ticket Lifecycle plays a crucial role in incident management processes, guiding the efficient handling and resolution of customer inquiries, service requests, and technical issues. By following clear procedures and workflows for ticket creation, assignment, and resolution, organizations can ensure timely response and resolution, minimize disruptions to business operations, and deliver exceptional customer service. Additionally, by leveraging ticket data and analytics to track performance, identify opportunities for improvement, and drive continuous enhancement, organizations can optimize support operations and enhance the overall customer experience.

Utilizing Ticketing Systems for Documentation and Reporting is an integral aspect of efficient incident management and service delivery processes, enabling organizations to capture, track, and analyze critical information related to customer inquiries, service requests, and technical issues. Ticketing systems serve as centralized repositories for recording and managing all communication and activities associated with incidents, providing a comprehensive record of interactions, resolutions, and outcomes. By leveraging ticketing systems for documentation and reporting, organizations can enhance transparency, accountability, and knowledge sharing, while also facilitating continuous improvement and decision-making based on data-driven insights. CLI commands such as "grep" on Linux or "Select-String" on Windows can be used to search for specific keywords or phrases in ticketing system logs or databases, enabling organizations to retrieve relevant information for documentation and reporting purposes.

Moreover, one of the primary functions of ticketing systems for documentation is to capture detailed information about incidents or service requests, including the nature of the issue, relevant context or background information, and any troubleshooting steps taken. When creating tickets, support agents should ensure that all pertinent details are documented accurately and comprehensively to facilitate efficient resolution and future reference. This documentation serves as a valuable knowledge base for support teams, enabling them to leverage past experiences and solutions to expedite problem-solving and enhance customer satisfaction. Additionally, organizations may use ticketing system features such as custom fields, templates, or forms to standardize data collection and ensure consistency in documentation practices. CLI commands such as "awk" on Linux or "Select-Object" on Windows can be used to filter and extract specific fields or attributes from ticket data, enabling organizations to customize documentation templates or reports based on their requirements.

Furthermore, ticketing systems play a crucial role in facilitating communication and collaboration among stakeholders involved in incident management and resolution processes. By recording all interactions and updates related to incidents within tickets, ticketing systems enable real-time communication and information sharing among support teams, management personnel, and other relevant parties. This ensures that everyone has access to the latest information and progress updates, facilitating collaboration and decision-making based on shared understanding and context. Additionally, organizations may use ticketing system features such as comments, attachments, or internal notes to facilitate communication within support teams and document key decisions or actions taken during incident resolution. CLI commands such as "sort" on Linux or "Sort-Object" on Windows can be used to organize and prioritize tickets based on communication history or update timestamps, enabling organizations to track progress and facilitate collaboration effectively.

Moreover, ticketing systems serve as valuable tools for tracking and monitoring key performance metrics related to incident management and service delivery. By capturing data on ticket volume, response times, resolution times, and customer satisfaction scores, ticketing systems enable organizations to measure and analyze their performance against predefined service level agreements (SLAs) or performance targets. This data provides valuable insights into support team efficiency, customer service quality, and areas for improvement, enabling organizations to identify trends, address bottlenecks, and optimize support processes. Additionally, organizations may use ticketing system reports or dashboards to visualize performance metrics, track trends over time, and communicate insights to stakeholders effectively. CLI commands such as "cut" on Linux or "Select-Object" on Windows can be used to extract specific fields or attributes from ticket data or reports, enabling organizations to generate customized performance reports or analytics based on their requirements.

Furthermore, ticketing systems facilitate compliance with regulatory requirements and industry standards by providing documentation and audit trails of incident management activities. By recording all actions taken and decisions made during incident resolution processes, ticketing systems enable organizations to demonstrate adherence to internal policies, external regulations, and best practices. This documentation is invaluable for compliance audits, regulatory inspections, or internal reviews, providing evidence of due diligence and accountability in managing incidents and ensuring data security and privacy. Additionally, organizations may use ticketing system features such as access controls, audit trails, or encryption to enhance security and integrity of incident documentation and protect sensitive information from unauthorized access or tampering. CLI commands such as "uniq" on Linux or "Group-Object" on Windows can be used to identify and aggregate similar incidents or patterns, enabling organizations to analyze incident data and identify compliance risks or issues proactively.

Moreover, ticketing systems support continuous improvement efforts by enabling organizations to analyze incident data, identify trends or recurring issues, and implement corrective actions or preventive measures to enhance service quality and efficiency. By conducting root cause analysis and trend analysis on ticket data, organizations can identify underlying causes of problems, address systemic issues, and implement proactive measures to prevent future incidents from occurring. Additionally, organizations may use ticketing system data to identify opportunities for automation, process optimization, or knowledge management initiatives that can streamline operations and improve overall service delivery. CLI commands such as "uniq -c" on Linux or "Group-Object" on Windows can be used to count and aggregate similar tickets or patterns, enabling organizations to prioritize improvement efforts based on impact and frequency.

In summary, Utilizing Ticketing Systems for Documentation and Reporting is essential for organizations to capture, track, and analyze critical information related to incident management and service delivery processes. By leveraging ticketing systems for documentation, organizations can maintain comprehensive records of incidents, facilitate communication and collaboration among stakeholders, and support compliance with regulatory requirements and industry standards. Additionally, by using ticketing system data for performance monitoring and analysis, organizations can identify opportunities for improvement, implement corrective actions, and drive continuous enhancement of service quality and efficiency.

Chapter 9: Basic Network Concepts for Service Desk Analysts

Network Topologies, including LAN (Local Area Network), WAN (Wide Area Network), and WLAN (Wireless Local Area Network), form the foundation of modern networking infrastructure, providing the framework for communication and data exchange among devices and systems across various geographic locations and environments. LAN, as the most common type of network topology, is characterized by its limited geographic scope, typically spanning a single building or campus, and interconnected devices such as computers, printers, and servers. LANs use Ethernet cables or wireless connections to facilitate communication and data transfer among devices within the same physical location. To deploy a LAN, organizations typically configure network switches, routers, and access points to establish connectivity and ensure seamless communication among devices. CLI commands such as "ipconfig" on Windows or "ifconfig" on Linux can be used to view network interface configurations and verify connectivity within a LAN environment.

Moreover, WAN extends the concept of LAN to a larger geographic area, connecting multiple LANs across different locations or regions, often spanning cities, countries, or continents. WANs utilize various networking technologies such as leased lines, fiber optics, or satellite links to establish connections between geographically dispersed sites and enable data exchange and communication over long distances. To deploy a WAN, organizations may use networking equipment such as routers, switches, and multiplexers to interconnect LANs and establish wide-reaching communication channels. Additionally, WANs may leverage technologies such as virtual private networks (VPNs) or dedicated circuits to ensure secure and reliable connectivity between remote sites. CLI commands such as "traceroute" on Linux or "tracert" on Windows can be used to trace the route of data packets across WAN links and diagnose connectivity issues between remote locations.

Furthermore, WLAN, also known as Wi-Fi, enables wireless connectivity within a local area, allowing devices to connect to a network without the need for physical cables or wired connections. WLANs use radio frequency signals to transmit data between devices and access points, providing flexibility and mobility for users to access network resources from anywhere within the coverage area. To deploy a WLAN, organizations typically install wireless access points strategically throughout the premises to provide seamless coverage and ensure reliable connectivity. Additionally, WLANs may implement security measures such as encryption, authentication, and access control to protect against unauthorized access and ensure data confidentiality. CLI commands such as "iwconfig" on Linux or "netsh wlan show networks" on Windows can be used to view wireless network configurations and troubleshoot connectivity issues within a WLAN environment.

Moreover, each network topology offers distinct advantages and considerations based on its design, scalability, performance, and security characteristics. LANs are ideal for connecting devices within a single location or building, offering high-speed communication and low latency for applications such as file sharing, printing, and collaborative work environments. WANs, on the other hand, provide connectivity between geographically dispersed sites, enabling organizations to establish wide-reaching communication links and facilitate centralized management and resource sharing across multiple locations. WLANs offer flexibility and mobility for users to connect to the network from anywhere within the coverage area, supporting mobile devices, IoT devices, and emerging technologies such as augmented reality and smart home devices.

Furthermore, organizations must carefully design and configure network topologies to meet their specific requirements, considering factors such as network bandwidth, reliability, security, and scalability. LAN designs may include Ethernet-based architectures such as star, bus, or ring topologies, each offering unique advantages and considerations in terms of performance, cost, and ease of deployment. WAN designs may incorporate technologies such as MPLS (Multiprotocol Label Switching), SD-WAN (Software-Defined Wide Area Network), or VPNs to optimize connectivity, enhance security, and improve application performance across distributed sites. WLAN designs may involve site surveys, channel planning, and access point placement to optimize coverage, minimize interference, and ensure seamless connectivity for users throughout the premises.

Moreover, organizations must implement robust network management and monitoring practices to ensure the optimal performance and reliability of their network infrastructures. This includes monitoring network traffic, analyzing performance metrics, and identifying potential bottlenecks or security vulnerabilities that may impact network operations. Network management tools such as SNMP (Simple Network Management Protocol), NMS (Network Management System), or packet analyzers can be used to monitor network activity, detect anomalies, and troubleshoot issues in real-time. Additionally, organizations may implement network security measures such as firewalls, intrusion detection systems (IDS), and access control lists

(ACLs) to protect against unauthorized access, malware threats, and data breaches across LANs, WANs, and WLANs. Furthermore, as organizations embrace digital transformation and adopt emerging technologies such as cloud computing, IoT (Internet of Things), and edge computing, network topologies will continue to evolve to meet the demands of modern business environments. This includes the adoption of hybrid network architectures that combine traditional on-premises infrastructure with cloud-based services and distributed edge computing resources. Organizations must adapt their network designs and configurations to accommodate these changes, ensuring seamless integration, interoperability, and security across LANs, WANs, and WLANs. Additionally, organizations must prioritize ongoing training and skill development for network administrators and IT professionals to stay abreast of evolving technologies, best practices, and security threats in the ever-changing landscape of network topologies.

IP Addressing and Subnetting Basics are fundamental concepts in computer networking, providing the framework for identifying and communicating with devices on a network. An IP (Internet Protocol) address serves as a unique identifier assigned to each device connected to a network, enabling communication between devices across different networks. IPv4 (Internet Protocol version 4) addresses are commonly used in networking and consist of four octets separated by periods, with each octet represented by a decimal number ranging from 0 to 255. To view the IP address configuration of a device in a network, one can use the "ipconfig" command in Windows or the "ifconfig" command in Linux. These commands display information about the device's IP address, subnet mask, default gateway, and other network settings.

Moreover, IP addresses are divided into two main categories: public IP addresses and private IP addresses. Public IP addresses are globally unique addresses assigned to devices connected to the Internet, allowing them to communicate with other devices across the Internet. Private IP addresses, on the other hand, are used within private networks such as home or corporate networks and are not routable on the Internet. Private IP addresses are defined by RFC 1918 and include ranges such as 10.0.0.0/8, 172.16.0.0/12, and 192.168.0.0/16. These addresses enable devices within the same network to communicate with each other without being directly accessible from the Internet.

Furthermore, subnetting is the process of dividing a large network into smaller, more manageable subnetworks, or subnets, to improve efficiency and scalability. Subnetting allows organizations to allocate IP addresses more efficiently and reduce network congestion by segmenting large networks into smaller, more manageable units. Subnets are defined by a subnet mask, which determines the network portion and host portion of an IP address. A subnet mask consists of a series of binary ones (1s) followed by a series of binary zeros (0s), with the number of ones indicating the length of the network portion. For example, a subnet mask of 255.255.255.0, commonly referred to as a /24 subnet, indicates that the first 24 bits of the IP address represent the network portion, while the remaining 8 bits represent the host portion.

Moreover, subnetting allows organizations to optimize network resources, improve security, and enhance network performance by logically grouping devices based on their geographic location, department, or function. For example, an organization may use subnetting to create separate subnets for different departments within the company, such as sales, marketing, and finance, to segregate network traffic and implement access controls based on departmental policies. Additionally, subnetting enables organizations to conserve IP address space by allocating smaller blocks of addresses to each subnet, reducing the overall number of addresses required for the network.

Furthermore, subnetting is essential for routing traffic efficiently within a network and between different networks. Routers use subnet information to determine the most appropriate path for forwarding data packets based on their destination IP addresses. Subnetting allows routers to divide network traffic into smaller, more manageable segments, reducing the broadcast domain and minimizing network congestion. By subnetting a network, organizations can optimize routing tables, reduce broadcast traffic, and improve overall network performance. To calculate the number of subnets and hosts per subnet in a subnetted network, one can use the subnetting formula and binary arithmetic. For example, to subnet a network with a given IP address and subnet mask, one can use the "ipcalc" command in Linux or online subnet calculators to determine the subnet ranges, broadcast addresses, and available host addresses for each subnet.

Moreover, subnetting introduces the concept of subnet masks and subnetting boundaries, which define the range of IP addresses available within each subnet. Subnet masks are used to identify the network portion and host portion of an IP address, while subnetting boundaries define the boundaries between different subnets within a larger network. For example, a subnet mask of 255.255.255.0, or /24 in CIDR notation, indicates that the first three octets of the IP address represent the network portion, while the last octet represents the host portion. Subnetting boundaries are typically defined by the number of bits borrowed from the host portion of the IP address to create subnets, known as subnet bits.

Furthermore, organizations must carefully plan and design their subnetting schemes to ensure scalability, flexibility, and ease of management. This includes determining the number of subnets required, the number of hosts per subnet, and the subnetting boundaries based on current and future network requirements. Additionally, organizations must consider factors such as network topology, traffic patterns, and security requirements when designing subnetting schemes to ensure optimal performance and security. By carefully planning and implementing subnetting schemes, organizations can optimize network resources, improve scalability, and enhance overall network efficiency and performance.

Chapter 10: Essential Security Principles for Service Desk Operations

Importance of Data Security Awareness cannot be overstated in today's digital age, where data breaches, cyber attacks, and privacy violations have become prevalent threats to organizations and individuals alike. Data security awareness refers to the understanding and consciousness of potential risks and best practices for protecting sensitive information from unauthorized access, disclosure, or misuse. It encompasses a wide range of concepts, including cybersecurity, privacy protection, regulatory compliance, and risk management, and is essential for safeguarding valuable data assets and mitigating the impact of security incidents. Organizations must prioritize data security awareness initiatives to educate employees, stakeholders, and customers about the importance of data protection and empower them to take proactive measures to safeguard sensitive information.

Moreover, data security awareness is critical for maintaining trust and credibility with customers, partners, and stakeholders who entrust organizations with their personal and confidential information. A data breach or security incident can have severe consequences for an organization's reputation, leading to loss of customer trust, financial repercussions, and legal liabilities. By raising awareness about data security risks and best practices, organizations can demonstrate their commitment to protecting sensitive information and instill confidence in their ability to safeguard customer data. Additionally, organizations can differentiate themselves from competitors by implementing robust data security measures and transparent communication practices, thereby enhancing their brand reputation and market credibility.

Furthermore, data security awareness is essential for compliance with regulatory requirements and industry standards governing the protection of sensitive information. Numerous regulations, such as the General Data Protection Regulation (GDPR), the Health Insurance Portability and Accountability Act (HIPAA), and the Payment Card Industry Data Security Standard (PCI DSS), impose stringent requirements on organizations to ensure the confidentiality, integrity, and availability of data. Compliance with these regulations requires organizations to implement comprehensive data security policies, procedures, and controls, as well as provide ongoing training and awareness programs to employees and stakeholders. Failure to comply with regulatory requirements can result in severe penalties, fines, and legal sanctions, making data security awareness a critical component of regulatory compliance efforts.

Moreover, data security awareness is vital for protecting against evolving cyber threats and vulnerabilities that pose significant risks to organizations' data assets and operations. Cybercriminals are constantly developing new techniques and tactics to exploit weaknesses in organizations' networks, systems, and applications, with phishing attacks, malware infections, ransomware, and social engineering scams being among the most common threats. By educating employees and stakeholders about the latest cybersecurity threats and attack vectors, organizations can empower them to recognize and respond effectively to suspicious activities, phishing emails, and potential security breaches. Additionally, organizations can implement security awareness training programs, phishing simulations, and incident response exercises to reinforce cybersecurity best practices and enhance the overall security posture.

Furthermore, data security awareness is essential for fostering a culture of security within organizations, where employees are actively engaged and committed to protecting sensitive information and mitigating security risks. A security-aware culture emphasizes the importance of data protection as a shared responsibility among all employees, regardless of their role or level within the organization. It encourages open communication, collaboration, and accountability for maintaining data security standards and adhering to established policies and procedures. Organizations can promote a security-aware culture by integrating data security awareness into employee onboarding and training programs, conducting regular security awareness campaigns and events, and recognizing and rewarding employees for their contributions to maintaining data security.

Moreover, data security awareness is crucial for mitigating insider threats and inadvertent data breaches caused by employee negligence, errors, or malicious intent. Insider threats pose significant risks to organizations' data security, as employees often have access to sensitive information and systems that can be exploited for personal gain or malicious purposes. By educating employees about the potential consequences of insider threats and the importance of following data security policies and procedures, organizations can reduce the likelihood of insider incidents and minimize the impact of insider-related data breaches. Additionally, organizations can implement security controls such as access controls, data encryption, and monitoring solutions to detect and prevent unauthorized access or misuse of sensitive information by insiders.

Furthermore, data security awareness is essential for empowering individuals to protect their personal information and privacy in an increasingly digital and interconnected world. With the proliferation of online services, social media platforms, and e-commerce transactions, individuals are constantly sharing personal information and sensitive data with various organizations and service providers. It is essential for individuals to understand the risks associated with sharing personal information online and take proactive measures to safeguard their privacy. By educating individuals about data privacy rights, security best practices, and privacy-enhancing technologies, organizations can empower them to make informed decisions about sharing their personal information and minimize the risk of unauthorized access, identity theft, and other privacy violations. Additionally, organizations can provide resources such as privacy policies, data protection tips, and privacy settings guides to help individuals protect their privacy online and maintain control over their personal information.

In summary, data security awareness is a critical component of effective cybersecurity and privacy protection efforts, enabling organizations and individuals to safeguard sensitive information from unauthorized access, disclosure, or misuse. By raising awareness about data security risks, regulatory requirements, and best practices, organizations can promote a culture of security, foster trust with customers and stakeholders, comply with regulatory requirements, mitigate cyber threats, and protect individuals' privacy rights. Data security awareness must be integrated into organizational culture, employee training programs, and customer engagement initiatives to ensure that everyone understands their role and responsibilities in maintaining data security and privacy in an increasingly digital and interconnected world.

Password Management Best Practices are essential for

ensuring the security of sensitive information and protecting against unauthorized access to accounts, systems, and data. Effective password management encompasses a range of strategies, policies, and techniques designed to create strong, unique passwords, securely store and manage passwords, and minimize the risk of password-related security incidents. Passwords serve as the primary means of authentication for accessing digital resources, making them a critical line of defense against unauthorized access and cyber threats. Therefore, organizations and individuals must adopt and adhere to password management best practices to enhance security posture and mitigate the risk of password-related security breaches.

One of the fundamental password management best practices is to create strong, complex passwords that are difficult for attackers to guess or brute-force. Strong passwords typically consist of a combination of uppercase and lowercase letters, numbers, and special characters and are at least eight characters long. To generate strong passwords, individuals can use password generators or passphrase techniques to create random strings of characters that are unique and difficult to guess. Additionally, individuals should avoid using easily guessable passwords such as "123456" or "password" and refrain from using dictionary words or common phrases that can be easily cracked by attackers.

Moreover, it is crucial to use unique passwords for each online account or system to prevent credential reuse attacks and minimize the impact of a compromised password. Reusing passwords across multiple accounts increases the risk of unauthorized access if one account is breached, as attackers can use the same credentials to gain access to other accounts belonging to the same user. To manage multiple passwords effectively, individuals can use password managers, which are software tools designed to securely store and manage passwords for various accounts. Password managers encrypt passwords and store them in a centralized vault, requiring users to authenticate with a master password or biometric authentication to access their stored credentials.

Furthermore, individuals should regularly update their passwords and change them periodically to reduce the likelihood of password-based attacks and ensure continued security. Password expiration policies can be enforced to prompt users to change their passwords at regular intervals, such as every 90 days, to mitigate the risk of compromised passwords being used maliciously over time. Additionally, individuals should change their passwords immediately if they suspect that their accounts may have been compromised or if they receive notifications of unauthorized access attempts. To change passwords on systems or accounts, individuals can use account settings or administration interfaces to update their credentials securely.

Moreover, organizations should implement strong password policies and enforce password complexity requirements to ensure that users create and maintain secure passwords. Password policies may include minimum length requirements, complexity rules, and expiration intervals to enforce strong password practices across the organization. For example, organizations may require passwords to be at least 12 characters long and contain a combination of uppercase and lowercase letters, numbers, and special characters. Additionally, organizations can implement multi-factor authentication (MFA) to add an extra layer of security beyond passwords, requiring users to provide additional verification, such as a one-time code sent to their mobile device, to access accounts or systems.

Furthermore, organizations should educate employees about password security best practices and provide training on how to create strong passwords, securely store and manage passwords, and recognize common password-related threats such as phishing scams and social engineering attacks. Training programs should emphasize the importance of protecting sensitive information and the role that strong passwords play in maintaining data security. Additionally, organizations can conduct simulated phishing exercises to test employees' awareness of phishing scams and reinforce training on how to identify and avoid suspicious emails or messages.

Moreover, organizations should implement measures to protect passwords and prevent unauthorized access to stored credentials, such as encrypting password databases and using secure authentication protocols. Password hashes should be used to store passwords securely, ensuring that even if a password database is compromised, attackers cannot easily decrypt or reverse-engineer stored passwords. Additionally, organizations should implement strong access controls and audit trails to monitor and track user access to password repositories and detect unauthorized attempts to access or modify stored credentials.

Furthermore, organizations should regularly audit and review their password management practices to identify weaknesses or vulnerabilities and implement corrective actions to address them. Regular password audits can help organizations identify outdated or weak passwords, detect unauthorized access attempts, and ensure compliance with password policies and regulatory requirements. Additionally, organizations can leverage automated tools and vulnerability scanners to assess the strength of passwords, identify misconfigured systems or applications, and remediate security gaps proactively.

In summary, Password Management Best Practices are essential for enhancing security posture, protecting sensitive information, and mitigating the risk of password-related security incidents. By creating strong, unique passwords, securely storing and managing passwords, and enforcing password policies and training programs, organizations and individuals can reduce the likelihood of unauthorized access and data breaches. Additionally, organizations should implement technical controls, such as encryption and access controls, to protect stored passwords and prevent unauthorized access to sensitive information. Password management is a critical component of effective cybersecurity practices and requires ongoing vigilance, education, and enforcement to maintain the integrity and confidentiality of digital assets.

BOOK 2
MASTERING SERVICE DESK TROUBLESHOOTING
CONFIGURING SOFTWARE FOR EFFICIENCY

ROB BOTWRIGHT

Chapter 1: Understanding Service Desk Troubleshooting

Root Cause Analysis (RCA) Methods play a crucial role in identifying the underlying causes of problems or incidents and implementing effective solutions to prevent recurrence. RCA is a systematic approach used to investigate and analyze the root causes of issues, failures, or deviations from expected performance in various domains, including engineering, manufacturing, healthcare, and information technology. By identifying the root causes of problems, organizations can address underlying issues, improve processes, and enhance overall performance. Several methods and techniques are commonly used to conduct root cause analysis, each with its unique approach and tools for identifying and addressing root causes effectively.

One widely used method for root cause analysis is the "5 Whys" technique, which involves asking a series of "why" questions to explore the underlying causes of a problem. The 5 Whys technique is based on the premise that by asking "why" multiple times, one can uncover deeper layers of causality and identify the root cause of an issue. To perform a 5 Whys analysis, individuals or teams start by identifying the problem or incident and then ask "why" it occurred. For example, if the problem is a machine breakdown, the first "why" question may be "Why did the machine stop working?" The process continues iteratively, with each subsequent "why" question probing deeper into the underlying factors contributing to the problem until the root cause is identified.

Moreover, another commonly used RCA method is the Fishbone Diagram, also known as the Ishikawa Diagram or Cause-and-Effect Diagram, which visually represents the various factors contributing to a problem or outcome. The Fishbone Diagram organizes potential causes into categories such as people, process, equipment, environment, and management, resembling the skeleton of a fish. To create a Fishbone Diagram, individuals or teams start by defining the problem or effect they want to analyze and then brainstorm potential causes within each category. The resulting diagram helps visualize the relationships between different factors and identify potential root causes that require further investigation.

Furthermore, Failure Mode and Effects Analysis (FMEA) is a systematic method for identifying and prioritizing potential failure modes in a process, system, or product and assessing their potential impact on performance or outcomes. FMEA involves analyzing each potential failure mode to determine its likelihood of occurrence, severity of impact, and detectability before prioritizing actions to address high-risk failure modes. To conduct an FMEA, individuals or teams typically create a table or spreadsheet to document potential failure modes, their causes, effects, and corresponding risk scores based on predefined criteria. The resulting analysis helps prioritize corrective actions and preventive measures to mitigate the risk of failures and improve overall performance.

Additionally, Root Cause Analysis can be conducted using statistical methods such as Pareto Analysis, which prioritizes the most significant contributing factors based on their frequency or impact on a given outcome. Pareto Analysis is based on the Pareto Principle, also known as the 80/20 rule, which states that roughly 80% of effects come from 20% of causes. To perform Pareto Analysis, individuals or teams collect data on contributing factors or categories related to a problem or outcome and then rank them in descending order based on their frequency or impact. The analysis helps identify the critical few factors that account for the majority of problems or issues, allowing organizations to focus resources on addressing the most significant root causes.

Moreover, Root Cause Analysis can benefit from the use of various quality management tools and techniques, such as Statistical Process Control (SPC), Control Charts, and Histograms, to analyze process data and identify patterns, trends, or anomalies that may indicate underlying causes of variation or nonconformity. SPC techniques involve monitoring process performance over time and using statistical methods to distinguish between common cause variation (inherent to the process) and special cause variation (due to specific factors or events). Control Charts and Histograms are graphical tools used to visualize process data and identify trends, shifts, or outliers that may signal potential root causes requiring further investigation.

Furthermore, Root Cause Analysis can be enhanced through the use of advanced analytical techniques such as Data Mining, Machine Learning, and Predictive Analytics, which leverage large datasets and algorithms to identify patterns, correlations, and causal relationships within data. Data Mining techniques involve extracting insights from structured and unstructured data sources to uncover hidden patterns or associations that may reveal underlying causes of problems or deviations. Machine Learning algorithms can analyze historical data to predict future outcomes or identify factors contributing to specific outcomes, while Predictive Analytics techniques use statistical models to forecast trends, risks, or opportunities based on historical data.

Additionally, Root Cause Analysis can be complemented by Human Factors Analysis, which focuses on understanding the role of human factors, behaviors, and interactions in contributing to problems or incidents. Human Factors Analysis examines factors such as communication breakdowns, decision-making errors, cognitive biases, and organizational culture to identify underlying causes of human error or performance deficiencies. By considering human factors alongside technical, procedural, and environmental factors, organizations can develop more comprehensive root cause analyses and implement targeted interventions to address systemic issues and improve overall performance.

Moreover, Root Cause Analysis should be conducted in a collaborative and multidisciplinary manner, involving stakeholders from different departments, functions, and levels of the organization to gain diverse perspectives and insights into the problem or issue. Cross-functional teams can bring together expertise from various disciplines, such as engineering, operations, quality assurance, and risk management, to analyze root causes comprehensively and develop holistic solutions that address underlying issues from multiple angles. Collaboration fosters transparency, communication, and accountability, enabling organizations to implement more effective corrective and preventive actions and drive continuous improvement.

Furthermore, Root Cause Analysis should be followed by action planning and implementation to address identified root causes and prevent recurrence of problems or incidents. Action plans should be specific, measurable, achievable, relevant, and time-bound (SMART), outlining concrete steps, responsibilities, and timelines for implementing corrective and preventive actions. Organizations should track progress, monitor outcomes, and evaluate the effectiveness of interventions to ensure that root causes are addressed effectively and sustained improvements are achieved over time. Continuous monitoring and review of performance metrics and key performance indicators (KPIs) can help organizations identify emerging issues, track trends, and make data-driven decisions to maintain process stability and reliability.

In summary, Root Cause Analysis Methods are essential tools for identifying underlying causes of problems or incidents and implementing effective solutions to prevent recurrence and drive continuous improvement. By applying systematic approaches such as the 5 Whys technique, Fishbone Diagrams, FMEA, Pareto Analysis, statistical methods, quality management tools, advanced analytical techniques, and human factors analysis, organizations can gain insights into root causes, develop targeted interventions, and improve overall performance. Collaboration, action planning, and continuous monitoring are key elements of successful root cause analysis efforts, enabling organizations to address systemic issues, mitigate risks, and achieve sustainable improvements in quality, reliability, and efficiency.

Common Troubleshooting Frameworks are structured methodologies used to systematically diagnose and resolve technical issues, problems, or malfunctions in various domains, including information technology, engineering, healthcare, and manufacturing. These frameworks provide a systematic approach for identifying symptoms, analyzing potential causes, and implementing solutions to restore normal operation. By following a structured troubleshooting process, individuals or teams can reduce the time and effort required to resolve issues, minimize downtime, and improve overall efficiency and reliability. Several widely used troubleshooting frameworks exist, each with its unique approach and steps for diagnosing and resolving problems effectively.

One of the most commonly used troubleshooting frameworks is the OSI Model, which stands for Open Systems Interconnection Model, a conceptual framework that defines the seven layers of networking protocols and their interactions. The OSI Model provides a structured framework for troubleshooting network connectivity issues by dividing the network communication process into distinct layers, each responsible for specific functions such as data encapsulation, routing, and error detection. To troubleshoot network connectivity issues using the OSI Model, individuals or teams start by identifying the symptoms of the problem, such as slow performance or network outages, and then systematically work through each layer of the OSI Model to isolate potential causes and implement solutions.

Moreover, another widely used troubleshooting framework is the Six Sigma DMAIC methodology, which stands for Define, Measure, Analyze, Improve, and Control. DMAIC is a structured problem-solving approach used to identify, analyze, and eliminate defects or variations in processes, products, or services. To apply the DMAIC methodology, individuals or teams start by defining the problem or opportunity for improvement, gathering data to quantify the extent of the problem, and analyzing root causes using statistical tools and techniques such as Pareto Analysis, Fishbone Diagrams, and Control Charts. Once root causes are identified, improvements are implemented, and controls are established to sustain gains and prevent recurrence of issues.

Furthermore, the PDCA Cycle, also known as the Deming Cycle or Plan-Do-Check-Act Cycle, is a continuous improvement framework used to solve problems, optimize processes, and drive organizational change. The PDCA Cycle consists of four iterative steps: Plan, Do, Check, and Act. In the Plan phase, individuals or teams identify the problem or objective, gather data, and develop a plan for improvement. In the Do phase, the plan is executed, and changes are implemented according to the defined objectives. In the

Check phase, the results of the implementation are evaluated, and performance metrics are analyzed to determine whether the desired outcomes were achieved. In the Act phase, adjustments are made based on the findings of the Check phase, and the cycle repeats iteratively to drive continuous improvement.

Additionally, the Kepner-Tregoe Problem Analysis (KTPA) framework is a structured problem-solving methodology used to identify, analyze, and resolve complex issues or decisions. KTPA consists of four key steps: Situation Appraisal, Problem Analysis, Decision Analysis, and Potential Problem Analysis. In the Situation Appraisal phase, individuals or teams gather information about the problem, its impact, and potential causes. In the Problem Analysis phase, the root causes of the problem are systematically analyzed using tools such as Cause-and-Effect Diagrams or the 5 Whys technique. In the Decision Analysis phase, potential solutions are evaluated based on their feasibility, impact, and risks, and a decision is made on the best course of action. In the Potential Problem Analysis phase, proactive measures are taken to anticipate and prevent potential issues or risks associated with the chosen solution.

Moreover, the ITIL (Information Technology Infrastructure Library) framework provides a comprehensive set of best practices for managing IT services and processes, including incident management, problem management, and change management. ITIL defines a structured approach for diagnosing and resolving IT issues through the Incident Management and Problem Management processes. In the Incident Management process, ITIL outlines procedures for logging, categorizing, prioritizing, and resolving incidents to restore normal service operation as quickly as possible. In the Problem Management process, ITIL focuses on identifying root causes of recurring incidents, implementing permanent fixes, and preventing future incidents from occurring.

Furthermore, the Microsoft Windows Troubleshooting Framework provides a structured approach for diagnosing and resolving common issues encountered in Windows operating systems. Windows Troubleshooting Tools such as Event Viewer, Task Manager, and System File Checker are used to gather diagnostic information, analyze system performance, and identify potential causes of problems. Additionally, built-in troubleshooting wizards and utilities such as the Windows Troubleshooting Packager (WTP) and Windows Diagnostic Data Viewer (WDDV) help guide users through the troubleshooting process and provide step-by-step instructions for resolving issues.

Additionally, the Cisco Troubleshooting Methodology is a structured approach used to diagnose and resolve network-related issues in Cisco networking environments. The Cisco Troubleshooting Methodology consists of seven sequential steps: Define the Problem, Gather Information, Analyze Information, Eliminate Possible Causes, Test Hypotheses, Document Findings, and Implement Solutions. Each step involves specific actions and techniques for identifying symptoms, collecting data, analyzing network traffic, and implementing corrective actions to restore network performance.

Chapter 2: Diagnostic Tools and Techniques

Network diagnostic tools play a pivotal role in troubleshooting and maintaining the health of computer networks. In the realm of information technology, where networks serve as the backbone for communication and data exchange, the ability to swiftly identify and rectify issues is paramount. These tools encompass a wide array of software and utilities designed to diagnose various network-related problems, ranging from connectivity issues to performance bottlenecks. They empower network administrators and engineers with insights into the functioning of network components, aiding in the swift resolution of issues and ensuring optimal network performance.

One of the fundamental tasks in network diagnostics is determining the connectivity between network devices. Ping, a ubiquitous command-line utility, serves as a cornerstone for assessing network connectivity. By sending ICMP (Internet Control Message Protocol) echo request packets to a specified destination, the Ping tool measures the round-trip time for packets to reach the destination and return. This simple yet powerful tool enables administrators to verify whether a network device is reachable and assess the latency between endpoints. To utilize Ping, one simply needs to open the command prompt or terminal and type the command followed by the IP address or hostname of the target device, such as "ping 192.168.1.1" in the case of an IPv4 address.

Traceroute, another invaluable network diagnostic tool, provides insights into the routing path packets take from the source to the destination. By sending a series of UDP or ICMP packets with incrementally increasing TTL (Time-to-

Live) values, Traceroute records the IP addresses of intermediary routers traversed by the packets en route to the destination. This information helps pinpoint the specific hop where connectivity issues or delays occur, facilitating targeted troubleshooting efforts. Executing Traceroute entails entering the command followed by the destination IP address or hostname, such as "traceroute example.com" for a domain name resolution.

Network scanning tools play a crucial role in identifying active hosts, open ports, and services running on a network. Nmap (Network Mapper), a versatile and feature-rich network scanner, stands out as a prominent choice for comprehensive network reconnaissance. With its ability to perform host discovery, port scanning, version detection, and OS fingerprinting, Nmap equips administrators with detailed insights into network topology and security posture. Utilizing Nmap involves specifying the target IP range or hostname along with desired scan options, such as "nmap -sV 192.168.1.0/24" to perform a service version detection scan on all hosts within the specified subnet.

Wireshark, a powerful packet analysis tool, enables deep inspection of network traffic at the packet level. By capturing and analyzing packets traversing a network interface, Wireshark facilitates the identification of anomalies, protocol errors, and malicious activities. Its intuitive graphical interface displays captured packets in a readable format, allowing administrators to dissect network communications and pinpoint aberrations. Deploying Wireshark involves installing the software on a workstation or server and launching the application to start packet capture on the desired network interface.

Bandwidth monitoring tools play a vital role in assessing network performance and utilization. Tools like SNMP (Simple Network Management Protocol) monitoring software and NetFlow analyzers provide real-time visibility into bandwidth consumption, traffic patterns, and network usage trends. By collecting and analyzing network traffic data, these tools enable administrators to identify bandwidth-intensive applications, detect anomalies, and optimize network resources. Deploying SNMP monitoring involves configuring SNMP agents on network devices and using SNMP management software like Nagios or Cacti to collect and visualize performance metrics.

In addition to reactive troubleshooting, proactive network diagnostics involve continuous monitoring and analysis of network health. Network monitoring solutions such as Zabbix, PRTG Network Monitor, and SolarWinds Network Performance Monitor offer comprehensive monitoring capabilities, including device availability, performance metrics, and alerting mechanisms. These tools empower administrators to preemptively identify and address potential issues before they escalate, ensuring uninterrupted network operation. Deploying network monitoring solutions typically entails installing monitoring agents or probes on network devices and configuring monitoring policies and thresholds.

DNS (Domain Name System) diagnostic tools play a crucial role in resolving domain name resolution issues and verifying DNS configurations. Tools like nslookup and dig enable administrators to query DNS servers, retrieve DNS records, and troubleshoot DNS-related problems. By analyzing DNS responses and resolving domain names to IP addresses, these tools facilitate the resolution of DNS misconfigurations, cache poisoning, and DNSSEC (Domain Name System Security Extensions) issues. Executing nslookup or dig commands involves specifying the domain name or DNS server to query, such as "nslookup example.com" or "dig @8.8.8.8 example.com".

Firewall diagnostic tools aid in assessing firewall configurations, rule effectiveness, and traffic filtering policies. Tools like hping and Firewalk enable administrators to test firewall rulesets, detect open ports, and assess firewall traversal capabilities. By crafting custom packets and analyzing firewall responses, these tools help identify potential security vulnerabilities and misconfigurations in firewall implementations. Using hping or Firewalk involves specifying packet parameters and target hosts to conduct firewall penetration testing and analysis.

In summary, network diagnostic tools serve as indispensable assets in the arsenal of network administrators and engineers, empowering them to troubleshoot, analyze, and optimize computer networks effectively. From assessing connectivity and routing to monitoring performance and security, these tools play a multifaceted role in ensuring the reliability, performance, and security of modern networks. By leveraging a diverse array of diagnostic utilities and techniques, administrators can proactively identify and resolve network issues, thereby minimizing downtime, enhancing user experience, and maximizing the resilience of network infrastructure.

Hardware diagnostic utilities play a pivotal role in ensuring the reliability, performance, and longevity of computer hardware components. In the dynamic landscape of technology, where hardware forms the backbone of computing systems, the ability to swiftly identify and rectify hardware issues is paramount. These utilities encompass a diverse range of software tools and techniques designed to diagnose various hardware-related problems, ranging from hardware failures to performance degradation. They empower system administrators, technicians, and end-users with insights into the health and functionality of hardware components, facilitating timely maintenance and troubleshooting efforts.

One of the fundamental tasks in hardware diagnostics is assessing the overall health of system components, including the CPU, memory, storage devices, and peripherals. CPU stress testing utilities, such as Prime95 for Windows or stress for Linux, subject the CPU to intensive computational workloads to evaluate its stability and thermal performance. These utilities are invaluable for identifying CPU overheating issues, hardware defects, and system instability under heavy computational loads. To deploy CPU stress testing, users can download and install the respective utility for their operating system and execute the stress test command, such as "prime95 -t" in the case of Prime95.

Memory diagnostic tools play a crucial role in identifying and troubleshooting memory-related issues, such as faulty RAM modules or memory corruption. Memtest86, a popular memory testing utility, boots independently of the operating system and performs thorough memory tests to detect errors and inconsistencies. Users can create a bootable Memtest86 USB drive or CD/DVD and boot their system from it to initiate memory testing. Once booted, Memtest86 automatically runs a series of memory tests, displaying detailed results and error reports for analysis. This allows users to pinpoint defective memory modules and take appropriate corrective actions.

Storage diagnostic utilities enable users to assess the health, performance, and reliability of storage devices, including hard disk drives (HDDs), solid-state drives (SSDs), and external storage media. SMART (Self-Monitoring, Analysis, and Reporting Technology) diagnostic tools, such as smartctl for Linux or CrystalDiskInfo for Windows, provide detailed information about the SMART attributes and health status of storage devices. By analyzing SMART data, users can identify warning signs of imminent drive failure, such as bad sectors, reallocated sectors, or excessive spin-up counts. To utilize SMART diagnostic tools, users can install the respective utility for their operating system and execute the SMART query command, such as "smartctl -a /dev/sda" for a detailed SMART report of the first SATA drive on a Linux system.

Graphics card stress testing utilities, such as FurMark or MSI Kombustor, assess the stability and thermal performance of GPU (Graphics Processing Unit) components under heavy graphical workloads. These utilities subject the GPU to intense rendering tasks, pushing it to its limits to evaluate its cooling efficiency and overall stability. GPU stress testing is particularly useful for overclocking enthusiasts, system builders, and gamers seeking to maximize the performance of their graphics hardware. To deploy GPU stress testing, users can download and install the respective utility for their platform and initiate the stress test command, such as "furmark --fullscreen" for FurMark.

Peripheral diagnostic utilities aid in assessing the functionality and connectivity of external hardware peripherals, such as keyboards, mice, printers, and USB devices. Device Manager in Windows and lsusb in Linux provide detailed information about connected USB devices, including vendor IDs, product IDs, and device status. By inspecting device properties and status indicators, users can troubleshoot connectivity issues, driver conflicts, and hardware malfunctions affecting peripheral devices. To access Device Manager in Windows, users can right-click on the Start menu, select "Device Manager," and navigate to the "Universal Serial Bus controllers" section for USB device information.

Temperature monitoring utilities enable users to track the thermal performance of hardware components, including the CPU, GPU, motherboard, and hard drives. Applications like Core Temp for Windows or lm-sensors for Linux provide real-time temperature readings and thermal sensors data, allowing users to monitor system temperatures and detect overheating issues. By setting temperature thresholds and alarms, users can receive notifications when temperatures exceed safe limits, preventing potential hardware damage or system instability. To deploy temperature monitoring, users can install the respective utility for their operating system and launch the application to view temperature readings in real-time.

Power supply diagnostic tools facilitate the assessment of power delivery and voltage stability from the power supply unit (PSU) to system components. Power supply testers, such as PSU testers or multimeters, enable users to measure voltages, current, and power output from the PSU connectors. By performing voltage and continuity tests on various PSU rails, users can verify proper power delivery and identify potential issues, such as voltage fluctuations or faulty connectors. To deploy power supply testing, users can use a PSU tester device or a multimeter to measure voltages across PSU connectors while the system is powered on.

In summary, hardware diagnostic utilities serve as indispensable tools for diagnosing, troubleshooting, and maintaining computer hardware components. From assessing CPU stability and memory integrity to evaluating storage health and peripheral connectivity, these utilities empower users to identify and address hardware issues effectively. By leveraging a diverse array of diagnostic techniques and tools, users can ensure the reliability, performance, and longevity of their computing systems, thereby enhancing productivity, minimizing downtime, and maximizing the lifespan of hardware components.

Chapter 3: Advanced Software Configuration Strategies

Software deployment automation is a critical component of modern software development practices, streamlining the process of distributing and installing software across various environments. In today's fast-paced digital landscape, where agility, scalability, and efficiency are paramount, automation plays a pivotal role in accelerating the deployment lifecycle and ensuring consistency and reliability across deployments. Deploying software manually can be time-consuming, error-prone, and labor-intensive, particularly in large-scale enterprise environments or cloud-based infrastructures. However, by leveraging automation tools and techniques, organizations can automate repetitive deployment tasks, minimize human intervention, and enhance deployment speed, accuracy, and repeatability.

One of the key aspects of software deployment automation is the use of configuration management tools to define and manage infrastructure and application configurations. Tools like Ansible, Puppet, and Chef enable administrators and developers to codify infrastructure as code (IaC) and automate the provisioning, configuration, and management of servers, virtual machines, and cloud instances. By writing declarative configuration files or scripts, users can define the desired state of infrastructure components and ensure consistency and reproducibility across environments. Deploying infrastructure with Ansible involves creating YAML (YAML Ain't Markup Language) playbooks that specify tasks and configurations and executing them using the ansible-playbook command, such as "ansible-playbook site.yml" to apply configurations defined in the site.yml playbook.

Containerization technologies, such as Docker and Kubernetes, revolutionize software deployment by encapsulating applications and their dependencies into lightweight, portable containers. Containers provide a consistent runtime environment across different platforms, enabling developers to build, ship, and run applications seamlessly across development, testing, and production environments. Docker, a leading containerization platform, simplifies the process of packaging applications into containers and automating their deployment using Dockerfiles and Docker Compose. To deploy a Docker container, users can write a Dockerfile that specifies the application's dependencies and runtime environment and build the image using the docker build command, followed by deploying the container using the docker run command, such as "docker run -d -p 8080:80 myapp:latest" to run a containerized application on port 8080.

Continuous Integration (CI) and Continuous Deployment (CD) pipelines automate the process of building, testing, and deploying software changes across development and production environments. CI/CD pipelines enable organizations to accelerate software delivery, improve code quality, and minimize the risk of introducing defects into production systems. Jenkins, GitLab CI/CD, and CircleCI are popular CI/CD platforms that facilitate the automation of build, test, and deployment workflows. By configuring pipeline scripts or YAML files, users can define stages and tasks for building, testing, and deploying applications automatically. Deploying a CI/CD pipeline involves setting up the pipeline configuration in the chosen CI/CD platform and triggering pipeline execution either manually or automatically upon code changes or commits.

Configuration management tools play a crucial role in automating the deployment of software applications and services across distributed environments. Tools like Ansible, Puppet, and Chef enable administrators to define and manage application configurations, dependencies, and deployment settings in a centralized manner. By writing configuration files or scripts, users can automate the installation, configuration, and orchestration of software components across multiple servers or virtual machines. Deploying software with Ansible involves writing YAML playbooks that define tasks and configurations for deploying applications and executing them using the ansible-playbook command, such as "ansible-playbook deploy.yml" to deploy an application defined in the deploy.yml playbook.

Container orchestration platforms, such as Kubernetes, simplify the management and scaling of containerized applications in production environments. Kubernetes automates various deployment tasks, including container scheduling, scaling, and load balancing, to ensure high availability, reliability, and scalability of applications. Deploying applications with Kubernetes involves defining deployment manifests or YAML files that specify container configurations, replica counts, and resource requirements. Users can apply these manifests using the kubectl apply command, such as "kubectl apply -f deployment.yaml" to create or update deployments in a Kubernetes cluster.

Infrastructure as Code (IaC) frameworks, such as Terraform and CloudFormation, automate the provisioning and management of cloud infrastructure resources using code-based configuration files. These frameworks enable users to define infrastructure components, such as virtual machines, networks, and storage, in a declarative manner and provision them automatically across cloud providers like AWS, Azure, and Google Cloud Platform. Deploying infrastructure with Terraform involves writing Terraform configuration files (HCL) that describe the desired state of infrastructure resources and executing Terraform commands, such as "terraform apply" to provision or update infrastructure according to the defined configuration.

Deployment pipelines automate the process of releasing software changes into production environments, ensuring a smooth and consistent deployment experience. Continuous Integration (CI) and Continuous Deployment (CD) pipelines automate various stages of the deployment lifecycle, including code integration, testing, and deployment, to deliver software changes rapidly and reliably. Tools like Jenkins, GitLab CI/CD, and CircleCI provide robust pipeline automation capabilities, allowing organizations to define, execute, and monitor deployment workflows seamlessly. Deploying a CI/CD pipeline involves configuring pipeline scripts or YAML files that define build, test, and deployment stages and executing them using the chosen CI/CD platform's interface or command-line interface.

Version control systems, such as Git and Subversion, play a crucial role in automating software deployment by facilitating collaboration, versioning, and release management. Version control systems enable developers to manage code changes, track revisions, and coordinate software releases across distributed teams effectively. By using branching, tagging, and merging workflows, developers can automate the process of integrating and deploying code changes into production environments. Deploying software with Git involves creating feature branches, committing code changes, and merging them into the main branch using Git commands, such as "git checkout -b feature-branch" to create a new feature branch and "git merge feature-branch" to merge changes into the main branch.

In summary, software deployment automation is a cornerstone of modern software development practices, enabling organizations to accelerate the delivery of software changes, enhance deployment consistency, and improve operational efficiency. By leveraging configuration management tools, containerization technologies, CI/CD pipelines, and infrastructure as code frameworks, organizations can automate the provisioning, configuration, and deployment of software applications and infrastructure components across diverse environments. Automation streamlines deployment workflows, minimizes human errors, and enhances collaboration, thereby enabling organizations to deliver high-quality software products rapidly and reliably.

Configuration management tools are essential components of modern IT infrastructure management, facilitating the automation, standardization, and control of configuration settings across diverse environments. In the dynamic landscape of technology, where organizations operate complex and distributed IT infrastructures, configuration management tools play a pivotal role in ensuring consistency, reliability, and scalability. These tools encompass a wide array of software solutions and techniques designed to streamline configuration tasks, enforce policy compliance, and mitigate configuration drift. Deploying configuration management tools enables organizations to automate repetitive tasks, minimize human errors, and enhance operational efficiency across servers, networking devices, and cloud environments.

One of the primary functions of configuration management tools is to automate the provisioning and configuration of infrastructure components, including servers, virtual machines, and cloud instances. Tools like Ansible, Puppet, and Chef enable administrators to define infrastructure configurations as code and automate the deployment and management of servers and services. Ansible, a popular configuration management tool, utilizes SSH (Secure Shell) to execute tasks on remote hosts and YAML (YAML Ain't Markup Language) to define configurations in human-readable format. To deploy configurations with Ansible, users write YAML playbooks that specify tasks and configurations and execute them using the ansible-playbook command, such as "ansible-playbook site.yml" to apply configurations defined in the site.yml playbook.

Configuration management tools also facilitate the enforcement of configuration standards and best practices across IT environments. By defining configuration policies and templates, organizations can ensure consistency and compliance with security, regulatory, and operational requirements. Tools like Puppet Enterprise provide policy-based management capabilities, allowing administrators to define configuration rules and apply them to managed nodes automatically. Deploying configuration policies with Puppet involves writing Puppet manifests that describe desired configurations and deploying them using the puppet apply command, such as "puppet apply site.pp" to enforce configurations defined in the site.pp manifest.

Another key aspect of configuration management tools is the ability to track and manage configuration changes over time. Version control systems, such as Git, enable organizations to track changes to configuration files, collaborate on configuration management tasks, and revert to previous configurations if necessary. By storing configuration files in version control repositories, organizations can maintain an audit trail of configuration changes, track configuration drift, and ensure accountability for configuration modifications. Deploying configuration files with Git involves creating a Git repository, adding configuration files to the repository, committing changes using Git commands, such as "git add" and "git commit," and pushing changes to a remote repository using "git push."

Configuration management tools also facilitate the automation of software deployment and configuration updates across distributed environments. Continuous Integration (CI) and Continuous Deployment (CD) pipelines automate the process of building, testing, and deploying software changes, ensuring rapid and reliable delivery of applications and services. Tools like Jenkins, GitLab CI/CD, and CircleCI provide robust pipeline automation capabilities, allowing organizations to define, execute, and monitor deployment workflows seamlessly. Deploying applications with Jenkins involves configuring pipeline scripts or YAML files that define build, test, and deployment stages and executing them using the Jenkins interface or CLI (Command Line Interface).

Infrastructure as Code (IaC) frameworks, such as Terraform and AWS CloudFormation, enable organizations to automate the provisioning and management of cloud infrastructure resources using code-based configuration files. These frameworks provide declarative syntax for defining infrastructure components, such as virtual machines, networks, and storage, and automate the deployment and scaling of cloud resources. Deploying infrastructure with Terraform involves writing Terraform configuration files (HCL) that describe the desired state of infrastructure resources and executing Terraform commands, such as "terraform apply" to provision or update infrastructure according to the defined configuration.

Configuration management tools play a crucial role in automating the deployment and management of containerized applications in production environments. Container orchestration platforms, such as Kubernetes, enable organizations to automate various deployment tasks, including container scheduling, scaling, and load balancing, to ensure high availability and scalability of containerized applications. Tools like Helm simplify the management of Kubernetes applications by providing package management capabilities and templating support for defining application configurations. Deploying applications with Kubernetes involves creating deployment manifests or YAML files that specify container configurations, replica counts, and resource requirements and applying these manifests using the kubectl apply command, such as "kubectl apply -f deployment.yaml" to deploy applications to a Kubernetes cluster.

In summary, configuration management tools are indispensable assets for organizations seeking to automate and streamline IT infrastructure management processes. By leveraging configuration management tools, organizations can automate the provisioning, configuration, and management of infrastructure components, enforce configuration standards and best practices, and ensure consistency and compliance across distributed environments. Whether automating server configurations with Ansible, enforcing policies with Puppet, or provisioning cloud resources with Terraform, configuration management tools empower organizations to achieve operational excellence, enhance security, and accelerate the delivery of IT services and applications.

Chapter 4: Analyzing Error Messages and Logs

Log analysis techniques are vital for gaining insights into system behavior, diagnosing issues, and enhancing security in complex computing environments. In today's digital age, where vast amounts of data are generated daily by various systems and applications, log analysis serves as a cornerstone for understanding the operational status and performance of IT infrastructure. These techniques encompass a diverse array of methodologies, tools, and approaches designed to parse, interpret, and derive meaningful information from log files. Deploying log analysis techniques enables organizations to identify patterns, detect anomalies, and make informed decisions based on actionable insights derived from log data.

One of the fundamental log analysis techniques involves parsing and extracting relevant information from log files using specialized tools and utilities. Command-line tools like grep, awk, and sed are commonly used to search, filter, and manipulate log data based on specific criteria. For instance, the grep command allows users to search for specific patterns or keywords within log files, such as "grep 'error' logfile.txt" to find all occurrences of the word 'error' in the logfile.txt file. Similarly, the awk command enables users to extract and manipulate fields from log entries, such as "awk '{print $4}' logfile.txt" to extract the fourth field from each line of the logfile.txt file.

Log aggregation tools play a crucial role in consolidating and centralizing log data from multiple sources for analysis and monitoring purposes. Platforms like Elasticsearch, Logstash, and Kibana (ELK stack) provide a comprehensive solution for collecting, parsing, and visualizing log data in real-time. By ingesting log data into a centralized repository, organizations can perform advanced analytics, correlation, and visualization to gain insights into system performance, security events, and operational trends. Deploying the ELK stack involves installing and configuring Elasticsearch, Logstash, and Kibana components, and setting up data pipelines to ingest, process, and visualize log data effectively.

Machine learning and artificial intelligence techniques are increasingly being utilized in log analysis to automate anomaly detection, pattern recognition, and predictive analytics. Supervised and unsupervised machine learning algorithms can be trained on historical log data to identify abnormal behavior, detect security threats, and predict future trends. Platforms like Splunk and IBM QRadar leverage machine learning capabilities to analyze log data at scale and provide actionable insights into system health and security posture. Deploying machine learning-based log analysis involves training machine learning models on labeled datasets, evaluating model performance, and integrating them into log analysis workflows for automated anomaly detection and prediction.

Log correlation techniques involve correlating events and log entries from multiple sources to identify relationships, patterns, and dependencies between different systems and applications. Correlation rules and algorithms can be applied to log data to detect security incidents, performance bottlenecks, and operational issues. Security Information and Event Management (SIEM) solutions like Splunk Enterprise Security and ArcSight utilize correlation engines to analyze log data in real-time and generate alerts for suspicious activities or policy violations. Deploying log correlation techniques involves defining correlation rules, configuring correlation engines, and fine-tuning alert thresholds to minimize false positives and false negatives.

Log visualization techniques play a crucial role in presenting log data in a meaningful and intuitive manner to facilitate analysis and decision-making. Data visualization tools like Grafana, Kibana, and Tableau enable organizations to create interactive dashboards, charts, and graphs to visualize log data trends, anomalies, and patterns. By visualizing log data, organizations can identify performance trends, troubleshoot issues, and communicate insights effectively across teams. Deploying log visualization techniques involves connecting data sources to visualization platforms, designing dashboards, and configuring data visualizations to represent log data effectively.

Forensic analysis techniques are used to investigate security incidents, data breaches, and system compromises by analyzing log data to reconstruct events and identify root causes. Forensic analysis tools like Volatility, The Sleuth Kit, and Autopsy enable forensic investigators to extract, analyze, and interpret log data to uncover evidence and establish timelines of events. By examining log entries, file metadata, and system artifacts, forensic analysts can piece together the sequence of events leading up to a security incident and attribute actions to specific users or attackers. Deploying forensic analysis techniques involves collecting and preserving log data in a forensically sound manner, analyzing log files using forensic tools, and documenting findings for legal or investigative purposes.

Real-time log monitoring techniques involve continuously monitoring log data streams for critical events, errors, or anomalies to enable proactive alerting and response. Log monitoring tools like Nagios Log Server, Graylog, and Splunk Real-time Monitoring enable organizations to monitor log data in real-time, set up alerts for specific conditions, and take automated actions based on predefined thresholds. By monitoring log data in real-time, organizations can detect and respond to security incidents, system failures, and performance issues promptly. Deploying real-time log monitoring techniques involves configuring log monitoring agents or collectors, defining alert rules, and setting up notification channels to receive alerts and notifications in real-time.

In summary, log analysis techniques are indispensable for organizations seeking to gain insights into system behavior, enhance security, and optimize performance in today's complex computing environments. Whether parsing log files with command-line tools, aggregating log data with centralized platforms like the ELK stack, or leveraging machine learning for anomaly detection, log analysis enables organizations to derive actionable insights from vast amounts of log data. By deploying a combination of parsing, aggregation, correlation, visualization, forensic analysis, and real-time monitoring techniques, organizations can effectively harness the power of log data to improve operational efficiency, enhance security posture, and drive informed decision-making.

Error message deciphering methods are essential skills for IT professionals and developers, enabling them to diagnose and resolve issues effectively in software systems. In the dynamic landscape of technology, where software complexity continues to grow, understanding error messages is crucial for troubleshooting problems, identifying root causes, and implementing corrective actions. These methods encompass a variety of techniques, tools, and approaches designed to interpret error messages, extract meaningful information, and provide insights into the underlying issues. Deploying error message deciphering methods empowers individuals and teams to overcome challenges, minimize downtime, and ensure the reliability and performance of software applications.

One of the fundamental techniques in error message deciphering is understanding the structure and format of error messages issued by software systems. Error messages typically consist of descriptive text, error codes, and contextual information that provide clues about the nature and cause of the problem. By analyzing the content and syntax of error messages, IT professionals can gain insights into the underlying issues and take appropriate actions to resolve them. For example, parsing error messages with command-line tools like grep, awk, or sed can help extract relevant information and identify patterns or keywords indicative of specific error conditions.

Error code lookup tools and databases are invaluable resources for deciphering error messages and understanding their meanings and implications. Platforms like Microsoft's MSDN, Linux Error Codes, and ErrorDecoder provide comprehensive databases of error codes and their corresponding explanations, causes, and resolutions. By searching error codes or error messages in these databases, IT professionals can quickly find relevant information and guidance on troubleshooting steps and potential solutions. Deploying error code lookup tools involves querying the database with the error code or error message using the search functionality provided by the platform, such as entering the error code "404" to retrieve information about the "Not Found" error in HTTP protocols.

Contextual analysis of error messages involves examining the surrounding circumstances, events, and system configurations to understand the context in which errors occur. By correlating error messages with system logs, event traces, and user actions, IT professionals can identify patterns, dependencies, and contributing factors leading to error conditions. Tools like log aggregation platforms (e.g., ELK stack) enable organizations to centralize and analyze log data from various sources to gain insights into system behavior and error patterns. Deploying contextual analysis techniques involves collecting and aggregating log data, correlating error messages with relevant events, and analyzing system configurations to identify potential causes and mitigating factors.

Troubleshooting error messages often involves replicating the error condition in a controlled environment to isolate and diagnose the problem effectively. By recreating the steps or conditions leading to the error, IT professionals can observe the behavior of the system, reproduce the error message, and identify factors contributing to the issue. Tools like virtualization platforms (e.g., VMware, VirtualBox) enable organizations to create isolated test environments for replicating software configurations and testing error scenarios. Deploying error replication techniques involves setting up a test environment with similar configurations to the production environment, executing the steps or actions leading to the error, and observing the behavior of the system to reproduce the error condition.

Error message debugging techniques involve using debugging tools and techniques to trace the execution flow of software applications and identify the origins of error messages. Debuggers like GDB (GNU Debugger) for C/C++ programs or pdb for Python enable developers to step through code, inspect variables, and analyze program state during runtime. By setting breakpoints, stepping through code, and examining stack traces and variable values, developers can pinpoint the location and cause of errors in their applications. Deploying error debugging techniques involves attaching a debugger to the software application, setting breakpoints at relevant locations, and analyzing program execution to identify the source of error messages.

Another approach to deciphering error messages is conducting online research and leveraging community forums, knowledge bases, and discussion groups for guidance and insights. Platforms like Stack Overflow, Reddit, and Quora provide forums where developers and IT professionals can ask questions, share experiences, and seek assistance with error messages and troubleshooting challenges. By searching for error messages or specific symptoms, individuals can find relevant discussions, articles, and solutions contributed by the community. Deploying online research techniques involves querying search engines with error messages or keywords, reviewing relevant articles and forum discussions, and applying insights and recommendations to resolve the issue.

Collaborative problem-solving techniques involve seeking assistance from colleagues, peers, or subject matter experts to brainstorm solutions and troubleshoot error messages collaboratively. Team collaboration platforms like Slack, Microsoft Teams, and Jira facilitate communication and collaboration among team members, allowing them to share insights, exchange ideas, and coordinate efforts to address issues. By leveraging the collective expertise and perspectives of team members, organizations can accelerate problem resolution and foster knowledge sharing and collaboration. Deploying collaborative problem-solving techniques involves creating a dedicated channel or forum for discussing the error message, sharing relevant information and insights, and soliciting input and feedback from team members.

In summary, error message deciphering methods are essential skills for IT professionals and developers tasked with troubleshooting issues and maintaining the reliability of software systems. Whether parsing error messages, looking up error codes, analyzing system logs, replicating error conditions, debugging code, conducting online research, or collaborating with colleagues, these methods enable individuals and teams to identify, diagnose, and resolve errors effectively. By deploying a combination of techniques and leveraging tools, resources, and expertise, organizations can overcome challenges, minimize downtime, and ensure the continued performance and stability of their software applications.

Chapter 5: Remote Troubleshooting Methods

Remote desktop tools and techniques are indispensable for facilitating remote access, collaboration, and support in modern computing environments. In today's interconnected world, where remote work and telecommuting are becoming increasingly prevalent, remote desktop solutions play a pivotal role in enabling users to access and control computers and devices from anywhere, at any time. These tools encompass a variety of software applications, protocols, and technologies designed to provide remote access to desktops, servers, and virtual machines. Deploying remote desktop tools and techniques empowers individuals and organizations to enhance productivity, streamline IT support, and facilitate seamless collaboration across geographically dispersed teams.

One of the most widely used remote desktop protocols is Remote Desktop Protocol (RDP), developed by Microsoft, which enables users to remotely access and control Windows-based computers over a network. To initiate an RDP session from a Windows-based client to a remote host, users can use the Remote Desktop Connection application, accessible via the Start menu or by running the "mstsc" command in the Run dialog box. Upon launching the Remote Desktop Connection application, users enter the hostname or IP address of the remote computer, along with their credentials, to establish a secure connection. Once connected, users can interact with the remote desktop as if they were physically present at the machine, accessing files, running applications, and performing administrative tasks.

Another popular remote desktop protocol is Virtual Network Computing (VNC), which provides cross-platform remote access to graphical desktop environments. VNC servers, such as TightVNC, RealVNC, and UltraVNC, run on remote computers and allow users to access the desktop remotely using VNC client software installed on their local machines. To connect to a remote desktop using VNC, users launch the VNC client application and enter the hostname or IP address of the remote computer, along with any authentication credentials required. Once connected, users can view and interact with the remote desktop in real-time, controlling mouse and keyboard input and viewing the screen output.

SSH (Secure Shell) is another powerful remote access tool widely used in Unix and Linux environments for secure command-line access to remote systems. While SSH is primarily used for command-line access, it also supports X11 forwarding, allowing users to run graphical applications remotely and display them on their local desktops. To establish an SSH session to a remote server, users can run the "ssh" command followed by the hostname or IP address of the remote server, along with their username, such as "ssh username@hostname". Once authenticated, users can run commands, transfer files, and tunnel other protocols securely over the SSH connection. For X11 forwarding, users can enable the "-X" or "-Y" option when establishing the SSH session to enable X11 forwarding, allowing remote display of graphical applications.

Remote desktop software solutions, such as TeamViewer, AnyDesk, and Splashtop, provide comprehensive remote access capabilities for desktops, servers, and mobile devices across platforms. These software applications offer features such as screen sharing, file transfer, remote printing, and remote reboot, making them ideal for remote support, collaboration, and troubleshooting. To initiate a remote desktop session using TeamViewer, users launch the TeamViewer application and enter the partner's ID or hostname provided by the remote user, along with any required authentication credentials. Once connected, users can view and control the remote desktop in real-time, collaborate on tasks, and provide remote assistance as needed.

Remote desktop virtualization technologies, such as Citrix Virtual Apps and Desktops (formerly XenDesktop/XenApp) and VMware Horizon, enable organizations to deliver virtual desktops and applications to users across distributed environments. These solutions centralize desktop and application delivery, providing users with secure, consistent access to their desktop environments from any device, anywhere. To access a virtual desktop or application using Citrix Virtual Apps and Desktops, users launch the Citrix Workspace application or web portal and log in with their credentials. Once authenticated, users can access their assigned virtual desktop or applications, which are hosted and managed centrally by the virtualization infrastructure.

Web-based remote desktop solutions, such as Microsoft Remote Desktop Web Access (RD Web Access) and Guacamole, provide browser-based access to remote desktops and applications without requiring client-side software installation. These solutions leverage web technologies like HTML5 and WebSocket to deliver remote access capabilities directly within a web browser, making them accessible from any device with an internet connection. To access a remote desktop or application using RD Web Access, users navigate to the RD Web Access portal URL in their web browser and log in with their credentials. Once authenticated, users can launch remote desktop sessions or access published applications directly from the web portal interface.

Remote desktop access control techniques involve implementing security measures and access controls to protect remote desktops and systems from unauthorized access and malicious activity. Techniques such as network segmentation, firewall rules, VPN (Virtual Private Network) access, multi-factor authentication (MFA), and role-based access control (RBAC) help organizations enforce security policies and mitigate risks associated with remote access. Deploying access control techniques involves configuring network devices, firewalls, VPN gateways, and authentication systems to restrict access to remote desktops and systems based on user identity, device posture, and security posture.

In summary, remote desktop tools and techniques play a vital role in enabling remote access, collaboration, and support in today's interconnected world. Whether using protocols like RDP, VNC, and SSH for remote command-line access, or leveraging remote desktop software solutions and virtualization technologies for desktop and application delivery, these tools empower organizations to enhance productivity, streamline IT support, and facilitate seamless collaboration across distributed teams. By deploying a combination of remote desktop tools, protocols, and access control techniques, organizations can ensure secure, reliable, and efficient remote access to desktops, servers, and applications, enabling users to work from anywhere, at any time.

Troubleshooting remote access issues is a critical skill for IT professionals and system administrators tasked with maintaining the accessibility and reliability of remote systems and services. In today's interconnected world, where remote work and telecommuting have become prevalent, ensuring seamless remote access to networks, applications, and data is essential for business continuity and productivity. Remote access issues can manifest in various forms, including connectivity problems, authentication failures, performance issues, and security concerns. Deploying effective troubleshooting techniques enables IT professionals to identify, diagnose, and resolve remote access issues promptly, minimizing downtime and ensuring uninterrupted access for remote users.

One of the first steps in troubleshooting remote access issues is to verify network connectivity between the remote client and the target system or service. The ping command is a useful tool for testing network connectivity by sending ICMP (Internet Control Message Protocol) echo requests to the target host and waiting for a response. To perform a basic connectivity test using the ping command, users can open a command prompt or terminal window and run the command "ping hostname" or "ping IP_address", where "hostname" is the hostname or domain name of the target system and "IP_address" is its IP address. If the ping command returns successful responses, it indicates that there is network connectivity between the client and the target system. However, if the ping command fails to receive responses, it suggests a network connectivity issue that needs to be investigated further.

Once network connectivity has been confirmed, the next step is to troubleshoot authentication issues that may prevent remote users from accessing the target system or service. Authentication failures can occur due to incorrect credentials, expired passwords, misconfigured authentication settings, or account lockout policies. To diagnose authentication issues, IT professionals can review authentication logs on both the client and server sides to identify error messages or events indicating authentication failures. In Windows environments, the Event Viewer application provides access to authentication logs, while in Unix/Linux environments, authentication logs are typically stored in files like /var/log/auth.log or /var/log/secure. By examining authentication logs, IT professionals can determine the cause of authentication failures and take appropriate corrective actions, such as resetting passwords, updating authentication settings, or unlocking user accounts. Performance issues are another common type of remote access problem that can affect the user experience and productivity of remote workers. Performance issues may manifest as slow response times, high latency, or intermittent connectivity problems when accessing remote systems or applications. To troubleshoot performance issues, IT professionals can use network monitoring tools to analyze network traffic, identify bottlenecks, and measure network performance metrics like latency, packet loss, and throughput. Tools like Wireshark, tcpdump, or PerfMon (on Windows) can capture and analyze network traffic to identify performance issues and anomalies. By analyzing network performance metrics, IT professionals can pinpoint the root cause of performance problems and implement optimization strategies such as network bandwidth upgrades, traffic prioritization, or Quality of Service (QoS) policies to improve remote access performance.

Security concerns are another important aspect of troubleshooting remote access issues, as unauthorized access or compromised credentials can pose significant risks to the confidentiality, integrity, and availability of remote systems and data. Security issues may arise from weak authentication mechanisms, unsecured network connections, or vulnerabilities in remote access protocols and services. To address security concerns, IT professionals can conduct security assessments and audits to identify security vulnerabilities and compliance gaps in remote access infrastructure. Vulnerability scanning tools like Nessus, OpenVAS, or Qualys can scan remote systems and networks for security vulnerabilities and misconfigurations. By remediating identified vulnerabilities and implementing security best practices such as strong authentication, encryption, and access controls, IT professionals can mitigate security risks and enhance the security posture of remote access infrastructure.

Firewall and routing issues can also cause remote access problems by blocking or restricting network traffic between remote clients and target systems or services. Firewalls, routers, and network access control devices may inadvertently block or filter traffic, leading to connectivity issues for remote users. To troubleshoot firewall and routing issues, IT professionals can inspect firewall and routing configuration settings to ensure that they permit traffic to and from remote clients and target systems. Command-line tools like iptables (on Linux) or netsh (on Windows) can display firewall rules and configuration settings. By reviewing firewall logs and analyzing packet flow, IT professionals can identify and resolve firewall and routing issues that may be impacting remote access.

DNS (Domain Name System) resolution issues can also contribute to remote access problems by preventing remote clients from resolving hostnames or domain names to IP addresses. DNS resolution issues may occur due to misconfigured DNS servers, DNS cache poisoning, or DNS server unavailability. To troubleshoot DNS resolution issues, IT professionals can use command-line tools like nslookup or dig to query DNS servers and verify hostname resolution. For example, running the command "nslookup hostname" or "dig hostname" can query DNS servers to resolve the hostname to its corresponding IP address. By verifying DNS configuration settings, checking DNS server availability, and troubleshooting DNS resolution errors, IT professionals can resolve DNS-related remote access issues and ensure proper hostname resolution for remote clients.

In summary, troubleshooting remote access issues requires a systematic approach and a combination of techniques to identify, diagnose, and resolve problems effectively. By verifying network connectivity, diagnosing authentication issues, analyzing network performance, addressing security concerns, troubleshooting firewall and routing issues, and resolving DNS resolution problems, IT professionals can overcome remote access challenges and ensure seamless access to remote systems and services for users. By deploying robust remote access infrastructure, implementing security best practices, and proactively monitoring and maintaining remote access systems, organizations can enhance productivity, enable remote work flexibility, and support business continuity in today's interconnected world.

Chapter 6: Automation for Efficient Troubleshooting

Scripting and task automation are indispensable techniques for streamlining repetitive tasks, increasing productivity, and improving efficiency in IT operations and software development. In today's fast-paced and dynamic environment, where organizations face growing demands for agility and scalability, scripting and automation play a crucial role in automating routine tasks, reducing manual effort, and accelerating the delivery of products and services. These techniques encompass a variety of scripting languages, frameworks, and tools designed to automate tasks ranging from system administration and configuration management to software deployment and testing. Deploying scripting and task automation techniques empowers IT professionals and developers to automate complex workflows, standardize processes, and achieve operational excellence.

One of the most widely used scripting languages for task automation is Python, renowned for its simplicity, versatility, and readability. Python's rich standard library and extensive ecosystem of third-party packages make it well-suited for automating a wide range of tasks, from file manipulation and system administration to web scraping and data analysis. To create and execute Python scripts, users can use a text editor or Integrated Development Environment (IDE) to write Python code and save it with a ".py" extension. Once saved, Python scripts can be executed from the command line using the "python" command followed by the script filename, such as "python script.py" to run the script named "script.py".

Bash (Bourne Again Shell) scripting is another powerful tool for task automation, particularly in Unix and Linux environments. Bash scripts enable users to automate system administration tasks, file management operations, and process automation using shell commands and utilities. To create a Bash script, users can use a text editor like Vim or Nano to write shell commands and save the script with a ".sh" extension. Once saved, Bash scripts can be executed from the command line using the "bash" command followed by the script filename, such as "bash script.sh" to run the script named "script.sh".

PowerShell is a scripting language developed by Microsoft for task automation and configuration management in Windows environments. PowerShell provides powerful scripting capabilities and tight integration with the Windows operating system, allowing users to automate administrative tasks, manage system configurations, and interact with Windows services and components. To create and execute PowerShell scripts, users can use the PowerShell Integrated Scripting Environment (ISE) or a text editor to write PowerShell code and save it with a ".ps1" extension. Once saved, PowerShell scripts can be executed from the PowerShell console or command prompt using the "&" (call operator) followed by the script filename, such as "& script.ps1" to run the script named "script.ps1".

Task scheduling and automation tools, such as cron (on Unix/Linux) and Task Scheduler (on Windows), enable users to automate the execution of scripts and commands at predefined intervals or specified times. Cron is a Unix/Linux utility for scheduling recurring tasks and automation jobs using cron jobs, which are defined in cron configuration files called "crontabs". To schedule a task using cron, users can use the "crontab" command to edit their crontab file and define the schedule and command to be executed. For example, to run a Python script named "script.py" every day at 3:00 AM, users can add the following line to their crontab file: "0 3 * * * python /path/to/script.py".

Task Scheduler is a built-in Windows utility for scheduling tasks and automation jobs on Windows-based systems. Users can use Task Scheduler to create and manage scheduled tasks that execute programs, scripts, or commands at specified times or intervals. To create a scheduled task using Task Scheduler, users can open the Task Scheduler application, create a new task, and configure the task settings, including the trigger (e.g., time-based or event-based) and action (e.g., running a program or script). For example, users can create a new task to run a PowerShell script named "script.ps1" daily at 3:00 AM.

Configuration management tools, such as Ansible, Puppet, and Chef, provide powerful automation capabilities for managing and configuring infrastructure resources across distributed environments. These tools enable users to define infrastructure configurations as code and automate the deployment and management of servers, networking devices, and cloud resources. Ansible, for example, uses YAML (YAML Ain't Markup Language) to define infrastructure configurations in human-readable format and SSH (Secure Shell) to execute tasks on remote hosts. To deploy configurations with Ansible, users can write YAML playbooks that specify tasks and configurations and execute them using the "ansible-playbook" command, such as "ansible-playbook site.yml" to apply configurations defined in the "site.yml" playbook.

Continuous Integration (CI) and Continuous Deployment (CD) pipelines automate the process of building, testing, and deploying software changes, enabling organizations to deliver software updates rapidly and reliably. CI/CD pipelines integrate with version control systems like Git and automate tasks such as code compilation, testing, and deployment using tools like Jenkins, GitLab CI/CD, and CircleCI. To deploy applications using Jenkins, for example, users can configure pipeline scripts or YAML files that define build, test, and deployment stages and execute them using the Jenkins interface or command-line interface.

Container orchestration platforms, such as Kubernetes and Docker Swarm, automate the deployment, scaling, and management of containerized applications in production environments. These platforms enable organizations to orchestrate containerized workloads across clusters of servers and ensure high availability and scalability of applications. To deploy applications to a Kubernetes cluster, users can create deployment manifests or YAML files that specify container configurations and apply these manifests using the "kubectl apply" command, such as "kubectl apply -f deployment.yaml" to deploy applications.

In summary, scripting and task automation are essential techniques for automating repetitive tasks, increasing efficiency, and improving productivity in IT operations and software development. Whether using scripting languages like Python, Bash, or PowerShell, task scheduling tools like cron and Task Scheduler, configuration management tools like Ansible and Puppet, or CI/CD pipelines and container orchestration platforms, organizations can leverage automation to streamline workflows, standardize processes, and accelerate the delivery of products and services. By deploying scripting and automation techniques effectively, IT professionals and developers can focus on high-value tasks, minimize manual effort, and drive innovation and growth in today's fast-paced and competitive business environment.

Implementing automated monitoring systems is essential for ensuring the reliability, performance, and security of IT infrastructure and applications. In today's digital landscape, where organizations rely heavily on technology to support their operations and deliver services, proactive monitoring is critical for detecting issues, identifying trends, and preventing potential disruptions. Automated monitoring systems leverage a combination of monitoring tools, agents, and sensors to collect, analyze, and visualize data from various sources, including servers, networks, applications, and databases. Deploying automated monitoring systems enables organizations to gain real-time insights into the health and performance of their IT environment, enabling them to respond promptly to issues and optimize resource utilization.

One of the key components of automated monitoring systems is monitoring agents, which are lightweight software components installed on target systems to collect and transmit monitoring data to centralized monitoring servers or platforms. Monitoring agents are responsible for gathering performance metrics, log data, and system information from the underlying infrastructure and transmitting it to the monitoring server for analysis. To deploy monitoring agents, organizations can use package management tools like apt, yum, or Chocolatey to install agent software on target systems. For example, to install the Prometheus Node Exporter agent on a Linux system using apt, users can run the command "sudo apt install prometheus-node-exporter".

Centralized monitoring servers or platforms serve as the core infrastructure for collecting, storing, and analyzing monitoring data from distributed systems and applications. These servers provide a centralized interface for managing monitoring configurations, viewing real-time metrics, and generating alerts and reports. Popular monitoring platforms include Prometheus, Grafana, Nagios, Zabbix, and Splunk, each offering unique features and capabilities for monitoring different aspects of IT infrastructure. To deploy a monitoring platform like Prometheus and Grafana, users can use containerization tools like Docker or Kubernetes to run containerized instances of the monitoring software. For example, users can create a Docker-compose file that defines services for Prometheus and Grafana and use the "docker-compose up" command to deploy the monitoring stack.

Once monitoring agents are deployed and centralized monitoring servers or platforms are set up, organizations can configure monitoring checks and alerts to monitor key performance indicators (KPIs), metrics, and thresholds relevant to their infrastructure and applications. Monitoring checks can include system resource utilization (e.g., CPU, memory, disk), network traffic, application response times, error rates, and security events. Alerts can be configured to trigger notifications via email, SMS, or integration with collaboration platforms like Slack or Microsoft Teams when predefined thresholds are exceeded or anomalies are detected. To configure monitoring checks and alerts in Prometheus, users can define alerting rules in Prometheus configuration files (prometheus.yml) and configure alert notification settings using the Alertmanager component. For example, users can define a rule to alert when CPU usage exceeds a certain threshold and specify notification recipients and channels for alert notifications.

In addition to basic monitoring checks and alerts, organizations can implement advanced monitoring techniques such as anomaly detection, predictive analytics, and machine learning-based monitoring to proactively identify and mitigate issues before they impact operations. Anomaly detection algorithms analyze historical monitoring data to identify patterns and deviations from normal behavior, enabling organizations to detect abnormal trends or behaviors indicative of potential problems. Predictive analytics techniques use statistical models and machine learning algorithms to forecast future trends and predict potential issues based on historical data and current conditions. Machine learning-based monitoring solutions, such as Amazon CloudWatch anomaly detection, use machine learning models to analyze telemetry data and identify anomalies in real-time. To implement anomaly detection and predictive analytics, organizations can leverage specialized monitoring tools and platforms that offer built-in support for these techniques or develop custom solutions using machine learning frameworks like TensorFlow or PyTorch.

Automated remediation and self-healing capabilities are another advanced feature of automated monitoring systems, enabling organizations to automate the resolution of common issues and reduce manual intervention. Remediation actions can include restarting services, scaling resources, adjusting configurations, or triggering automated workflows to resolve detected problems automatically. For example, in a Kubernetes cluster, organizations can implement auto-scaling policies to dynamically adjust the number of pods based on resource utilization metrics monitored by Kubernetes Horizontal Pod Autoscaler (HPA). Similarly, in cloud environments, organizations can use Infrastructure as Code (IaC) tools like Terraform or AWS CloudFormation to automatically provision and configure resources based on predefined templates and policies.

Continuous monitoring and feedback loops are essential for maintaining the effectiveness and relevance of automated monitoring systems over time. Organizations should regularly review monitoring configurations, thresholds, and alerts to ensure they align with changing business requirements and evolving technology landscapes.

Additionally, organizations should collect feedback from users, operators, and stakeholders to identify areas for improvement and optimize monitoring processes and workflows. Continuous monitoring and feedback loops enable organizations to adapt and refine their monitoring strategies, ensuring they remain effective in detecting and responding to emerging threats and challenges.

In summary, implementing automated monitoring systems is crucial for organizations seeking to maintain the reliability, performance, and security of their IT infrastructure and applications. By deploying monitoring agents, centralized monitoring servers or platforms, and configuring monitoring checks, alerts, and remediation actions, organizations can gain real-time insights into the health and performance of their IT environment and respond promptly to issues. Advanced monitoring techniques such as anomaly detection, predictive analytics, and automated remediation enable organizations to proactively identify and mitigate issues before they impact operations, while continuous monitoring and feedback loops ensure the effectiveness and relevance of monitoring strategies over time. By embracing automated monitoring systems, organizations can optimize resource utilization, enhance operational efficiency, and deliver seamless experiences to users and customers.

Chapter 7: Managing Software Updates and Patching

Patch management strategies are essential for maintaining the security, stability, and performance of IT systems and applications. In today's interconnected world, where cyber threats are constantly evolving, keeping systems up-to-date with the latest security patches and software updates is crucial for mitigating vulnerabilities and protecting against potential security breaches. Patch management encompasses a set of processes, policies, and tools designed to identify, deploy, and manage software patches and updates across an organization's IT infrastructure. Deploying effective patch management strategies enables organizations to minimize security risks, ensure compliance with regulatory requirements, and maintain operational continuity.

One of the key components of patch management strategies is vulnerability assessment, which involves identifying security vulnerabilities and weaknesses in IT systems and applications. Vulnerability scanning tools, such as Nessus, OpenVAS, and Qualys, enable organizations to scan their infrastructure for known vulnerabilities and assess the overall security posture. To conduct a vulnerability scan using Nessus, for example, users can run the "nessus" command followed by the IP address or hostname of the target system, such as "nessus -scan 192.168.1.1". The vulnerability scanner then scans the target system for known vulnerabilities and generates a report detailing the findings, including severity ratings and recommended remediation actions.

Patch prioritization is another critical aspect of patch management strategies, as organizations often face limited resources and need to prioritize patch deployment based on risk and impact. Patch prioritization involves assessing the severity, exploitability, and potential impact of vulnerabilities and prioritizing patches accordingly. Vulnerability management platforms like Tenable.io or Qualys Vulnerability Management provide risk-based prioritization features that help organizations prioritize patches based on factors such as severity ratings, exploitability, and asset criticality. To prioritize patches using Tenable.io, for example, users can view vulnerability dashboards and reports that highlight high-risk vulnerabilities and prioritize remediation efforts accordingly.

Patch testing is an essential step in the patch management process, as deploying untested patches can potentially introduce new issues or disrupt existing systems and applications. Before deploying patches to production environments, organizations should conduct thorough testing in a controlled environment to ensure compatibility and stability. Patch testing involves deploying patches to a test environment that mirrors the production environment and evaluating their impact on system performance, functionality, and interoperability. Configuration management tools like Ansible or Puppet can automate patch deployment and testing processes, enabling organizations to streamline testing workflows and ensure consistent testing practices across environments.

Once patches have been tested and validated, organizations can proceed with patch deployment to production environments. Patch deployment involves distributing and applying patches to target systems and applications while minimizing disruption to operations. Configuration management tools like Ansible, Puppet, or Chef provide automation capabilities for patch deployment, allowing organizations to automate the rollout of patches across distributed environments. For example, organizations can use Ansible playbooks or Puppet manifests to define patching tasks and configurations and execute them across fleets of servers or endpoints. By automating patch deployment, organizations can accelerate the patching process, reduce human error, and ensure consistent patching practices across environments.

Patch tracking and reporting are essential for maintaining visibility and accountability throughout the patch management lifecycle. Organizations should track patch deployment status, monitor compliance with patching policies, and generate reports to document patching activities and outcomes. Patch management platforms like SolarWinds Patch Manager or ManageEngine Patch Manager Plus provide centralized dashboards and reporting features that enable organizations to track patching progress, monitor patch compliance, and generate audit-ready reports. To track patch deployment using SolarWinds Patch Manager, for example, users can view patch status reports and deployment summaries that provide insights into patching activities and compliance levels.

Regular patch management audits and reviews are essential for evaluating the effectiveness of patch management strategies and identifying areas for improvement. Organizations should conduct periodic audits to assess patching practices, identify gaps or deficiencies, and implement corrective actions as needed. Patch management audits can include reviewing patching policies and procedures, analyzing patching metrics and trends, and conducting vulnerability assessments to identify unpatched systems or critical vulnerabilities. By conducting regular audits and reviews, organizations can ensure compliance with patching policies, enhance patching effectiveness, and mitigate security risks effectively.

In summary, patch management strategies are critical for maintaining the security, stability, and performance of IT systems and applications. By implementing comprehensive patch management processes, organizations can identify, deploy, and manage software patches and updates efficiently, reducing security risks, ensuring compliance with regulatory requirements, and maintaining operational continuity. Key components of patch management strategies include vulnerability assessment, patch prioritization, patch testing, patch deployment automation, patch tracking and reporting, and regular audits and reviews. By deploying effective patch management strategies, organizations can proactively address security vulnerabilities, minimize downtime, and safeguard against potential security breaches.

Risk assessment in patch deployment is a crucial aspect of maintaining the security and stability of IT systems and applications. In today's dynamic threat landscape, where cyber threats continue to evolve and exploit vulnerabilities, organizations must assess the risks associated with deploying patches to mitigate potential adverse impacts on system functionality, performance, and security. Risk assessment involves evaluating the potential risks and benefits of applying patches, weighing the likelihood of adverse outcomes against the potential benefits of patching, and making informed decisions based on risk analysis. Deploying patches without conducting a thorough risk assessment can lead to unintended consequences, including system downtime, application compatibility issues, and security breaches.
One of the primary considerations in risk assessment is understanding the impact of applying patches on system functionality and performance. Patching can introduce

changes to system configurations, libraries, and dependencies that may impact the behavior and performance of applications and services. Organizations should assess the potential impact of patches on critical systems and applications to determine the level of risk associated with patch deployment. This assessment may involve reviewing patch release notes, testing patches in a controlled environment, and evaluating the compatibility of patches with existing software and configurations.

To assess the impact of patches on system functionality and performance, organizations can conduct testing and validation exercises to simulate patch deployment in a controlled environment. Configuration management tools like Ansible, Puppet, or Chef can automate the process of deploying patches to test environments, enabling organizations to evaluate the impact of patches on system behavior and performance. For example, organizations can use Ansible playbooks or Puppet manifests to deploy patches to a test environment that mirrors the production environment and monitor the effects of patch deployment on system performance and application behavior.

Another critical aspect of risk assessment in patch deployment is evaluating the security risks associated with unpatched vulnerabilities. Vulnerability management tools like Nessus, OpenVAS, or Qualys enable organizations to scan their infrastructure for known vulnerabilities and assess the severity and exploitability of vulnerabilities. To conduct a vulnerability scan using Nessus, for example, users can run the "nessus" command followed by the IP address or hostname of the target system, such as "nessus -scan 192.168.1.1". The vulnerability scanner then scans the target system for known vulnerabilities and generates a report detailing the findings, including severity ratings and recommended remediation actions.

Based on the results of vulnerability scans and risk assessments, organizations can prioritize patches based on the severity and exploitability of vulnerabilities. Patch prioritization involves categorizing patches into critical, high, medium, and low severity categories based on the potential impact of vulnerabilities on system security. Vulnerability management platforms like Tenable.io or Qualys Vulnerability Management provide risk-based prioritization features that help organizations prioritize patches based on factors such as severity ratings, exploitability, and asset criticality. To prioritize patches using Tenable.io, for example, users can view vulnerability dashboards and reports that highlight high-risk vulnerabilities and prioritize remediation efforts accordingly.

Risk assessment in patch deployment also involves evaluating the potential risks of applying patches versus the risks of leaving systems unpatched. While patching is essential for addressing security vulnerabilities and mitigating risks, deploying patches can introduce new issues or disrupt existing systems and applications. Organizations must weigh the potential benefits of patching, such as improved security and reduced risk of exploitation, against the potential risks, such as system downtime, application compatibility issues, and unintended consequences. This evaluation should consider factors such as the criticality of systems and applications, the availability of mitigating controls, and the likelihood of exploitation.

To mitigate the risks associated with patch deployment, organizations can implement risk mitigation strategies such as phased deployment, rollback procedures, and backup and recovery plans. Phased deployment involves deploying patches to a subset of systems or users initially and gradually expanding deployment based on feedback and monitoring. This approach allows organizations to identify and address issues in a controlled manner, minimizing the impact on operations. Rollback procedures enable organizations to revert to previous configurations or versions in the event of issues or adverse outcomes resulting from patch deployment. Backup and recovery plans ensure that organizations can restore systems and applications to a known good state in the event of data loss or corruption resulting from patch deployment.

Continuous monitoring and feedback are essential for assessing the effectiveness of patch deployment and identifying emerging risks and issues. Organizations should monitor patch deployment status, track system performance and security metrics, and collect feedback from users and stakeholders to evaluate the impact of patches and identify areas for improvement. Continuous monitoring enables organizations to detect and respond to issues promptly, optimize patching processes, and ensure compliance with patching policies and procedures.

In summary, risk assessment is a critical aspect of patch deployment that enables organizations to evaluate the potential risks and benefits of applying patches and make informed decisions based on risk analysis. By assessing the impact of patches on system functionality and performance, evaluating the security risks associated with unpatched vulnerabilities, prioritizing patches based on severity and exploitability, and weighing the risks of patching versus leaving systems unpatched, organizations can mitigate the risks associated with patch deployment effectively. By implementing risk mitigation strategies, such as phased deployment, rollback procedures, and backup and recovery plans, and continuously monitoring and evaluating patching processes, organizations can maintain the security, stability, and performance of their IT systems and applications.

Chapter 8: Data Backup and Recovery Strategies

Backup types and rotation schedules are fundamental aspects of data protection and disaster recovery strategies, crucial for ensuring the resilience and availability of critical information in the event of data loss or system failure. Organizations employ various backup types and rotation schedules to balance data retention requirements, storage efficiency, and recovery objectives. Backup types encompass full backups, incremental backups, and differential backups, each offering unique advantages and trade-offs in terms of backup speed, storage space requirements, and recovery granularity. Rotation schedules dictate the frequency and timing of backups, determining how often backups are created, retained, and rotated to ensure data integrity and compliance with retention policies.

Full backups are comprehensive copies of entire data sets, capturing all files, folders, and system configurations at a specific point in time. Full backups provide complete data protection and enable fast and straightforward restores, making them ideal for disaster recovery scenarios. To create a full backup using a command-line interface, organizations can use backup utilities like rsync, tar, or Windows Backup (wbadmin) to copy all files and directories to a backup destination. For example, to create a full backup of a directory named "data" using rsync, users can run the command "rsync -av /path/to/source /path/to/destination".

Incremental backups capture only the changes made since the last backup, reducing backup time and storage space requirements compared to full backups. Incremental backups store only the data that has changed since the last backup, enabling organizations to optimize backup storage and network bandwidth usage. To create an incremental backup using a command-line interface, organizations can use backup utilities like rsync or tar with the appropriate flags to perform incremental backups. For example, to perform an incremental backup of a directory named "data" using rsync, users can run the command "rsync -av --backup --backup-dir=/path/to/incremental /path/to/source /path/to/destination".

Differential backups capture changes made since the last full backup, providing a balance between backup speed and storage efficiency compared to full and incremental backups. Differential backups store all changes made since the last full backup, enabling organizations to reduce backup time and storage space requirements compared to full backups while maintaining faster restore times compared to incremental backups. To create a differential backup using a command-line interface, organizations can use backup utilities like rsync or tar with the appropriate flags to perform differential backups. For example, to perform a differential backup of a directory named "data" using rsync, users can run the command "rsync -av --backup --backup-dir=/path/to/differential /path/to/source /path/to/destination".

Rotation schedules dictate how often backups are created, retained, and rotated to ensure data integrity, compliance with retention policies, and efficient use of storage resources. Common rotation schedules include daily, weekly, monthly, and yearly backups, each defining the frequency and timing of backup creation and retention periods. Daily backups capture changes made within a single day and are typically retained for a short period, such as one week, to provide recent recovery points for fast restores. Weekly backups capture changes made within a week and are retained for a longer period, such as one month, to provide recovery points spanning multiple days.

Monthly backups capture changes made within a month and are retained for an extended period, such as one year, to provide recovery points spanning multiple weeks or months. Yearly backups capture changes made within a year and are retained for archival purposes, providing long-term retention of historical data. To implement a rotation schedule using a command-line interface, organizations can use backup utilities with scheduling capabilities or custom scripts to automate backup creation, retention, and rotation tasks. For example, organizations can use cron (on Unix/Linux) or Task Scheduler (on Windows) to schedule backup jobs at predefined intervals and configure backup rotation policies based on retention requirements.

Grandfather-father-son (GFS) backup rotation is a popular backup rotation scheme that combines daily, weekly, and monthly backups to provide a balance between recent recovery points and long-term retention. In a GFS backup rotation scheme, daily backups (sons) capture changes made within a single day and are retained for a short period, such as one week. Weekly backups (fathers) capture changes made within a week and are retained for a longer period, such as one month. Monthly backups (grandfathers) capture changes made within a month and are retained for an extended period, such as one year, to provide historical recovery points.

To implement a GFS backup rotation scheme using a command-line interface, organizations can use backup utilities with support for GFS rotation or custom scripts to automate backup creation, retention, and rotation tasks according to the GFS rotation schedule. For example, organizations can use rsync or tar with custom scripts to create daily, weekly, and monthly backups and configure retention policies based on the GFS rotation scheme. By implementing backup types and rotation schedules effectively, organizations can ensure data protection, compliance with retention policies, and efficient use of storage resources, mitigating the risks of data loss and maximizing data availability and recoverability in the event of disasters or system failures.

Disaster recovery planning is a critical aspect of business continuity management, aimed at minimizing the impact of disasters or disruptions on organizational operations and ensuring the timely recovery of critical systems and services. Disaster recovery planning encompasses a comprehensive set of processes, procedures, and technologies designed to mitigate risks, prioritize recovery efforts, and restore normal operations following a disaster or disruptive event. Organizations develop disaster recovery plans to define roles and responsibilities, establish recovery objectives, and outline strategies for responding to various types of disasters, including natural disasters, cyber-attacks, hardware failures, and human errors.

One of the first steps in disaster recovery planning is conducting a risk assessment to identify potential threats and vulnerabilities that could impact organizational operations. Risk assessment involves evaluating the likelihood and potential impact of various disaster scenarios on critical systems, applications, and data, as well as assessing the effectiveness of existing controls and mitigation measures. Organizations can use risk assessment methodologies such as the risk matrix or risk heat maps to prioritize risks based on severity and likelihood. To conduct a risk assessment, organizations can use risk assessment tools or frameworks such as ISO 31000 or NIST SP 800-30 to identify, analyze, and evaluate risks systematically.

Based on the results of the risk assessment, organizations can develop disaster recovery plans that outline strategies and procedures for responding to different types of disasters. These plans typically include predefined steps for activating the disaster recovery process, notifying key stakeholders, and initiating recovery operations. Organizations should define recovery objectives, such as Recovery Time Objectives (RTOs) and Recovery Point Objectives (RPOs), which specify the maximum tolerable downtime and data loss acceptable during a disaster recovery event. To develop a disaster recovery plan, organizations can use templates or frameworks provided by industry standards such as ISO 22301 or the Disaster Recovery Institute International (DRII).

A key component of disaster recovery planning is defining roles and responsibilities for key personnel involved in the recovery process. Organizations should identify individuals or teams responsible for coordinating recovery efforts, communicating with stakeholders, and executing recovery tasks. Roles and responsibilities should be clearly defined in the disaster recovery plan, including contact information, escalation procedures, and decision-making authority. To define roles and responsibilities, organizations can use organizational charts or matrices to map out the structure of the disaster recovery team and assign specific tasks and responsibilities to team members based on their expertise and availability.

Once roles and responsibilities are defined, organizations should establish communication protocols and procedures for notifying key stakeholders and coordinating recovery efforts. Effective communication is essential during a disaster recovery event to ensure timely decision-making, resource allocation, and coordination of recovery activities. Organizations should establish communication channels, such as phone trees, email distribution lists, or collaboration platforms, and define procedures for activating communication protocols during emergencies. To test communication protocols, organizations can conduct tabletop exercises or simulations to simulate various disaster scenarios and evaluate the effectiveness of communication strategies.

Another critical aspect of disaster recovery planning is defining recovery strategies and solutions for restoring critical systems and services following a disaster or disruptive event. Recovery strategies may include data backup and restoration, failover and redundancy, cloud-based recovery services, and alternate site recovery. Organizations should identify recovery solutions that align with their recovery objectives, budget constraints, and technical requirements. To implement data backup and restoration, organizations can use backup solutions such as tape backup, disk backup, or cloud backup to create copies of critical data and applications and store them in offsite locations. To deploy failover and redundancy solutions, organizations can use high-availability clusters, redundant hardware, or virtualization technologies to ensure continuous operation of critical systems and services.

In addition to defining recovery strategies, organizations should develop testing and validation procedures to verify the effectiveness of their disaster recovery plans and solutions. Testing and validation involve conducting regular drills, exercises, or simulations to assess the readiness of the disaster recovery team and validate the functionality of recovery systems and processes. Organizations can use testing methodologies such as tabletop exercises, functional testing, or full-scale simulations to evaluate different aspects of the disaster recovery plan, including response times, recovery objectives, and communication protocols. To conduct testing and validation, organizations should establish testing schedules, document test results, and identify areas for improvement based on lessons learned from testing exercises.

Continuous monitoring and maintenance are essential for ensuring the effectiveness and relevance of disaster recovery plans over time. Organizations should regularly review and update their disaster recovery plans to reflect changes in business requirements, technology environments, and regulatory requirements. Continuous monitoring involves monitoring key performance indicators (KPIs), such as RTOs and RPOs, and conducting periodic audits or assessments to identify gaps or deficiencies in the disaster recovery process. Organizations should also conduct regular training and awareness programs to ensure that all personnel are familiar with their roles and responsibilities during a disaster recovery event.

In summary, disaster recovery planning is a critical component of business continuity management, essential for minimizing the impact of disasters or disruptions on organizational operations and ensuring the timely recovery of critical systems and services. By conducting risk assessments, developing comprehensive disaster recovery plans, defining roles and responsibilities, establishing communication protocols, and implementing recovery strategies and solutions, organizations can enhance their resilience and preparedness to respond to various types of disasters effectively. Continuous testing, monitoring, and maintenance are essential for ensuring the effectiveness and relevance of disaster recovery plans and solutions over time, enabling organizations to mitigate risks and maintain business continuity in the face of adversity.

Chapter 9: Performance Tuning for Software Systems

Performance monitoring tools play a crucial role in assessing the health, efficiency, and reliability of IT systems and applications, enabling organizations to identify performance bottlenecks, optimize resource utilization, and ensure optimal user experiences. These tools provide real-time insights into system performance metrics, such as CPU usage, memory utilization, disk I/O, network traffic, and application response times, allowing IT teams to proactively monitor and troubleshoot performance issues. Performance monitoring tools come in various forms, including system monitoring tools, application performance monitoring (APM) solutions, network monitoring tools, and log management platforms, each offering unique features and capabilities for monitoring different aspects of IT infrastructure and applications.

System monitoring tools are designed to monitor and analyze the performance of servers, operating systems, and hardware components, providing insights into system resource utilization, performance metrics, and system health status. These tools collect data from system-level metrics, such as CPU usage, memory utilization, disk I/O, and network activity, and present it in a centralized dashboard or interface for analysis and visualization. Popular system monitoring tools include Nagios, Zabbix, Prometheus, and SolarWinds Server & Application Monitor (SAM). To deploy system monitoring tools, organizations can use package management tools like apt, yum, or Chocolatey to install monitoring agents on target systems and configure monitoring checks and alerts using the tools' configuration interfaces.

Application performance monitoring (APM) solutions focus on monitoring the performance and availability of applications and services, providing insights into application response times, transaction throughput, error rates, and user experiences. APM tools capture data from application logs, transaction traces, and infrastructure metrics, enabling organizations to identify performance issues, diagnose root causes, and optimize application performance. Popular APM solutions include New Relic, AppDynamics, Dynatrace, and Datadog APM. To deploy APM solutions, organizations can integrate monitoring agents or instrumentation libraries into their applications and configure monitoring dashboards and alerts using the APM platforms' web-based interfaces.

Network monitoring tools are designed to monitor and analyze network traffic, bandwidth utilization, and network device performance, providing insights into network latency, packet loss, and traffic patterns. These tools capture data from network devices, such as routers, switches, and firewalls, and analyze it to detect anomalies, troubleshoot network issues, and optimize network performance. Popular network monitoring tools include Wireshark, PRTG Network Monitor, Nagios Network Analyzer, and SolarWinds Network Performance Monitor (NPM). To deploy network monitoring tools, organizations can install monitoring agents or sensors on network devices or deploy network monitoring appliances and configure monitoring policies using the tools' web-based interfaces.

Log management platforms are designed to collect, aggregate, and analyze log data from various sources, including servers, applications, network devices, and security appliances, providing insights into system events, error messages, and security incidents. Log management platforms enable organizations to centralize log data, perform log analysis, and generate alerts and reports to detect and respond to operational issues and security threats. Popular log management platforms include Splunk, ELK Stack (Elasticsearch, Logstash, Kibana), Graylog, and Sumo Logic. To deploy log management platforms, organizations can install log collectors or agents on target systems to forward log data to a centralized log repository and configure log parsing rules and alerting thresholds using the platforms' configuration interfaces.

In addition to standalone performance monitoring tools, organizations can also leverage cloud-based monitoring services and platforms offered by cloud service providers (CSPs) to monitor and manage their IT infrastructure and applications in the cloud. Cloud monitoring services, such as Amazon CloudWatch, Microsoft Azure Monitor, and Google Cloud Monitoring, provide built-in monitoring capabilities for monitoring cloud resources, services, and applications, enabling organizations to gain visibility into cloud performance, scalability, and security. To deploy cloud monitoring services, organizations can enable monitoring features in their cloud accounts and configure monitoring policies and alerts using the cloud provider's management console or APIs.

Continuous monitoring and proactive alerting are essential for effective performance monitoring, enabling organizations to detect and respond to performance issues in real-time before they impact operations or user experiences. Organizations should configure monitoring checks, thresholds, and alerts based on key performance indicators (KPIs) and service level objectives (SLOs) to ensure timely detection and resolution of performance issues. By leveraging performance monitoring tools and platforms effectively, organizations can optimize resource utilization, improve system reliability, and deliver seamless experiences to users and customers, thereby enhancing overall business performance and competitiveness.

Optimization techniques for resource-intensive applications are essential for maximizing performance, scalability, and efficiency while minimizing resource consumption and operational costs. Resource-intensive applications, such as database servers, web servers, and big data analytics platforms, often require significant computational, memory, and storage resources to handle large workloads and process complex data sets. Optimizing resource-intensive applications involves identifying performance bottlenecks, fine-tuning system configurations, and implementing best practices to improve performance, scalability, and reliability.

One optimization technique for resource-intensive applications is code optimization, which involves optimizing application code to improve performance and reduce resource consumption. Code optimization techniques include reducing unnecessary code execution, optimizing algorithms and data structures, and minimizing resource-intensive operations. Organizations can use profiling tools such as Gprof, Perf, or Valgrind to analyze application performance and identify hotspots or bottlenecks in the code. To optimize code performance, developers can use compiler optimizations, such as loop unrolling, function inlining, and vectorization, to generate optimized machine code that executes more efficiently on target hardware architectures.

Another optimization technique for resource-intensive applications is memory optimization, which involves optimizing memory usage to reduce memory footprint and improve memory efficiency. Memory optimization techniques include minimizing memory leaks, reducing memory fragmentation, and optimizing memory allocation and deallocation patterns. Organizations can use memory profiling tools such as Valgrind, Massif, or Memcheck to analyze memory usage and identify memory-related issues in applications. To optimize memory usage, developers can use techniques such as object pooling, lazy loading, and memory reuse to minimize memory overhead and improve overall memory efficiency.

Concurrency optimization is another important technique for resource-intensive applications, particularly those that require parallel processing or multi-threaded execution. Concurrency optimization involves maximizing parallelism and minimizing contention to improve scalability and performance. Techniques for concurrency optimization include fine-grained locking, lock-free data structures, and asynchronous programming models. Organizations can use profiling tools such as ThreadSanitizer, Helgrind, or Intel Inspector to analyze thread behavior and identify concurrency issues in applications. To optimize concurrency, developers can use thread pooling, task parallelism, and parallel algorithms to maximize parallelism and minimize synchronization overhead.

Storage optimization is crucial for resource-intensive applications that rely on disk storage or database systems to store and retrieve data. Storage optimization techniques include optimizing data access patterns, reducing disk I/O latency, and minimizing storage space usage. Organizations can use storage profiling tools such as iostat, blktrace, or Dstat to analyze disk I/O performance and identify storage-related bottlenecks in applications. To optimize storage performance, developers can use techniques such as data partitioning, indexing, and caching to improve data access efficiency and reduce disk I/O overhead.

Network optimization is important for resource-intensive applications that rely on network communication to exchange data with clients or other systems. Network optimization techniques include optimizing network protocols, reducing network latency, and minimizing network bandwidth usage. Organizations can use network profiling tools such as Wireshark, tcpdump, or Netdata to analyze network traffic and identify network-related issues in applications. To optimize network performance, developers can use techniques such as connection pooling, protocol optimization, and content compression to improve network efficiency and reduce latency.

Database optimization is critical for resource-intensive applications that rely on database systems to store and retrieve data efficiently. Database optimization techniques include optimizing database schema design, indexing, query optimization, and database configuration tuning. Organizations can use database profiling tools such as EXPLAIN, SQL Profiler, or Database Engine Tuning Advisor to analyze database performance and identify database-related bottlenecks in applications. To optimize database performance, developers can use techniques such as denormalization, query caching, and database partitioning to improve query performance and reduce database contention.

Resource utilization monitoring and management are essential for optimizing resource-intensive applications in real-time. Organizations can use system monitoring tools such as top, htop, or nmon to monitor CPU, memory, disk, and network usage in real-time and identify resource bottlenecks or anomalies. To manage resource utilization, organizations can use resource management techniques such as workload balancing, resource prioritization, and auto-scaling to allocate resources dynamically based on demand. Cloud computing platforms such as Amazon Web Services (AWS), Microsoft Azure, and Google Cloud Platform

(GCP) provide auto-scaling features that enable organizations to scale resources up or down automatically based on predefined thresholds or policies.

Continuous performance testing and optimization are essential for maintaining the performance, scalability, and efficiency of resource-intensive applications over time. Organizations should conduct regular performance tests, load tests, and stress tests to identify performance bottlenecks, validate performance improvements, and ensure that applications meet performance requirements under various workloads and conditions. By implementing optimization techniques for resource-intensive applications and continuously monitoring and fine-tuning application performance, organizations can maximize performance, scalability, and efficiency while minimizing resource consumption and operational costs.

Chapter 10: Implementing Best Practices for Software Configuration

Version control systems (VCS) play a pivotal role in configuration management, providing organizations with the ability to track, manage, and version control changes to configuration files, scripts, and infrastructure code. Configuration management involves maintaining consistency and integrity across IT environments by managing configurations, automating deployment processes, and enforcing configuration policies. Version control systems enable organizations to store configuration files in a central repository, track changes over time, and collaborate effectively on configuration management tasks.

One of the most widely used version control systems for configuration management is Git, a distributed version control system designed for managing source code but widely adopted for managing configuration files and infrastructure as code. Git provides features such as branching and merging, distributed repositories, and decentralized workflows, making it suitable for managing configurations across distributed teams and environments. To use Git for configuration management, organizations can create a Git repository to store configuration files, add files to the repository using the "git add" command, commit changes using the "git commit" command, and push changes to a remote repository using the "git push" command.

Another popular version control system for configuration management is Subversion (SVN), a centralized version control system that provides features such as versioned directories, atomic commits, and branching and tagging. SVN is well-suited for managing configuration files and scripts in centralized environments where strict access controls and centralized administration are required. To use SVN for configuration management, organizations can create an SVN repository using the "svnadmin create" command, import configuration files into the repository using the "svn import" command, and commit changes using the "svn commit" command.

Mercurial is another distributed version control system similar to Git, designed for managing source code but also suitable for managing configuration files and infrastructure code. Mercurial provides features such as branching and merging, lightweight branches, and easy collaboration, making it suitable for managing configurations across distributed teams and environments. To use Mercurial for configuration management, organizations can create a Mercurial repository using the "hg init" command, add files to the repository using the "hg add" command, commit changes using the "hg commit" command, and push changes to a remote repository using the "hg push" command.

Configuration management tools such as Ansible, Puppet, and Chef also provide version control capabilities for managing configuration files and infrastructure code. These tools integrate with version control systems such as Git and SVN to fetch configuration files from repositories, track changes, and enforce configuration policies. To use Ansible with Git for configuration management, organizations can configure Ansible playbooks to fetch configuration files from a Git repository using the "git" module, apply configurations using the "ansible-playbook" command, and manage inventory files and variables using Git branches and tags.

Configuration management with Puppet involves storing configuration files, modules, and manifests in a version control repository and deploying configurations using Puppet agents. Organizations can use Puppet with Git to manage Puppet manifests and modules in a Git repository, track changes over time, and enforce configuration policies using Puppet's declarative language. To use Puppet with Git for configuration management, organizations can create a Puppet environment in a Git repository, push changes to the repository using the "git push" command, and deploy configurations to Puppet agents using the "puppet apply" command.

Chef provides similar version control capabilities for managing infrastructure code and configuration files in a Git repository. Organizations can use Chef with Git to store cookbooks, recipes, and attributes in a version-controlled repository, track changes over time, and enforce configuration policies using Chef's infrastructure as code approach. To use Chef with Git for configuration management, organizations can create a Chef repository in a Git repository, push changes to the repository using the "git push" command, and deploy configurations to Chef nodes using the "chef-client" command.

In addition to version control systems and configuration management tools, organizations can also leverage continuous integration and continuous delivery (CI/CD) pipelines for managing configuration changes and automating deployment processes. CI/CD pipelines integrate with version control systems to trigger automated builds, tests, and deployments whenever changes are pushed to a repository. By using CI/CD pipelines for configuration management, organizations can enforce code quality standards, automate testing, and ensure consistent deployment of configurations across different environments. Continuous monitoring and auditing are essential for ensuring the integrity and compliance of configurations managed using version control systems. Organizations should implement monitoring and auditing mechanisms to track configuration changes, detect unauthorized modifications, and enforce configuration policies. Version control systems provide features such as access controls, audit logs, and change tracking to help organizations monitor and audit configuration changes effectively. By implementing version control systems for configuration management and leveraging automation, organizations can improve collaboration, enforce configuration policies, and ensure the consistency and reliability of IT environments.

Configuration auditing and compliance verification are critical processes in ensuring the integrity, security, and compliance of IT systems and infrastructure. Configuration auditing involves assessing and validating the configuration settings of systems, applications, and network devices against predefined standards, policies, and best practices. Compliance verification entails ensuring that IT systems adhere to regulatory requirements, industry standards, and internal security policies. These processes help organizations identify configuration drift, mitigate security risks, and maintain compliance with legal and regulatory obligations.

To perform configuration auditing and compliance verification, organizations utilize a variety of tools and techniques tailored to their specific requirements and regulatory frameworks. One common approach is to use configuration management tools such as Ansible, Puppet, or Chef, which provide capabilities for automating configuration checks, enforcing configuration policies, and remediating non-compliant configurations. These tools allow organizations to define configuration baselines, deploy configuration changes consistently, and monitor compliance in real-time.

For example, with Ansible, organizations can create Ansible playbooks to perform configuration audits against a set of predefined rules or standards. Ansible playbooks leverage modules such as **ansible-lint** and **ansible-review** to check configuration files for compliance with best practices and security guidelines. By running the **ansible-playbook** command with appropriate parameters and playbook files, organizations can execute configuration audits across multiple systems simultaneously and generate detailed reports on configuration compliance status.

Similarly, Puppet provides a framework for defining configuration policies using Puppet manifests and modules. Organizations can use Puppet's built-in reporting capabilities to assess the compliance of managed nodes against predefined configuration standards. By running the **puppet agent -t** command on Puppet agents, organizations can trigger configuration audits and receive real-time feedback on compliance violations. Puppet also integrates with external compliance frameworks such as CIS benchmarks, enabling organizations to evaluate configurations against industry-standard benchmarks.

Another approach to configuration auditing and compliance verification involves using specialized auditing tools and vulnerability scanners designed to assess the security posture of IT systems and infrastructure. Tools such as Nessus, OpenSCAP, and Lynis provide capabilities for scanning systems for vulnerabilities, misconfigurations, and compliance violations. These tools leverage predefined audit policies and security checks to identify potential security risks and non-compliant configurations.

For instance, organizations can use Nessus to perform vulnerability scans and configuration audits across their IT infrastructure. By running Nessus scans with appropriate scan policies and target hosts, organizations can identify security vulnerabilities, weak configurations, and compliance violations. Nessus generates detailed reports with prioritized findings, enabling organizations to remediate identified issues and improve overall security posture.

OpenSCAP is another tool commonly used for configuration auditing and compliance verification, particularly in environments requiring compliance with government regulations and security standards such as NIST SP 800-53, PCI DSS, or HIPAA. OpenSCAP provides a set of predefined security policies and checks for assessing the compliance of systems against regulatory requirements. Organizations can use OpenSCAP to scan systems for compliance deviations, generate compliance reports, and remediate non-compliant configurations using recommended remediation steps.

Lynis is a lightweight auditing tool that specializes in security audits and hardening assessments for Unix/Linux-based systems. Organizations can use Lynis to perform security audits, identify security vulnerabilities, and validate system configurations against security best practices. By running the **lynis audit system** command on target systems, organizations can initiate system audits and receive recommendations for improving system security and compliance.

Continuous monitoring and periodic audits are essential components of configuration auditing and compliance verification. Organizations should establish processes for regularly reviewing and assessing the configuration settings of IT systems and infrastructure to ensure ongoing compliance with security policies and regulatory requirements. Automated monitoring solutions such as Security Information and Event Management (SIEM) platforms, log management systems, and intrusion detection systems (IDS) can provide real-time visibility into configuration changes and security events, enabling organizations to detect and respond to security incidents promptly.

Furthermore, organizations should implement change management processes to manage configuration changes effectively and maintain an audit trail of configuration modifications. Change management processes help organizations track changes to configurations, assess the impact of changes on security and compliance, and ensure that changes are implemented in a controlled and documented manner. Version control systems such as Git or SVN can be used to manage configuration files, track changes, and facilitate collaboration among team members during the configuration change process.

In summary, configuration auditing and compliance verification are essential practices for maintaining the security, integrity, and compliance of IT systems and infrastructure. By leveraging configuration management tools, auditing tools, and automated monitoring solutions, organizations can assess configuration settings, identify security vulnerabilities, and ensure compliance with regulatory requirements and security standards. Continuous monitoring, periodic audits, and change management processes are key elements of effective configuration auditing and compliance verification strategies, enabling organizations to mitigate security risks, detect configuration drift, and maintain a strong security posture.

BOOK 3
ADVANCED SERVICE DESK TECHNIQUES
HARDWARE MAINTENANCE AND OPTIMIZATION

ROB BOTWRIGHT

Chapter 1: Advanced Hardware Components Overview

Cutting-edge CPU architectures represent the forefront of innovation in the design and development of central processing units (CPUs), driving advancements in performance, power efficiency, and scalability. These architectures embody the latest technologies, methodologies, and design principles aimed at pushing the boundaries of computing performance and addressing emerging challenges in various application domains. From traditional desktop and server processors to specialized accelerators for artificial intelligence (AI), machine learning (ML), and high-performance computing (HPC), cutting-edge CPU architectures play a pivotal role in shaping the future of computing.

One of the key trends in cutting-edge CPU architectures is the move towards heterogeneous computing, which combines diverse processing elements such as CPU cores, graphics processing units (GPUs), and accelerators on a single chip. Heterogeneous architectures leverage the strengths of different processing units to optimize performance, power efficiency, and flexibility for specific workloads. For example, AMD's Ryzen and EPYC processors feature a combination of CPU cores and Radeon Vega graphics cores, enabling high-performance computing and graphics processing in a single chip. To deploy systems with heterogeneous architectures, organizations can use system-on-chip (SoC) platforms such as AMD's Ryzen Embedded or Intel's Core and Xeon processors, which integrate CPU cores, graphics cores, and other specialized accelerators into a single package.

Another trend in cutting-edge CPU architectures is the adoption of advanced manufacturing processes and materials to enhance performance and energy efficiency. Leading semiconductor manufacturers such as Intel, AMD, and NVIDIA are leveraging technologies such as FinFET transistors, high-k metal gate (HKMG) materials, and 3D chip stacking to shrink transistor sizes, increase transistor density, and improve power efficiency. For example, Intel's 10nm and 7nm process technologies enable higher transistor density and lower power consumption, allowing for the development of more powerful and energy-efficient CPUs. To deploy systems with advanced CPU architectures, organizations can choose CPUs based on the latest manufacturing processes and architectures, such as Intel's Tiger Lake or AMD's Zen 3 processors, which offer improved performance and efficiency over previous generations.

Parallelism and scalability are also key considerations in cutting-edge CPU architectures, particularly in the context of multi-core and many-core processors designed to handle parallel workloads efficiently. Modern CPUs feature multiple CPU cores and hardware threads, enabling parallel execution of tasks across multiple cores for increased performance and responsiveness. Additionally, technologies such as simultaneous multithreading (SMT) and chip multiprocessing (CMP) further enhance parallelism by allowing multiple threads to execute concurrently on each CPU core. For example, Intel's Core i9 and Xeon processors feature multiple CPU cores and support Hyper-Threading technology, enabling parallel execution of multiple threads on each core. To deploy systems with scalable CPU architectures, organizations can use multi-core processors and server platforms such as Intel's Xeon Scalable processors or AMD's EPYC processors, which offer high core counts, large memory capacities, and support for advanced features such as NUMA and PCIe Gen4.

Specialized accelerators and coprocessors are becoming increasingly important in cutting-edge CPU architectures, particularly for accelerating specific tasks such as AI inference, ML training, and scientific computing. These accelerators offload compute-intensive workloads from the CPU cores, enabling higher performance and efficiency for specialized tasks. For example, NVIDIA's GPU accelerators such as the Tesla and Quadro series are widely used for deep learning, scientific simulations, and visualization tasks. To deploy systems with specialized accelerators, organizations can use heterogeneous computing platforms such as NVIDIA's CUDA or AMD's ROCm, which provide software frameworks and libraries for developing and deploying accelerated applications on GPUs and other accelerators.

In addition to traditional CPU architectures, emerging technologies such as neuromorphic computing, quantum computing, and photonic computing are pushing the boundaries of computing beyond the limitations of classical von Neumann architectures. Neuromorphic computing architectures, inspired by the structure and function of the human brain, aim to mimic the parallelism, plasticity, and energy efficiency of biological neural networks. IBM's TrueNorth and Intel's Loihi are examples of neuromorphic computing architectures designed for tasks such as pattern recognition, sensor processing, and autonomous navigation. Quantum computing architectures, based on the principles of quantum mechanics, promise to revolutionize computing by exploiting quantum phenomena such as superposition and entanglement to perform complex computations at unprecedented speeds. Companies such as IBM, Google, and D-Wave are developing quantum processors and cloud-based quantum computing platforms for applications such as cryptography, optimization, and material science. Photonic computing architectures, which use photons instead of electrons to carry and process information, offer the potential for ultrafast, low-power computing for tasks such as data transmission, signal processing, and optical computing. Research efforts such as Intel's Silicon Photonics and IBM's Holey Optochip are exploring the use of photonics for building high-speed interconnects and on-chip communication networks in future CPU architectures.

Overall, cutting-edge CPU architectures represent the culmination of years of research, development, and innovation in the field of computer architecture, driving advancements in performance, power efficiency, and scalability across a wide range of application domains. From heterogeneous computing and advanced manufacturing processes to parallelism and specialized accelerators, these architectures embody the latest technologies and methodologies for pushing the boundaries of computing and addressing emerging challenges in the era of big data, AI, and cloud computing. As technology continues to evolve, new paradigms such as neuromorphic computing, quantum computing, and photonic computing promise to further revolutionize computing and shape the future of CPU architectures.

Advanced storage technologies encompass a broad range of innovations and techniques aimed at improving the performance, capacity, reliability, and efficiency of storage systems in modern computing environments. These technologies address the growing demands for storing and managing ever-increasing volumes of data across diverse workloads and use cases, ranging from enterprise applications to cloud services and high-performance computing (HPC) environments. From solid-state drives

(SSDs) and non-volatile memory express (NVMe) to shingled magnetic recording (SMR) and storage-class memory (SCM), advanced storage technologies play a critical role in meeting the evolving storage needs of organizations and enabling new applications and services.

One of the key advancements in storage technology is the widespread adoption of solid-state drives (SSDs) as a replacement for traditional hard disk drives (HDDs) in storage systems. SSDs leverage flash memory technology to provide faster access times, lower latency, and higher throughput compared to HDDs, making them ideal for high-performance storage applications. To deploy SSDs, organizations can use storage management tools such as **fdisk**, **parted**, or **lsblk** to partition the SSDs and format them with a file system such as ext4 or XFS. They can then mount the SSDs to a directory using the **mount** command and configure them as primary or secondary storage devices for applications and databases.

Non-volatile memory express (NVMe) is another significant advancement in storage technology that improves the performance and efficiency of storage systems. NVMe is a high-performance, low-latency interface protocol designed specifically for SSDs, providing faster data transfer rates and lower overhead compared to traditional storage interfaces such as Serial ATA (SATA) and Serial Attached SCSI (SAS). To deploy NVMe SSDs, organizations can use NVMe management tools such as **nvme-cli** or **nvmeadm** to manage NVMe devices and monitor their performance. They can also configure NVMe over Fabrics (NVMe-oF) to enable remote access to NVMe SSDs over high-speed networks such as Ethernet or InfiniBand.

Shingled magnetic recording (SMR) is an emerging storage technology that increases the storage density of HDDs by overlapping or "shingling" data tracks on the disk platters.

SMR allows HDD manufacturers to achieve higher storage capacities without significantly increasing the physical size of the drives. To deploy SMR HDDs, organizations can use storage management tools such as **smartctl** or **hdparm** to monitor the health and performance of SMR drives. They can also use file system utilities such as **mkfs** or **fstrim** to create file systems optimized for SMR drives and maximize their storage efficiency.

Storage-class memory (SCM) is a revolutionary storage technology that bridges the gap between traditional memory and storage devices, providing high-speed, byte-addressable access to data with persistent storage capabilities. SCM devices, such as Intel Optane and Micron X100, combine the performance of DRAM with the persistence of NAND flash memory, enabling applications to access data at memory speeds while retaining data across power cycles. To deploy SCM devices, organizations can use storage management tools such as **ipmctl** or **ndctl** to manage SCM modules and configure them as block devices or persistent memory regions. They can also use operating system utilities such as **mount** or **mount-pmem** to mount SCM devices as file systems or block devices and leverage them for high-performance storage applications.

Storage virtualization is a key technique for optimizing storage resources and improving flexibility, scalability, and manageability in storage systems. Storage virtualization abstracts physical storage resources into logical pools, enabling administrators to allocate and manage storage dynamically according to application requirements. Technologies such as Storage Area Networks (SANs), Network Attached Storage (NAS), and software-defined storage (SDS) platforms provide storage virtualization capabilities for consolidating storage resources, optimizing storage utilization, and simplifying storage management tasks. To deploy storage virtualization, organizations can use storage management tools such as **lvm** or **mdadm** to create logical volumes or software RAID arrays from physical storage devices. They can also configure SAN or NAS protocols such as Fibre Channel (FC), iSCSI, or NFS to provide access to virtualized storage resources over network connections.

Data deduplication and compression are essential techniques for reducing storage costs and optimizing storage efficiency by eliminating redundant data and compressing data to reduce its size. Deduplication removes duplicate copies of data within storage systems, while compression algorithms such as LZ4, Zstandard, or gzip reduce the size of data blocks to save storage space. To deploy data deduplication and compression, organizations can use storage appliances or software-defined storage platforms that support these features out of the box. They can configure deduplication and compression policies using storage management interfaces or command-line tools provided by the storage systems.

Erasure coding is another important technique for improving data reliability and fault tolerance in storage systems by distributing data across multiple storage devices and encoding it with redundant information. Erasure coding algorithms such as Reed-Solomon, XOR-based codes, or RAID-Z provide redundancy and parity protection against data loss due to disk failures or data corruption. To deploy erasure coding, organizations can use storage systems or software-defined storage platforms that support erasure coding features. They can configure erasure coding schemes and redundancy levels to optimize data protection and storage efficiency according to their requirements.

In summary, advanced storage technologies offer a wide range of capabilities and benefits for organizations seeking to improve the performance, capacity, reliability, and efficiency of their storage infrastructure. From solid-state drives and NVMe to SMR and SCM, these technologies enable organizations to meet the evolving storage needs of modern computing environments and unlock new opportunities for innovation and growth. By leveraging storage virtualization, data deduplication, compression, erasure coding, and other techniques, organizations can optimize storage resources, reduce costs, and enhance data protection and availability across diverse workloads and use cases.

Chapter 2: Diagnostic Tools and Techniques for Hardware

Advanced hardware diagnostic utilities are indispensable tools for identifying, troubleshooting, and resolving hardware issues in modern computing systems. These utilities offer comprehensive capabilities for analyzing the health, performance, and reliability of hardware components such as processors, memory modules, storage devices, and peripherals. From built-in system diagnostics and vendor-specific tools to third-party diagnostics suites, advanced hardware diagnostic utilities provide organizations with the means to diagnose hardware problems accurately, minimize downtime, and optimize system performance.

One of the primary tools for hardware diagnostics is the built-in system diagnostic tool provided by the system firmware or BIOS (Basic Input/Output System). Most modern computers include a built-in diagnostics utility that performs comprehensive tests on hardware components during the boot process. These diagnostics utilities typically provide options for running quick tests or extended tests on CPU, memory, storage, and other hardware components to detect and report any issues. To access the built-in system diagnostics, users can enter the system firmware or BIOS setup utility during the boot process by pressing a specific key such as F2, Del, or Esc. Once in the setup utility, users can navigate to the diagnostics menu and initiate hardware tests.

Vendor-specific diagnostic tools provided by hardware manufacturers are another essential resource for diagnosing hardware issues. Companies such as Dell, HP, Lenovo, and IBM provide diagnostic utilities tailored to their specific hardware platforms, enabling users to perform detailed hardware tests and troubleshooting procedures. These diagnostic tools often include features such as system information gathering, component testing, error code interpretation, and firmware updates. To use vendor-specific diagnostic tools, users can download the appropriate utility from the manufacturer's support website and run it on the target system. For example, Dell provides the Dell Diagnostics utility, which users can run by pressing the F12 key during the boot process and selecting the diagnostics option from the boot menu.

Third-party hardware diagnostic suites offer advanced features and capabilities beyond those provided by built-in or vendor-specific tools. These diagnostic suites are designed to work with a wide range of hardware configurations and provide comprehensive testing and diagnostic capabilities for CPUs, memory, storage devices, graphics cards, and other hardware components. Popular third-party diagnostic suites include PassMark PerformanceTest, MemTest86, Prime95, and FurMark, which offer features such as benchmarking, stress testing, and component-specific diagnostics. To deploy third-party diagnostic suites, users can download the software from the vendor's website, install it on the target system, and run the appropriate tests or diagnostics modules as needed.

One of the key features of advanced hardware diagnostic utilities is the ability to perform stress testing on hardware components to identify stability issues and potential failures under heavy loads. Stress testing involves subjecting hardware components to intense workloads for an extended period to simulate real-world usage scenarios and uncover any weaknesses or defects. Stress testing utilities such as Prime95, FurMark, and MemTest86+ provide options for running stress tests on CPUs, GPUs, and memory modules to evaluate their stability and reliability. To perform stress testing, users can configure the stress testing parameters such as test duration, workload intensity, and monitoring options, and then run the stress test on the target hardware component.

Another important feature of advanced hardware diagnostic utilities is the ability to generate detailed reports and logs summarizing the results of diagnostic tests and hardware analysis. These reports provide valuable information about the health, performance, and reliability of hardware components, including any errors, warnings, or abnormalities detected during testing. Diagnostic utilities often generate reports in standard formats such as HTML, CSV, or text files, making it easy to review and analyze the results. To generate diagnostic reports, users can run the appropriate diagnostic tests or analyses using the diagnostic utility and then export the results to a report file using the utility's built-in reporting features.

Remote hardware diagnostics are becoming increasingly important for diagnosing hardware issues in distributed computing environments such as data centers, cloud infrastructure, and remote offices. Remote diagnostic tools such as Dell Remote Diagnostic Tool (DRAC), HP Integrated Lights-Out (iLO), and Intel Active Management Technology (AMT) enable administrators to perform hardware diagnostics and troubleshooting tasks remotely over the network. These remote diagnostic tools provide features such as remote access to system firmware, remote power control, and remote hardware monitoring, allowing administrators to diagnose and resolve hardware issues without physically accessing the target systems. To use remote diagnostic tools, administrators can connect to the target systems using a web browser or management console and initiate diagnostic tests or troubleshooting procedures remotely.

In summary, advanced hardware diagnostic utilities are essential tools for diagnosing and troubleshooting hardware issues in modern computing systems. Whether built-in system diagnostics, vendor-specific tools, third-party diagnostic suites, stress testing utilities, or remote diagnostic tools, these utilities provide organizations with comprehensive capabilities for analyzing hardware components, identifying potential issues, and optimizing system performance. By leveraging advanced hardware diagnostic utilities, organizations can minimize downtime, maximize system reliability, and ensure the smooth operation of their computing infrastructure.

Hardware troubleshooting methodologies are systematic approaches used to identify, isolate, and resolve hardware issues in computing systems. These methodologies encompass a variety of techniques, tools, and best practices aimed at diagnosing and fixing hardware problems efficiently and effectively. From basic troubleshooting steps to advanced diagnostic techniques, hardware troubleshooting methodologies provide a structured framework for IT professionals to address hardware-related issues in desktops, laptops, servers, and other electronic devices.

One of the fundamental principles of hardware troubleshooting is to start with the most basic and straightforward steps before moving on to more complex diagnostic procedures. This approach, often referred to as the "divide and conquer" method, involves breaking down the troubleshooting process into smaller, manageable steps to isolate the root cause of the problem. For example, when troubleshooting a desktop computer that fails to power on, IT professionals may begin by checking the power source, power cables, and power supply unit (PSU) to ensure that the system is receiving power. To verify the power source, IT professionals can use a multimeter to measure the voltage output of the power outlet or use a power supply tester to check the output voltage of the PSU.

Once basic hardware components such as power supply, cables, and connections have been verified, IT professionals can proceed to perform more advanced diagnostic tests to identify potential hardware failures. Diagnostic tools such as hardware diagnostic utilities, built-in system diagnostics, and vendor-specific diagnostic tools can help diagnose hardware issues by performing comprehensive tests on CPU, memory, storage, and other hardware components. For example, when troubleshooting a laptop that experiences frequent crashes or freezes, IT professionals may use a hardware diagnostic utility such as MemTest86 to test the integrity of the laptop's memory modules. To deploy MemTest86, IT professionals can create a bootable USB drive containing the MemTest86 image file using a tool such as Rufus or dd command, boot the laptop from the USB drive, and run the memory test.

In addition to diagnostic tools, hardware troubleshooting methodologies often involve visual inspection of hardware components to identify physical damage, loose connections, or other visible signs of malfunction. Visual inspection can help pinpoint hardware issues such as damaged cables, loose screws, or corroded connectors that may not be immediately apparent from diagnostic tests alone. For example, when troubleshooting a server that experiences intermittent network connectivity issues, IT professionals may visually inspect the network interface card (NIC) for loose or damaged cables, connectors, or components. To inspect hardware components visually, IT professionals can use a flashlight, magnifying glass, or digital camera to examine components closely and look for signs of damage or wear.

Another key aspect of hardware troubleshooting methodologies is the use of diagnostic logs, error messages, and system logs to identify and diagnose hardware issues. Operating systems and hardware components often generate error messages, warnings, and event logs that can provide valuable information about hardware failures, driver issues, and system errors. For example, when troubleshooting a server that experiences disk I/O errors, IT professionals may review the system logs and error messages in the event viewer or syslog to identify the cause of the disk errors. To view system logs and error messages, IT professionals can use command-line utilities such as dmesg, journalctl, or eventvwr to access and analyze diagnostic logs and event records.

Remote hardware troubleshooting methodologies involve diagnosing and resolving hardware issues in computing systems located in remote or inaccessible locations. Remote troubleshooting techniques such as remote desktop access, remote console access, and remote management interfaces enable IT professionals to diagnose and troubleshoot hardware issues without physically accessing the target systems. For example, when troubleshooting a server located in a remote data center, IT professionals may use remote desktop software such as Remote Desktop Protocol (RDP) or Virtual Network Computing (VNC) to connect to the server's desktop interface remotely and perform diagnostic tests. To access remote desktop interfaces, IT professionals can use RDP client software such as Microsoft Remote Desktop, Remmina, or TightVNC to connect to the target system's IP address or hostname.

Furthermore, hardware troubleshooting methodologies often involve the use of spare parts, replacement components, and test equipment to isolate and confirm hardware failures. Swapping out suspect components such as memory modules, hard drives, or expansion cards with known-good replacements can help determine whether a specific hardware component is causing the problem. For example, when troubleshooting a desktop computer that fails to boot, IT professionals may swap out the system's memory modules with known-good modules to determine whether the memory is faulty. To replace hardware components, IT professionals can use appropriate tools such as screwdrivers, pliers, and antistatic wrist straps to safely remove and install components in computing systems.

In summary, hardware troubleshooting methodologies provide a structured framework for diagnosing and resolving hardware issues in computing systems. By following basic troubleshooting steps, performing advanced diagnostic tests, visually inspecting hardware components, analyzing diagnostic logs, using remote troubleshooting techniques, and swapping out suspect components, IT professionals can identify and resolve hardware problems efficiently and effectively. Whether troubleshooting desktops, laptops, servers, or other electronic devices, applying hardware troubleshooting methodologies can help minimize downtime, optimize system performance, and ensure the reliability and stability of computing systems.

Chapter 3: Advanced Hardware Troubleshooting Strategies

Root cause analysis (RCA) in hardware failures is a systematic approach used to identify the underlying causes or factors contributing to hardware malfunctions, errors, or failures in computing systems. RCA methodologies aim to uncover the primary reason or reasons why hardware components fail, enabling organizations to implement corrective actions and prevent similar failures from occurring in the future. From analyzing error logs and diagnostic data to conducting physical inspections and conducting stress tests, RCA in hardware failures involves a series of steps and techniques to pinpoint the root cause of hardware issues accurately.

One of the initial steps in RCA is to gather information about the symptoms, behaviors, and events leading up to the hardware failure. This involves collecting data such as error messages, system logs, diagnostic reports, and user observations to understand the nature and extent of the hardware problem. For example, when troubleshooting a server that experiences intermittent crashes or freezes, IT professionals may review system logs using commands such as **journalctl** in Linux or **Event Viewer** in Windows to identify error messages, warnings, and critical events associated with the hardware failure.

Once sufficient data has been collected, the next step in RCA is to analyze the available information to identify potential causes or contributing factors to the hardware failure. This may involve examining error patterns, correlating events, and identifying commonalities among affected systems to narrow down the list of possible root causes. For example, when analyzing system logs, IT professionals may look for recurring error messages, abnormal system behaviors, or patterns of failure that could indicate underlying hardware issues. To analyze system logs, IT professionals can use command-line utilities such as **grep**, **awk**, or **sed** to search for specific keywords or patterns in log files and extract relevant information.

In addition to analyzing diagnostic data and system logs, conducting physical inspections of hardware components can provide valuable insights into potential root causes of hardware failures. Physical inspections involve visually examining hardware components such as CPUs, memory modules, storage drives, and expansion cards for signs of damage, overheating, corrosion, or other abnormalities. For example, when troubleshooting a desktop computer that fails to power on, IT professionals may visually inspect the power supply unit (PSU) for blown capacitors, loose connections, or burnt components. To conduct physical inspections, IT professionals can use tools such as flashlights, magnifying glasses, or thermal imaging cameras to examine hardware components closely and identify any visible defects or irregularities.

Once potential root causes have been identified through data analysis and physical inspections, the next step in RCA is to conduct diagnostic tests and experiments to validate hypotheses and confirm the root cause of the hardware failure. Diagnostic tests may involve running stress tests, hardware diagnostics, or performance benchmarks on suspect hardware components to simulate real-world usage scenarios and identify failure modes. For example, when diagnosing memory-related issues, IT professionals may use memory testing utilities such as MemTest86 or memtester to perform comprehensive tests on memory modules and identify faulty DIMMs. To run diagnostic tests, IT professionals can use command-line utilities or third-party diagnostic tools to initiate tests and analyze the results.

In addition to diagnostic tests, conducting controlled experiments and implementing temporary fixes or workarounds can help isolate the root cause of hardware failures and validate potential solutions. Controlled experiments involve systematically changing one variable at a time and observing the effects on system behavior to identify cause-and-effect relationships. For example, when troubleshooting a server that experiences network connectivity issues, IT professionals may disable specific network interfaces or change network configurations to determine whether the problem is related to hardware, software, or network settings. To conduct controlled experiments, IT professionals can use command-line utilities or configuration files to modify system settings and monitor the effects on system performance and behavior.

Once the root cause of the hardware failure has been identified and validated, the final step in RCA is to implement corrective actions and preventive measures to address the underlying issues and prevent similar failures from occurring in the future. Corrective actions may involve repairing or replacing faulty hardware components, updating device drivers or firmware, applying software patches or updates, or modifying system configurations to mitigate known issues. Preventive measures may include implementing redundant hardware configurations, implementing monitoring and alerting systems, conducting regular maintenance and inspections, or providing user training and education on proper hardware usage and maintenance practices.

In summary, root cause analysis in hardware failures is a systematic approach used to identify and address the underlying causes of hardware malfunctions, errors, or failures in computing systems. By collecting and analyzing diagnostic data, conducting physical inspections, running diagnostic tests and experiments, and implementing corrective actions and preventive measures, organizations can pinpoint the root cause of hardware issues accurately and prevent similar failures from occurring in the future. Whether troubleshooting desktops, laptops, servers, or other electronic devices, applying RCA methodologies can help minimize downtime, optimize system reliability, and ensure the smooth operation of computing systems.

Advanced hardware fault isolation techniques are essential methodologies used to identify, isolate, and resolve complex hardware issues in computing systems. These techniques go beyond basic troubleshooting methods and involve sophisticated diagnostic procedures, tools, and strategies to pinpoint the root cause of hardware faults accurately. From analyzing system logs and error messages to conducting stress tests and using diagnostic equipment, advanced hardware fault isolation techniques provide IT professionals with the means to diagnose and resolve hardware issues efficiently and effectively.

One of the key techniques in advanced hardware fault isolation is the analysis of system logs and error messages to identify patterns, trends, and anomalies that may indicate underlying hardware issues. System logs, error logs, and event logs generated by operating systems and hardware components contain valuable information about system events, errors, warnings, and failures. For example, when troubleshooting a server that experiences intermittent crashes or freezes, IT professionals may review system logs using commands such as **journalctl** in Linux or **Event Viewer** in Windows to identify error messages, warnings, and critical events associated with the hardware failure.

In addition to analyzing system logs, advanced hardware fault isolation techniques may involve the use of diagnostic tools and utilities to perform comprehensive tests on hardware components such as CPUs, memory modules, storage devices, and expansion cards. These diagnostic tools provide IT professionals with detailed information about the health, performance, and reliability of hardware components, enabling them to identify potential faults and failures. For example, when diagnosing memory-related issues, IT professionals may use memory testing utilities such as MemTest86 or memtester to perform extensive tests on memory modules and identify faulty DIMMs. To run diagnostic tests, IT professionals can use command-line utilities or third-party diagnostic tools to initiate tests and analyze the results.

Another important technique in advanced hardware fault isolation is the use of stress testing to identify stability issues and potential failures under heavy loads. Stress testing involves subjecting hardware components to intense workloads for an extended period to simulate real-world usage scenarios and uncover any weaknesses or defects. Stress testing utilities such as Prime95, FurMark, and MemTest86+ provide options for running stress tests on CPUs, GPUs, and memory modules to evaluate their stability and reliability. To perform stress testing, IT professionals can configure stress testing parameters such as test duration, workload intensity, and monitoring options and then run the stress test on the target hardware component.

Physical inspections of hardware components are also critical in advanced hardware fault isolation techniques, as they can provide valuable insights into potential root causes of hardware failures. Physical inspections involve visually examining hardware components such as CPUs, memory modules, storage drives, and expansion cards for signs of damage, overheating, corrosion, or other abnormalities. For example, when troubleshooting a desktop computer that fails to power on, IT professionals may visually inspect the power supply unit (PSU) for blown capacitors, loose connections, or burnt components. To conduct physical inspections, IT professionals can use tools such as flashlights, magnifying glasses, or thermal imaging cameras to examine hardware components closely and identify any visible defects or irregularities.

In addition to diagnostic tests and physical inspections, advanced hardware fault isolation techniques may involve the use of specialized diagnostic equipment and tools to diagnose complex hardware issues. Diagnostic equipment such as oscilloscopes, multimeters, logic analyzers, and thermal imaging cameras can provide IT professionals with detailed insights into the performance, signals, voltages, and temperatures of hardware components. For example, when diagnosing network connectivity issues, IT professionals may use a network analyzer to monitor network traffic, analyze packet data, and identify network errors or anomalies. To deploy diagnostic equipment, IT professionals can connect the diagnostic tools to the target hardware components using appropriate cables, connectors, and adapters and then use the tools to capture, analyze, and interpret diagnostic data.

Remote hardware fault isolation techniques are becoming increasingly important for diagnosing and resolving hardware issues in distributed computing environments such as data centers, cloud infrastructure, and remote offices. Remote troubleshooting techniques such as remote desktop access, remote console access, and remote management interfaces enable IT professionals to diagnose and troubleshoot hardware issues without physically accessing the target systems. For example, when troubleshooting a server located in a remote data center, IT professionals may use remote desktop software such as Remote Desktop

Protocol (RDP) or Virtual Network Computing (VNC) to connect to the server's desktop interface remotely and perform diagnostic tests. To access remote desktop interfaces, IT professionals can use RDP client software such as Microsoft Remote Desktop, Remmina, or TightVNC to connect to the target system's IP address or hostname.

In summary, advanced hardware fault isolation techniques are essential methodologies for identifying, isolating, and resolving complex hardware issues in computing systems. By analyzing system logs, using diagnostic tools, conducting stress tests, performing physical inspections, using specialized diagnostic equipment, and employing remote troubleshooting techniques, IT professionals can diagnose and resolve hardware faults efficiently and effectively. Whether troubleshooting desktops, laptops, servers, or other electronic devices, applying advanced hardware fault isolation techniques can help minimize downtime, optimize system reliability, and ensure the smooth operation of computing systems.

Chapter 4: Preventive Maintenance for Hardware Systems

Proactive hardware maintenance plans are structured strategies implemented by organizations to prevent hardware failures, optimize system performance, and maximize the lifespan of computing hardware. These plans involve regular inspections, preventive maintenance tasks, firmware updates, and performance optimizations to identify and address potential issues before they escalate into critical failures. From scheduling routine maintenance activities to monitoring hardware health metrics and implementing predictive analytics, proactive hardware maintenance plans aim to reduce downtime, improve system reliability, and minimize the total cost of ownership for computing infrastructure.

One of the key components of proactive hardware maintenance plans is the establishment of a regular maintenance schedule to ensure that hardware components are inspected, cleaned, and maintained at predefined intervals. This schedule may include tasks such as cleaning dust and debris from fans and heatsinks, checking cable connections, updating firmware and drivers, and replacing worn-out components. For example, IT professionals may schedule quarterly maintenance checks for servers, desktops, and networking equipment to inspect hardware components, apply firmware updates, and perform preventive maintenance tasks. To schedule maintenance activities, IT professionals can use calendar applications, task management tools, or IT service management (ITSM) software to create recurring maintenance tasks and reminders.

In addition to regular maintenance schedules, proactive hardware maintenance plans often include the implementation of monitoring and alerting systems to continuously monitor the health, performance, and reliability of hardware components in real-time. Monitoring tools such as Nagios, Zabbix, and SolarWinds provide IT professionals with visibility into key hardware metrics such as CPU utilization, memory usage, disk I/O, and temperature. These tools can alert IT staff to potential hardware issues such as overheating, high resource utilization, or imminent disk failures, allowing them to take proactive action before issues escalate. To deploy monitoring and alerting systems, IT professionals can install monitoring agents or sensors on hardware components and configure alerting rules to notify IT staff of abnormal conditions or events.

Another important aspect of proactive hardware maintenance plans is the implementation of predictive analytics and machine learning algorithms to forecast hardware failures and performance degradation based on historical data and usage patterns. Predictive analytics tools such as Splunk, Elasticsearch, and IBM Watson Analytics analyze historical data from monitoring systems, log files, and performance metrics to identify trends, patterns, and anomalies indicative of potential hardware issues. By leveraging predictive analytics, IT professionals can anticipate hardware failures, plan maintenance activities, and take preventive measures to mitigate risks and avoid unplanned downtime. To implement predictive analytics, organizations can collect and analyze historical data using data analytics platforms and machine learning algorithms and develop predictive models to forecast hardware failures. Furthermore, proactive hardware maintenance plans may involve the implementation of remote monitoring and management (RMM) solutions to monitor and manage hardware infrastructure across distributed environments such as remote offices, branch locations, and cloud platforms. RMM solutions such as ConnectWise Automate, Kaseya VSA, and SolarWinds RMM enable IT professionals to remotely monitor hardware health, deploy patches and updates, and perform troubleshooting tasks from a centralized management console. These solutions provide features such as remote desktop access, patch management, software deployment, and asset tracking, allowing IT staff to proactively manage hardware infrastructure and address issues remotely. To deploy RMM solutions, organizations can install RMM agents on target systems and configure them to communicate with a central management server or cloud-based dashboard.

Moreover, proactive hardware maintenance plans may include the implementation of hardware redundancy and fault-tolerant configurations to mitigate the impact of hardware failures and ensure high availability of critical systems. Redundant hardware configurations such as RAID (Redundant Array of Independent Disks), hot-swappable components, and clustering technologies provide resilience against hardware failures by automatically failing over to redundant components or systems in the event of a failure. For example, organizations may configure servers with RAID arrays to protect against disk failures or deploy high availability clusters to ensure continuous operation of mission-critical applications. To implement hardware redundancy, IT professionals can configure redundant components, set up failover mechanisms, and test failover procedures to ensure seamless failover in the event of a hardware failure.

In summary, proactive hardware maintenance plans are essential strategies for preventing hardware failures, optimizing system performance, and maximizing the lifespan of computing hardware. By establishing regular maintenance schedules, implementing monitoring and alerting systems, leveraging predictive analytics, deploying remote monitoring and management solutions, and implementing hardware redundancy, organizations can proactively manage hardware infrastructure, minimize downtime, and ensure the reliability and availability of critical systems. Whether managing on-premises infrastructure, cloud environments, or hybrid deployments, proactive hardware maintenance plans play a crucial role in maintaining the health and performance of computing systems. Predictive maintenance strategies are proactive approaches employed by organizations to anticipate and prevent equipment failures by leveraging data analytics, machine learning, and sensor technology to predict when maintenance is required based on the condition of the equipment. These strategies aim to optimize maintenance schedules, reduce downtime, extend equipment lifespan, and minimize maintenance costs by detecting potential issues before they lead to failures. From collecting and analyzing equipment data to developing predictive models and implementing automated maintenance workflows, predictive maintenance strategies enable organizations to transition from reactive to proactive maintenance practices. One of the fundamental components of predictive maintenance strategies is the collection of equipment data from various sources such as sensors, monitoring systems, and industrial IoT (Internet of Things) devices. This data includes information about equipment performance, operating conditions, environmental factors, and other relevant parameters that can be used to assess the health and condition of the equipment. For example, in manufacturing plants, sensors embedded in machinery can collect data on temperature, vibration, pressure, and other key indicators of equipment health. To collect equipment data, organizations can use data acquisition systems, sensor networks, or industrial control systems to capture data from sensors and other monitoring devices.

Once equipment data has been collected, the next step in predictive maintenance strategies is to analyze the data to identify patterns, trends, and anomalies that may indicate potential equipment failures or performance degradation. Data analysis techniques such as statistical analysis, machine learning, and anomaly detection algorithms can be used to process large volumes of data and extract actionable insights. For example, machine learning algorithms can analyze historical equipment data to identify correlations between equipment performance and maintenance events, allowing organizations to predict when maintenance is likely to be required. To analyze equipment data, organizations can use data analytics platforms such as Apache Spark, TensorFlow, or Microsoft Azure Machine Learning to develop and deploy predictive models.

In addition to analyzing equipment data, predictive maintenance strategies may involve the development of predictive models and algorithms to forecast equipment failures and performance degradation based on historical data and usage patterns. These predictive models use advanced statistical techniques, machine learning algorithms, and domain-specific knowledge to predict when equipment failures are likely to occur and recommend appropriate maintenance actions. For example, organizations may develop predictive models that use sensor data to predict when industrial machinery is at risk of failure and recommend maintenance tasks such as lubrication, calibration, or component replacement. To develop predictive models, organizations can use data science techniques such as regression analysis, time series analysis, and neural networks to train and validate predictive algorithms. Another important aspect of predictive maintenance strategies is the implementation of condition monitoring systems to continuously monitor the health and performance of equipment in real-time. Condition monitoring systems use sensors, telemetry, and monitoring devices to collect data on equipment condition, operating parameters, and environmental factors. This data is then analyzed to detect abnormal conditions, identify early signs of equipment degradation, and trigger maintenance alerts when intervention is required. For example, vibration sensors installed on rotating equipment can detect changes in vibration patterns that may indicate bearing wear or misalignment, prompting maintenance personnel to inspect and repair the equipment. To implement condition monitoring systems, organizations can deploy sensor networks, telemetry devices, and monitoring software to collect and analyze equipment data in real-time.

Furthermore, predictive maintenance strategies may involve the integration of predictive maintenance solutions with enterprise asset management (EAM) systems to automate maintenance workflows, prioritize maintenance tasks, and optimize maintenance schedules. Predictive maintenance solutions such as IBM Maximo Predictive Maintenance Insights, SAP Predictive Maintenance and Service, and GE Predix APM (Asset Performance Management) provide features such as predictive analytics, condition monitoring, and maintenance scheduling to help organizations streamline maintenance operations. These solutions leverage equipment data, predictive models, and maintenance rules to generate maintenance recommendations, create work orders, and assign tasks to maintenance personnel. To integrate predictive maintenance solutions with EAM systems, organizations can use application programming interfaces (APIs), web services, or middleware to exchange data between systems and automate maintenance workflows.

Moreover, predictive maintenance strategies may incorporate reliability-centered maintenance (RCM) principles to optimize maintenance strategies, prioritize critical equipment, and allocate resources effectively. RCM is a systematic approach to maintenance planning that focuses on identifying and addressing the root causes of equipment failures to improve reliability and performance. By analyzing equipment failure modes, consequences, and probabilities, organizations can develop maintenance strategies that maximize equipment uptime, minimize maintenance costs, and mitigate risks. To implement RCM principles, organizations can conduct failure mode and effects analysis (FMEA), develop maintenance plans based on equipment criticality, and continuously monitor equipment performance to identify opportunities for improvement.

In summary, predictive maintenance strategies are proactive approaches used by organizations to anticipate and prevent equipment failures by leveraging data analytics, machine learning, and condition monitoring technology. By collecting and analyzing equipment data, developing predictive models, implementing condition monitoring systems, integrating predictive maintenance solutions with EAM systems, and incorporating reliability-centered maintenance principles, organizations can optimize maintenance schedules, reduce downtime, extend equipment lifespan, and minimize maintenance costs. Whether in manufacturing plants, power plants, transportation fleets, or facilities management, predictive maintenance strategies play a crucial role in improving equipment reliability, performance, and efficiency.

Chapter 5: Hardware Upgrade Planning and Implementation

Strategic hardware upgrade assessments are systematic evaluations conducted by organizations to determine the necessity, feasibility, and impact of upgrading existing hardware infrastructure. These assessments involve analyzing various factors such as technological advancements, business requirements, budget constraints, and return on investment (ROI) considerations to make informed decisions about hardware upgrades. From conducting hardware audits and performance evaluations to assessing compatibility and scalability, strategic hardware upgrade assessments enable organizations to optimize their IT infrastructure, enhance system capabilities, and support business objectives effectively.

One of the initial steps in strategic hardware upgrade assessments is to conduct a comprehensive audit of existing hardware infrastructure to identify outdated, underperforming, or end-of-life components that may require upgrading. This involves inventorying hardware assets, documenting specifications, configurations, and usage patterns, and assessing the condition and reliability of hardware components. For example, IT professionals may use commands such as **lshw** or **hwinfo** in Linux or **Get-WmiObject** in PowerShell to gather detailed information about hardware components such as CPUs, memory, storage, and network interfaces. To conduct hardware audits, organizations can use asset management tools, configuration management databases (CMDBs), or inventory management systems to track hardware assets and maintain up-to-date records.

Once the existing hardware infrastructure has been audited, the next step in strategic hardware upgrade assessments is to evaluate the performance and capabilities of the current hardware against business requirements and future growth projections. This involves analyzing performance metrics such as CPU utilization, memory usage, disk I/O, and network throughput to identify bottlenecks, constraints, and limitations that may impact system performance and scalability. For example, IT professionals may use performance monitoring tools such as **top**, **htop**, or **perf** in Linux or **Performance Monitor** in Windows to measure and analyze system performance metrics in real-time. To evaluate hardware performance, organizations can conduct benchmark tests, load tests, and stress tests to simulate workload scenarios and assess system responsiveness and reliability.

In addition to performance evaluations, strategic hardware upgrade assessments may involve assessing the compatibility of existing hardware with new software applications, operating systems, or workload requirements. This includes verifying hardware specifications such as processor architecture, memory capacity, storage interfaces, and network connectivity to ensure compatibility with software requirements and standards. For example, organizations planning to upgrade to a new version of an operating system may need to verify that existing hardware meets the minimum system requirements and is compatible with device drivers and software dependencies. To assess compatibility, IT professionals can use tools such as **lspci**, **lsusb**, or **dmidecode** in Linux or **System Information** in Windows to gather hardware information and check compatibility with software requirements.

Furthermore, strategic hardware upgrade assessments may involve evaluating the scalability and future-proofing capabilities of existing hardware infrastructure to accommodate future growth and expansion. This includes assessing the ability of hardware components to scale up or scale out to support increasing workloads, user demands, and business requirements over time. For example, organizations may need to assess whether existing servers, storage arrays, and networking equipment can be upgraded or expanded to accommodate additional users, applications, or data volumes. To evaluate scalability, organizations can review hardware specifications, assess upgrade options, and consider factors such as compatibility, performance, and cost-effectiveness when planning hardware upgrades.

Moreover, strategic hardware upgrade assessments may involve conducting cost-benefit analyses and ROI calculations to determine the financial viability and potential return on investment of hardware upgrades. This includes estimating the costs associated with hardware procurement, installation, configuration, and maintenance, as well as quantifying the expected benefits in terms of improved performance, productivity, efficiency, and business outcomes. For example, organizations may calculate the total cost of ownership (TCO) of existing hardware infrastructure and compare it to the TCO of proposed hardware upgrades to assess cost-effectiveness and ROI. To conduct cost-benefit analyses, organizations can use financial modeling tools, ROI calculators, and investment appraisal techniques to evaluate the economic feasibility of hardware upgrades.

In summary, strategic hardware upgrade assessments are essential processes for evaluating the necessity, feasibility, and impact of upgrading existing hardware infrastructure. By conducting hardware audits, performance evaluations, compatibility assessments, scalability reviews, and cost-benefit analyses, organizations can make informed decisions about hardware upgrades that align with business objectives, support future growth, and maximize ROI. Whether upgrading servers, storage systems, networking equipment, or end-user devices, strategic hardware upgrade assessments enable organizations to optimize their IT infrastructure, enhance system capabilities, and maintain competitiveness in today's dynamic business environment.

Seamless hardware migration strategies are meticulously planned approaches employed by organizations to transition from legacy hardware to new hardware seamlessly while minimizing disruption to operations and ensuring continuity of services. These strategies encompass a range of tasks, including inventorying existing hardware, assessing compatibility and dependencies, planning migration procedures, executing migration tasks, and validating the success of the migration process. From identifying migration objectives and risks to implementing rollback plans and post-migration support, seamless hardware migration strategies are essential for organizations looking to upgrade their hardware infrastructure efficiently and effectively.

The first step in seamless hardware migration strategies is to conduct a thorough inventory of existing hardware assets to identify the scope and scale of the migration project. This involves compiling a comprehensive list of hardware components, including servers, networking equipment, storage devices, and end-user devices, along with their specifications, configurations, and dependencies. For example, IT professionals may use commands such as **lshw** or **Get-WmiObject** to gather detailed information about hardware assets in Linux or Windows environments, respectively. To streamline the inventory process, organizations can use asset management tools or configuration management databases (CMDBs) to track hardware assets and maintain up-to-date records of hardware configurations.

Once the inventory of existing hardware assets is complete, the next step in seamless hardware migration strategies is to assess compatibility and dependencies to identify potential challenges and risks associated with the migration process. This involves evaluating hardware specifications, device drivers, firmware versions, software dependencies, and interoperability requirements to ensure that new hardware is compatible with existing infrastructure and applications. For example, organizations may need to verify that new servers support the same operating systems, applications, and peripheral devices as the old servers to minimize compatibility issues. To assess compatibility, IT professionals can use tools such as **lspci, lsusb,** or **dmidecode** in Linux or **System Information** in Windows to gather hardware information and check compatibility with software requirements.

After assessing compatibility and dependencies, the next step in seamless hardware migration strategies is to plan migration procedures and develop a detailed migration plan outlining tasks, timelines, responsibilities, and contingencies. This involves defining migration objectives, setting migration priorities, and establishing communication channels to coordinate migration activities across teams and departments. For example, organizations may need to schedule downtime windows, allocate resources, and notify stakeholders of planned maintenance activities to minimize disruption to operations. To plan migration procedures, organizations can use project management tools, task management software, or collaboration platforms to create and manage migration plans collaboratively.

Once migration procedures are planned and documented, the next step in seamless hardware migration strategies is to

186

execute migration tasks according to the migration plan while adhering to best practices and industry standards. This involves tasks such as preparing new hardware, configuring network settings, transferring data and applications, testing migration procedures, and verifying the integrity and functionality of migrated systems. For example, organizations may need to use commands such as **scp**, **rsync**, or **robocopy** to transfer data and files between old and new hardware during the migration process. To execute migration tasks, organizations can use automation tools, deployment scripts, or migration utilities to streamline the migration process and reduce manual effort.

During the migration process, it is essential to monitor the progress of migration tasks, track key performance indicators, and address any issues or errors that arise promptly. This involves monitoring system logs, error messages, and performance metrics to identify anomalies, failures, or bottlenecks that may affect the success of the migration process. For example, organizations may use commands such as **tail**, **grep**, or **Event Viewer** to monitor logs and diagnose issues during the migration process. To monitor migration progress, organizations can use monitoring tools, dashboards, or alerting systems to track migration metrics such as data transfer rates, system uptime, and resource utilization.

After completing migration tasks, the next step in seamless hardware migration strategies is to validate the success of the migration process by conducting post-migration testing and verification activities. This involves testing migrated systems, applications, and services to ensure that they are functioning as expected and meeting performance and reliability requirements. For example, organizations may conduct functional testing, regression testing, and performance testing to verify the integrity and functionality of migrated systems. To validate migration success, organizations can use testing frameworks, automated testing tools, or manual testing procedures to assess the performance and reliability of migrated systems.

In summary, seamless hardware migration strategies are essential for organizations looking to upgrade their hardware infrastructure efficiently and effectively while minimizing disruption to operations. By conducting inventory assessments, assessing compatibility and dependencies, planning migration procedures, executing migration tasks, monitoring migration progress, and validating migration success, organizations can ensure a smooth and successful transition to new hardware while maintaining continuity of services and minimizing risks. Whether migrating servers, networking equipment, storage devices, or end-user devices, seamless hardware migration strategies enable organizations to optimize their IT infrastructure and support business objectives effectively.

Chapter 6: Performance Optimization Techniques for Hardware

Hardware performance monitoring tools are essential components of IT infrastructure management, providing insights into the health, utilization, and efficiency of hardware components such as CPUs, memory, storage, and network interfaces. These tools enable organizations to monitor hardware performance metrics in real-time, identify bottlenecks, troubleshoot issues, and optimize resource allocation to ensure optimal system performance and reliability. From command-line utilities to graphical user interfaces (GUIs) and cloud-based platforms, a variety of hardware performance monitoring tools are available to meet the diverse needs of IT professionals across different environments and use cases.

One of the commonly used hardware performance monitoring tools in the command-line interface (CLI) is **top**, which provides a dynamic, real-time view of system resource usage, including CPU utilization, memory usage, and process activity. By running the **top** command in a terminal window, IT professionals can monitor system performance metrics and identify processes or applications consuming excessive system resources. For example, typing **top** in the terminal window displays a continuously updating list of processes sorted by CPU usage, allowing IT professionals to identify resource-intensive processes and take appropriate actions such as terminating or prioritizing tasks.

Another CLI-based hardware performance monitoring tool is **vmstat**, which provides information about system memory, CPU, and disk I/O activity in a concise, tabular format. By running the **vmstat** command with appropriate options, IT professionals can monitor various system performance metrics, including memory usage, CPU utilization, disk I/O throughput, and paging activity. For example, typing **vmstat 1** in the terminal window displays system performance metrics updated every second, allowing IT professionals to monitor system behavior in real-time and identify performance bottlenecks or abnormalities.

Furthermore, the **iostat** command is another CLI-based hardware performance monitoring tool that provides insights into disk I/O activity, including disk utilization, throughput, and response times. By running the **iostat** command with appropriate options, IT professionals can monitor disk performance metrics for individual disks or disk partitions, identify I/O bottlenecks, and optimize disk usage. For example, typing **iostat -x 1** in the terminal window displays disk performance metrics updated every second, allowing IT professionals to identify disks with high utilization or latency and take corrective actions such as redistributing I/O load or upgrading storage hardware.

In addition to CLI-based tools, graphical user interface (GUI) tools such as **htop** provide a more user-friendly and interactive way to monitor hardware performance metrics. **htop** is an enhanced version of the **top** command that offers additional features such as color-coded display, mouse-based interaction, and customizable views. By launching **htop** in a terminal window, IT professionals can monitor system resource usage, CPU and memory utilization, and process activity in a visually appealing and intuitive interface. For example, launching **htop** displays a dynamic, color-coded view of system resource usage, allowing IT professionals to identify resource-intensive processes and manage system resources efficiently.

Moreover, cloud-based hardware performance monitoring platforms such as Datadog, New Relic, and Grafana provide scalable, centralized solutions for monitoring hardware performance metrics across distributed environments and cloud platforms. These platforms offer features such as real-time monitoring, customizable dashboards, alerting mechanisms, and historical data analysis, enabling organizations to monitor hardware performance metrics, track trends, and troubleshoot issues proactively. For example, organizations can use Datadog to monitor CPU utilization, memory usage, disk I/O, and network traffic across cloud instances, virtual machines, and containers, allowing IT professionals to detect anomalies, identify performance bottlenecks, and optimize resource allocation.

Furthermore, hardware performance monitoring tools often integrate with other monitoring and management systems such as network monitoring tools, application performance monitoring (APM) solutions, and infrastructure automation platforms to provide comprehensive visibility into system performance and health. For example, organizations may integrate hardware performance monitoring tools with network monitoring tools such as Nagios or Zabbix to correlate hardware performance metrics with network traffic and identify performance bottlenecks. Similarly, organizations may integrate hardware performance monitoring tools with APM solutions such as AppDynamics or Dynatrace to monitor hardware performance metrics in the context of application performance and user experience.

Additionally, hardware performance monitoring tools support the collection, aggregation, and visualization of hardware performance metrics over time, allowing organizations to track performance trends, analyze historical data, and forecast future resource requirements. By leveraging historical performance data, organizations can identify long-term trends, plan capacity upgrades, and optimize resource allocation to meet evolving business needs. For example, organizations can use Grafana to create custom dashboards that visualize CPU utilization, memory usage, disk I/O, and network throughput over time, allowing IT professionals to analyze performance trends and make data-driven decisions about hardware upgrades or optimizations.

In summary, hardware performance monitoring tools play a crucial role in ensuring the health, reliability, and efficiency of IT infrastructure by providing real-time insights into hardware performance metrics such as CPU utilization, memory usage, disk I/O, and network traffic. Whether using CLI-based tools such as **top**, **vmstat**, and **iostat**, GUI-based tools such as **htop**, or cloud-based platforms such as Datadog and New Relic, organizations can monitor hardware performance effectively, troubleshoot issues proactively, and optimize resource allocation to support business objectives. By integrating hardware performance monitoring tools with other monitoring and management systems and leveraging historical performance data, organizations can gain comprehensive visibility into system performance and make informed decisions about hardware upgrades, optimizations, and capacity planning.

Advanced hardware tuning methods are sophisticated techniques used by IT professionals to optimize the performance, reliability, and efficiency of hardware components in computer systems. These methods involve fine-tuning hardware settings, adjusting system configurations, and optimizing resource allocation to maximize system performance and meet specific workload requirements. From adjusting BIOS settings and firmware updates to optimizing hardware parameters and tuning kernel parameters, advanced hardware tuning methods require in-depth knowledge of hardware architecture, operating systems, and performance monitoring tools to achieve desired performance improvements and overcome performance bottlenecks.

One of the key aspects of advanced hardware tuning methods is adjusting BIOS (Basic Input/Output System) settings to optimize hardware performance and compatibility. The BIOS is firmware embedded in the motherboard that initializes hardware components during the boot process and provides basic input/output services to the operating system. By accessing the BIOS setup utility during system boot using a specific key (commonly Del, F2, or F10), IT professionals can adjust various hardware settings such as CPU clock speed, memory timings, power management options, and system voltages to optimize system performance and stability. For example, adjusting CPU settings such as multiplier, voltage, and frequency can overclock or underclock the CPU to achieve higher performance or lower power consumption, respectively.

Another aspect of advanced hardware tuning methods is applying firmware updates to hardware components such as CPUs, GPUs (Graphics Processing Units), storage controllers, and network interfaces to improve compatibility, reliability, and performance. Firmware updates, also known as BIOS updates, driver updates, or firmware upgrades, are software patches provided by hardware manufacturers to fix bugs, enhance functionality, and address security vulnerabilities in hardware components. By downloading and installing the latest firmware updates from the manufacturer's website or using firmware management tools provided by the operating system, IT professionals can ensure that hardware components are running the latest firmware versions with optimized performance and compatibility. For example, updating the firmware of a network interface card (NIC) can improve network performance, stability, and security by resolving compatibility issues with the operating system or network protocols.

Furthermore, advanced hardware tuning methods involve optimizing hardware parameters such as CPU cache size, memory interleaving, disk I/O scheduler, and network buffer size to improve system performance and responsiveness. These optimizations require modifying system configuration files or kernel parameters using text editors or system administration tools to fine-tune hardware settings according to workload characteristics and performance requirements. For example, adjusting the disk I/O scheduler algorithm from the default to a more suitable one such as deadline or noop can improve disk I/O performance for specific workloads such as database servers or virtualization hosts.

Moreover, advanced hardware tuning methods may involve tuning kernel parameters in the operating system to optimize hardware utilization, resource allocation, and system behavior. Kernel parameters, also known as sysctl parameters or kernel tunables, control various aspects of kernel behavior such as memory management, process scheduling, network stack, and file system caching. By modifying kernel parameters using the **sysctl** command or editing configuration files such as **/etc/sysctl.conf** or **/etc/sysctl.d/*.conf**, IT professionals can adjust system behavior to improve performance, scalability, and reliability. For example, increasing the maximum number of file descriptors or network connections can improve the scalability of web servers or database servers under heavy load.

Additionally, advanced hardware tuning methods may involve optimizing hardware virtualization settings such as CPU virtualization extensions (e.g., Intel VT-x, AMD-V), memory ballooning, and I/O virtualization to improve performance and efficiency in virtualized environments. Virtualization platforms such as VMware vSphere, Microsoft Hyper-V, and KVM (Kernel-based Virtual Machine) provide options to configure hardware virtualization features and allocate hardware resources to virtual machines (VMs) based on workload requirements. By adjusting virtualization settings and resource allocations using the management interface or CLI commands, IT professionals can optimize hardware utilization, improve VM performance, and achieve better consolidation ratios in virtualized environments. For example, enabling CPU virtualization extensions and hardware-assisted virtualization can improve the performance of CPU-bound workloads running in VMs by offloading virtualization tasks to the CPU hardware.

Furthermore, advanced hardware tuning methods may involve using performance monitoring tools such as **perf**, **sar**, and **dstat** to analyze hardware performance metrics, identify performance bottlenecks, and fine-tune hardware settings accordingly. These tools provide insights into hardware utilization, system resource usage, and performance metrics such as CPU utilization, memory usage, disk I/O throughput, and network traffic. By running performance monitoring tools in real-time or collecting performance data over time, IT professionals can identify performance bottlenecks, analyze performance trends, and optimize hardware configurations to achieve optimal performance and reliability. For example, analyzing CPU performance metrics using **sar -u** or **dstat --cpu** can identify CPU-bound processes or threads that may benefit from CPU affinity settings or task scheduling optimizations.

In summary, advanced hardware tuning methods are essential techniques used by IT professionals to optimize the performance, reliability, and efficiency of hardware components in computer systems. By adjusting BIOS settings, applying firmware updates, optimizing hardware parameters, tuning kernel parameters, optimizing hardware virtualization settings, and using performance monitoring tools, organizations can achieve significant performance improvements, overcome performance bottlenecks, and meet specific workload requirements effectively. Whether optimizing hardware for single-node systems, virtualized environments, or distributed systems, advanced hardware tuning methods enable organizations to maximize the value of their hardware investments and ensure optimal system performance and reliability.

Chapter 7: Managing Hardware Inventory and Assets

Advanced asset tracking systems are sophisticated solutions employed by organizations to monitor, manage, and optimize their assets efficiently and effectively. These systems utilize advanced technologies such as RFID (Radio Frequency Identification), GPS (Global Positioning System), IoT (Internet of Things), and cloud computing to track the location, status, and usage of assets in real-time. From inventory management and equipment tracking to fleet monitoring and supply chain optimization, advanced asset tracking systems enable organizations to improve operational efficiency, reduce costs, and enhance asset utilization across diverse industries and use cases.

One of the key components of advanced asset tracking systems is RFID technology, which enables organizations to identify and track assets using radio frequency signals transmitted between RFID tags and readers. RFID tags are small electronic devices containing a unique identifier that can be attached to assets such as inventory items, equipment, vehicles, and containers. RFID readers are devices that detect and read RFID tags within a specified range, allowing organizations to track the movement and location of assets as they pass through RFID reader zones. By deploying RFID tags and readers strategically in warehouses, distribution centers, manufacturing facilities, and transportation hubs, organizations can automate asset tracking processes, improve inventory visibility, and reduce manual labor associated with asset management tasks.

Another key component of advanced asset tracking systems is GPS technology, which enables organizations to track the location and movement of assets in real-time using satellite-based positioning systems. GPS tracking devices, also known as GPS trackers or GPS tags, are small electronic devices equipped with GPS receivers and cellular or satellite communication capabilities that transmit location data to central monitoring systems. By attaching GPS trackers to vehicles, equipment, containers, and high-value assets, organizations can monitor their location, route, speed, and status in real-time using web-based or mobile applications. By leveraging GPS technology, organizations can optimize fleet operations, improve asset security, and enhance logistics management by tracking assets' movements accurately and efficiently.

Additionally, IoT technology plays a significant role in advanced asset tracking systems by enabling organizations to connect and monitor assets remotely using sensors, actuators, and communication networks. IoT devices, such as environmental sensors, motion detectors, and vibration sensors, can be integrated with assets to monitor various parameters such as temperature, humidity, pressure, and motion. By collecting and analyzing sensor data in real-time, organizations can gain insights into asset condition, performance, and usage patterns, allowing them to optimize asset maintenance schedules, detect anomalies, and prevent equipment failures proactively. By deploying IoT-enabled asset tracking solutions, organizations can improve asset reliability, reduce downtime, and extend asset lifespan by implementing predictive maintenance strategies based on real-time sensor data.

Furthermore, cloud computing technology plays a crucial role in advanced asset tracking systems by providing scalable, centralized platforms for storing, processing, and analyzing asset data collected from diverse sources. Cloud-based asset tracking platforms offer features such as data storage, analytics, reporting, and integration with third-party systems, allowing organizations to manage their assets efficiently and securely from anywhere, at any time. By leveraging cloud-based asset tracking platforms, organizations can centralize asset data, gain actionable insights, and streamline asset management workflows across distributed locations and business units. By integrating cloud-based asset tracking platforms with enterprise resource planning (ERP) systems, warehouse management systems (WMS), and fleet management solutions, organizations can achieve end-to-end visibility and control over their assets throughout their lifecycle.

Moreover, advanced asset tracking systems may incorporate technologies such as barcode scanning, NFC (Near Field Communication), and Bluetooth Low Energy (BLE) to complement RFID, GPS, and IoT capabilities and provide additional functionalities for asset identification and tracking. Barcode scanning enables organizations to track assets using barcode labels affixed to assets, which can be scanned using handheld barcode scanners or mobile devices equipped with barcode scanning capabilities. NFC technology allows organizations to track assets using NFC-enabled smartphones or tablets, which can read NFC tags embedded in assets to retrieve asset information or trigger actions such as check-in/check-out operations. BLE technology enables organizations to track assets using low-power wireless beacons that broadcast their location and status to nearby BLE-enabled devices, allowing organizations to create proximity-based asset tracking solutions for indoor environments such as warehouses, retail stores, and manufacturing facilities.

Furthermore, advanced asset tracking systems may incorporate artificial intelligence (AI) and machine learning (ML) algorithms to analyze asset data, detect patterns, and predict future asset behavior. By applying AI and ML techniques to historical asset data, organizations can identify trends, anomalies, and correlations that may indicate potential issues or opportunities for optimization. For example, AI-powered predictive maintenance algorithms can analyze sensor data from equipment assets to predict when maintenance is required based on patterns of equipment degradation or failure. By deploying AI-enabled asset tracking solutions, organizations can optimize asset performance, reduce maintenance costs, and minimize downtime by proactively addressing asset issues before they escalate into critical failures.

In summary, advanced asset tracking systems leverage technologies such as RFID, GPS, IoT, cloud computing, barcode scanning, NFC, BLE, AI, and ML to monitor, manage, and optimize assets efficiently and effectively. By deploying advanced asset tracking systems, organizations can improve operational efficiency, reduce costs, and enhance asset utilization across diverse industries and use cases. Whether tracking inventory items, equipment, vehicles, or high-value assets, advanced asset tracking systems enable organizations to gain real-time visibility into asset location, status, and usage, empowering them to make data-driven decisions and achieve strategic business objectives. Hardware lifecycle management best practices encompass a comprehensive set of strategies and methodologies employed by organizations to effectively manage hardware assets throughout their lifecycle, from procurement and deployment to retirement and disposal. These best practices ensure that hardware assets are utilized efficiently, maintained properly, and retired responsibly, ultimately maximizing the return on investment (ROI) and minimizing risks associated with hardware ownership. By following established best practices for hardware lifecycle management, organizations can streamline operations, optimize resource utilization, and mitigate potential risks associated with hardware procurement, maintenance, and disposal.

The first phase of hardware lifecycle management is planning, which involves defining hardware requirements, evaluating technology options, and developing procurement strategies to acquire hardware assets that meet business needs and budget constraints. Organizations can use various methods to plan hardware procurement, including conducting needs assessments, analyzing usage patterns, and forecasting future demand for hardware resources. By defining hardware specifications, performance criteria, and budgetary constraints upfront, organizations can streamline the procurement process and ensure that hardware investments align with strategic business objectives.

Once hardware requirements are defined, the next phase of hardware lifecycle management is procurement, which involves sourcing hardware from vendors, negotiating contracts, and purchasing hardware assets according to established procurement policies and procedures. Organizations can use procurement tools and platforms to solicit bids from vendors, compare pricing and features, and select hardware suppliers based on factors such as cost, quality, and service level agreements (SLAs). By negotiating volume discounts, warranties, and service contracts, organizations can maximize the value of hardware purchases and minimize total cost of ownership (TCO) over the hardware lifecycle.

After procuring hardware assets, the next phase of hardware lifecycle management is deployment, which involves installing, configuring, and integrating hardware into existing IT infrastructure to support business operations and workflows. Organizations can use deployment tools and automation scripts to streamline the deployment process and ensure consistent configuration across multiple hardware assets. By following deployment best practices such as standardizing hardware configurations, documenting installation procedures, and conducting pilot testing before full-scale deployment, organizations can minimize deployment risks and ensure that hardware assets are deployed successfully.

Once hardware assets are deployed, the next phase of hardware lifecycle management is operation and maintenance, which involves monitoring hardware performance, applying software updates, and performing routine maintenance tasks to ensure optimal performance and reliability. Organizations can use monitoring tools and management platforms to track hardware health, detect performance anomalies, and proactively address issues before they escalate into critical failures. By implementing preventive maintenance schedules, performing regular inspections, and replacing worn-out components proactively, organizations can extend the lifespan of hardware assets and minimize unplanned downtime.

As hardware assets age and reach the end of their useful life, the next phase of hardware lifecycle management is retirement and disposal, which involves decommissioning hardware assets, securely wiping data, and disposing of hardware components in an environmentally responsible manner. Organizations can use decommissioning tools and data erasure software to wipe sensitive data from storage devices and ensure compliance with data privacy regulations. By recycling or refurbishing hardware components, organizations can recover valuable materials and reduce the environmental impact of hardware disposal.

Throughout the hardware lifecycle, organizations should also maintain accurate records of hardware assets, including inventory information, warranty status, maintenance history, and disposal records. By implementing asset management systems and inventory tracking tools, organizations can track hardware assets throughout their lifecycle, monitor asset utilization, and make informed decisions about hardware upgrades, replacements, and retirements. By maintaining comprehensive asset documentation and conducting regular audits, organizations can ensure compliance with regulatory requirements and minimize the risk of asset loss or theft.

Furthermore, organizations should periodically review and update their hardware lifecycle management processes to incorporate emerging technologies, industry best practices, and lessons learned from previous hardware lifecycle management initiatives. By conducting post-implementation reviews, soliciting feedback from stakeholders, and benchmarking against industry standards, organizations can identify areas for improvement and implement continuous process improvements to optimize hardware lifecycle management practices.

In summary, hardware lifecycle management best practices encompass a comprehensive set of strategies and methodologies employed by organizations to effectively manage hardware assets throughout their lifecycle. By following established best practices for hardware planning, procurement, deployment, operation and maintenance, retirement and disposal, organizations can optimize resource utilization, minimize risks, and maximize the return on investment from hardware assets. By maintaining accurate records, conducting regular audits, and incorporating continuous process improvements, organizations can ensure that hardware lifecycle management practices align with strategic business objectives and support long-term sustainability and growth.

Chapter 8: Advanced BIOS and Firmware Configuration

BIOS customization and optimization are critical processes in maximizing the performance, stability, and functionality of computer systems by fine-tuning settings in the Basic Input/Output System (BIOS) firmware. The BIOS, residing on a motherboard's firmware chip, initializes hardware components during boot-up and provides low-level system configuration options. Customizing and optimizing BIOS settings enable users to tailor system behavior to their specific requirements, whether it's overclocking hardware for enhanced performance, adjusting power management settings for energy efficiency, or configuring hardware compatibility options for stability. These processes involve accessing the BIOS setup utility, navigating through various settings, and adjusting parameters according to hardware specifications and performance goals.

One of the primary purposes of BIOS customization and optimization is overclocking, a technique used to increase the clock speed of hardware components such as CPUs, memory modules, and GPUs beyond their factory-set frequencies. Overclocking can result in significant performance gains for tasks that are CPU or GPU-bound, such as gaming, video editing, and scientific simulations. To overclock a CPU in the BIOS, users typically enter the BIOS setup utility by pressing a specific key during the boot process, such as Del, F2, or F10, depending on the motherboard manufacturer. Once in the BIOS setup utility, users navigate to the overclocking settings, which may be located under headings such as "Advanced," "CPU Configuration," or "Overclocking." From there, users can adjust parameters such as CPU multiplier, base clock frequency, and voltage settings to overclock the CPU safely within thermal and voltage limits.

Similarly, memory overclocking involves adjusting memory timings, frequencies, and voltages in the BIOS to achieve higher memory bandwidth and lower latency, resulting in improved system responsiveness and application performance. Memory overclocking can be done by accessing the memory settings in the BIOS setup utility and adjusting parameters such as memory frequency (MHz), memory voltage (V), and memory timings (CAS latency, tRCD, tRP, tRAS). By carefully tweaking memory settings and stress-testing the system for stability using tools like MemTest86 or Prime95, users can determine the optimal memory overclocking configuration for their hardware.

In addition to overclocking, BIOS customization and optimization encompass power management settings, which allow users to control system power consumption, heat generation, and battery life. Power management settings in the BIOS setup utility include options such as CPU power states (C-states), CPU voltage regulation (VRM), and fan control profiles. By adjusting power management settings, users can optimize system performance and energy efficiency based on workload characteristics and usage patterns. For example, enabling CPU power-saving features such as Intel SpeedStep or AMD Cool'n'Quiet can dynamically adjust CPU clock speeds and voltages to match processing demands, reducing power consumption and heat output during idle periods.

Furthermore, BIOS customization and optimization involve configuring hardware compatibility options to ensure system stability and compatibility with peripheral devices, storage drives, and expansion cards. Compatibility options in the BIOS setup utility include settings such as SATA mode (AHCI, IDE, RAID), USB legacy support, and PCI Express (PCIe) configuration. By selecting the appropriate compatibility options, users can resolve compatibility issues, enable advanced features, and optimize system performance. For example, setting the SATA mode to AHCI (Advanced Host Controller Interface) enables advanced features such as Native Command Queuing (NCQ) and hot-swappable SATA devices, improving storage performance and flexibility.

Moreover, BIOS customization and optimization extend to security settings, which allow users to enhance system security and protect against unauthorized access, malware, and data breaches. Security settings in the BIOS setup utility include options such as Secure Boot, TPM (Trusted Platform Module), and BIOS password protection. By enabling Secure Boot, users can ensure that only digitally signed operating system bootloaders and drivers are loaded during the boot process, preventing the execution of malicious code or unauthorized software. Similarly, enabling TPM support allows users to leverage hardware-based encryption and secure storage for sensitive data, enhancing system security and integrity.

Additionally, BIOS customization and optimization encompass fine-tuning advanced features and settings specific to certain motherboard models and hardware platforms. These features may include advanced chipset settings, hardware monitoring options, and BIOS firmware updates. Advanced chipset settings allow users to optimize system performance by adjusting parameters such as memory interleaving, PCI Express (PCIe) bandwidth allocation, and USB controller settings. Hardware monitoring options enable users to monitor system temperatures, voltages, and fan speeds in real-time, ensuring optimal system cooling and stability. BIOS firmware updates provide patches, bug fixes, and performance enhancements released by motherboard manufacturers to improve system compatibility, stability, and security over time.

Furthermore, BIOS customization and optimization require careful consideration of hardware compatibility, thermal constraints, and warranty implications when making changes to BIOS settings. Overclocking hardware beyond factory specifications may void warranty coverage and increase the risk of hardware damage or instability if not done cautiously. It's essential to research hardware specifications, consult manufacturer documentation, and follow best practices for overclocking and BIOS customization to ensure safe and effective results. By leveraging BIOS customization and optimization techniques, users can unlock the full potential of their hardware, achieve higher performance levels, and tailor system behavior to their specific needs and preferences.

Firmware security best practices are essential guidelines and methodologies employed by organizations to mitigate security risks associated with firmware vulnerabilities, exploits, and attacks on embedded systems, IoT devices, and hardware peripherals. Firmware, residing on non-volatile memory chips such as ROM (Read-Only Memory), EEPROM (Electrically Erasable Programmable Read-Only Memory), or flash memory, contains low-level software code that controls hardware initialization, device drivers, and system boot-up processes. Securing firmware is critical to prevent unauthorized access, data breaches, and malicious activities that could compromise system integrity, confidentiality, and availability. Firmware security best practices encompass a range of strategies, including secure boot, code signing, firmware updates, vulnerability management, and threat intelligence, to protect firmware assets and ensure their trustworthiness.

One of the fundamental aspects of firmware security is secure boot, a process that verifies the integrity and authenticity of firmware code during the system boot-up sequence to prevent unauthorized or tampered firmware from executing. Secure boot relies on cryptographic mechanisms such as digital signatures and hash functions to validate firmware images before loading them into memory. Organizations can enable secure boot functionality on supported hardware platforms by accessing the BIOS or UEFI (Unified Extensible Firmware Interface) setup utility and configuring secure boot options. By enabling secure boot and specifying trusted firmware sources, organizations can protect against firmware tampering, rootkits, and boot-time attacks that attempt to compromise system integrity by modifying firmware code.

Another key aspect of firmware security is code signing, a technique used to digitally sign firmware images and updates with cryptographic keys to verify their authenticity and integrity. Code signing ensures that firmware code comes from a trusted source and has not been altered or tampered with during transmission or storage. Organizations can generate digital signatures for firmware images using code signing tools and cryptographic algorithms such as RSA (Rivest-Shamir-Adleman) or ECDSA (Elliptic Curve Digital Signature Algorithm). By validating digital signatures during the firmware update process, devices can verify the authenticity of firmware images before applying updates, preventing the installation of malicious or unauthorized firmware.

Furthermore, firmware security best practices include implementing secure firmware update mechanisms to deliver patches, bug fixes, and security updates to devices in a timely and secure manner. Secure firmware updates rely on encrypted communication channels, authentication mechanisms, and integrity checks to protect firmware images during transmission and installation. Organizations can deploy secure firmware update mechanisms using protocols such as HTTPS (Hypertext Transfer Protocol Secure), TLS (Transport Layer Security), or proprietary update protocols. By encrypting firmware images, signing update packages, and verifying digital signatures during the update process, organizations can ensure the confidentiality, integrity, and authenticity of firmware updates, minimizing the risk of firmware-related security incidents.

Additionally, firmware security best practices involve vulnerability management processes to identify, assess, and remediate security vulnerabilities in firmware components and underlying hardware platforms. Vulnerability management encompasses activities such as vulnerability scanning, risk assessment, patch management, and vulnerability disclosure coordination. Organizations can use vulnerability scanning tools and security assessment frameworks to identify known vulnerabilities in firmware code, firmware dependencies, and third-party libraries. By prioritizing and addressing high-risk vulnerabilities through patch management processes, organizations can reduce the likelihood of firmware-related security breaches and minimize the impact of potential exploits.

Moreover, firmware security best practices include leveraging threat intelligence sources and security information sharing platforms to stay informed about emerging threats, attack vectors, and vulnerabilities affecting firmware ecosystems. Threat intelligence feeds provide organizations with timely information about known vulnerabilities, exploit techniques, and malware targeting firmware-based systems. By monitoring threat intelligence feeds, subscribing to security advisories, and participating in industry forums and mailing lists, organizations can proactively identify and respond to firmware-related security threats, enhancing their overall security posture and resilience against cyber attacks.

Furthermore, firmware security best practices encompass implementing hardware-based security features such as secure enclaves, trusted execution environments (TEEs), and hardware security modules (HSMs) to protect firmware assets from physical attacks, side-channel attacks, and hardware tampering. Hardware-based security features provide a secure execution environment for firmware code, cryptographic operations, and sensitive data storage, isolating critical components from unauthorized access and manipulation. By leveraging hardware-based security features in embedded systems, IoT devices, and hardware peripherals, organizations can enhance firmware security and defend against advanced threats targeting firmware vulnerabilities.

Additionally, firmware security best practices involve continuous monitoring, auditing, and logging of firmware-related activities to detect and respond to security incidents in real-time. Organizations can deploy monitoring tools, intrusion detection systems (IDS), and security information and event management (SIEM) solutions to monitor firmware integrity, analyze firmware behavior, and detect anomalous activities indicative of security breaches. By correlating firmware-related events with network traffic, system logs, and security alerts, organizations can identify signs of compromise, investigate security incidents, and implement response measures to contain and mitigate the impact of firmware-related attacks.

In summary, firmware security best practices are essential guidelines and methodologies employed by organizations to mitigate security risks associated with firmware vulnerabilities, exploits, and attacks on embedded systems,

IoT devices, and hardware peripherals. By implementing secure boot, code signing, secure firmware update mechanisms, vulnerability management processes, threat intelligence integration, hardware-based security features, and continuous monitoring, organizations can protect firmware assets and ensure their trustworthiness. By adopting a proactive approach to firmware security, organizations can reduce the likelihood of firmware-related security incidents, safeguard sensitive data, and maintain the integrity and availability of critical systems and infrastructure.

Chapter 9: Hardware Security Best Practices

Advanced hardware security mechanisms encompass a range of sophisticated techniques and technologies employed to protect hardware components, systems, and devices from cyber threats, physical attacks, and unauthorized access. These mechanisms leverage hardware-based security features, cryptographic algorithms, and specialized hardware components to enforce security policies, authenticate users, encrypt data, and safeguard sensitive information. From secure boot and trusted execution environments to hardware security modules and tamper-resistant chips, advanced hardware security mechanisms play a critical role in defending against evolving cyber threats and ensuring the integrity, confidentiality, and availability of hardware assets in various domains and applications.

One of the fundamental hardware security mechanisms is secure boot, a process that verifies the integrity and authenticity of firmware and operating system code during the system boot-up sequence to prevent unauthorized or tampered code from executing. Secure boot relies on cryptographic techniques such as digital signatures and hash functions to validate firmware and bootloader images before loading them into memory. Organizations can enable secure boot functionality on supported hardware platforms by configuring secure boot options in the BIOS or UEFI setup utility. By ensuring that only trusted firmware and operating system code are executed during boot-up, secure boot protects against boot-time attacks, rootkits, and malware that attempt to compromise system integrity by injecting malicious code into the boot process.

Another critical hardware security mechanism is trusted execution environments (TEEs), which provide isolated execution environments within the main processor or system-on-chip (SoC) to run trusted applications and cryptographic operations securely. TEEs use hardware-based isolation mechanisms such as secure enclaves, memory protection units (MPUs), and secure co-processors to prevent unauthorized access to sensitive data and code. Popular TEE implementations include Intel SGX (Software Guard Extensions) and ARM TrustZone, which provide secure execution environments for applications that require confidentiality, integrity, and authenticity guarantees. By leveraging TEEs, organizations can protect sensitive workloads, cryptographic keys, and intellectual property from unauthorized access and tampering, even in the presence of compromised operating systems or hypervisors.

Moreover, hardware security modules (HSMs) are specialized hardware devices or embedded components designed to perform cryptographic operations, key management, and secure storage of cryptographic keys and sensitive data. HSMs incorporate tamper-resistant hardware, secure firmware, and dedicated cryptographic processors to ensure the confidentiality, integrity, and availability of cryptographic operations and keys. Organizations can deploy HSMs in data centers, cloud environments, and IoT devices to protect cryptographic keys from unauthorized access, theft, or misuse. By offloading cryptographic operations to HSMs, organizations can achieve compliance with regulatory requirements, strengthen cryptographic security, and mitigate the risk of cryptographic key compromise.

Additionally, tamper-resistant chips and secure elements are hardware components designed to withstand physical attacks, reverse engineering, and tampering attempts aimed at extracting sensitive information or compromising device security. These chips integrate security features such as anti-tamper coatings, meshed metal layers, and secure storage elements to protect against invasive attacks, side-channel attacks, and fault injection techniques. Tamper-resistant chips are used in various applications, including smart cards, payment terminals, automotive systems, and industrial control systems, to protect against physical attacks and ensure the integrity and confidentiality of critical operations and data.

Furthermore, hardware-based random number generators (RNGs) are essential components of advanced hardware security mechanisms, providing a reliable source of entropy for cryptographic operations such as key generation, encryption, and digital signatures. Hardware RNGs leverage physical processes such as thermal noise, radioactivity, or electronic noise to generate random values with high entropy levels, ensuring unpredictability and randomness required for cryptographic security. Organizations can use hardware RNGs in cryptographic applications, secure communication protocols, and cryptographic algorithms to enhance security and protect against cryptographic attacks such as key guessing, brute force attacks, and cryptographic vulnerabilities resulting from weak entropy sources.

Moreover, hardware-based authentication mechanisms such as biometric sensors, hardware tokens, and secure authentication chips provide robust authentication and access control capabilities for user authentication, device authentication, and identity verification. Biometric sensors, such as fingerprint scanners, iris scanners, and facial recognition cameras, authenticate users based on unique physiological characteristics, providing strong authentication and reducing reliance on passwords or PINs. Hardware tokens, such as smart cards, USB security keys, and one-time password (OTP) tokens, generate cryptographic credentials or authentication codes to verify user identities and secure access to sensitive resources. Secure authentication chips, such as TPMs (Trusted Platform Modules) and secure elements, provide hardware-based authentication and key management capabilities to protect against credential theft, replay attacks, and impersonation attacks.

Additionally, hardware-based memory encryption and memory isolation mechanisms are essential components of advanced hardware security mechanisms, providing protection against memory-based attacks, buffer overflows, and code injection vulnerabilities. Memory encryption technologies such as Intel SGX, AMD SEV (Secure Encrypted Virtualization), and ARM Memory Tagging Extension (MTE) encrypt memory contents to protect against unauthorized access and tampering. Memory isolation mechanisms such as address space layout randomization (ASLR), data execution prevention (DEP), and memory protection units (MPUs) enforce memory access policies and prevent malicious code execution in privileged memory regions. By leveraging memory encryption and isolation mechanisms, organizations can mitigate the risk of memory-based attacks, data breaches, and memory corruption vulnerabilities in software applications and operating systems.

In summary, advanced hardware security mechanisms encompass a range of sophisticated techniques and technologies employed to protect hardware components, systems, and devices from cyber threats, physical attacks, and unauthorized access. From secure boot and trusted execution environments to hardware security modules and tamper-resistant chips, these mechanisms leverage hardware-based security features, cryptographic algorithms, and specialized hardware components to ensure the integrity, confidentiality, and availability of hardware assets in various domains and applications. By adopting advanced hardware security mechanisms, organizations can enhance their overall security posture, mitigate risks, and safeguard critical operations and data against emerging threats and vulnerabilities.

Hardware security auditing techniques are essential methodologies used to assess the security posture of hardware components, systems, and devices to identify vulnerabilities, weaknesses, and security gaps that could be exploited by attackers. These techniques involve evaluating hardware design, configuration, implementation, and operation to ensure compliance with security best practices, standards, and regulatory requirements. By conducting hardware security audits, organizations can proactively identify and address security risks, enhance their overall security posture, and protect against cyber threats and attacks targeting hardware assets. Hardware security auditing techniques encompass a range of methodologies, including vulnerability scanning, penetration testing, code review, firmware analysis, and physical security assessments, to evaluate hardware security controls and mitigate potential risks.

One of the fundamental hardware security auditing techniques is vulnerability scanning, a process that involves using automated tools and scanners to identify known vulnerabilities, misconfigurations, and security weaknesses in hardware components, firmware, and operating systems. Vulnerability scanning tools such as Nessus, OpenVAS, and Qualys Vulnerability Management scan devices and networks for known vulnerabilities based on predefined signatures, vulnerability databases, and Common Vulnerability Scoring System (CVSS) metrics. Organizations can deploy vulnerability scanning tools to assess the security posture of hardware assets, prioritize remediation efforts, and ensure compliance with security policies and standards. By regularly scanning hardware components for vulnerabilities and applying patches and updates, organizations can reduce the risk of exploitation and compromise by malicious actors.

Another critical hardware security auditing technique is penetration testing, a controlled process of simulating real-world cyber attacks to identify security weaknesses, exploit vulnerabilities, and assess the effectiveness of security controls in protecting hardware assets. Penetration testing, also known as ethical hacking, involves conducting security assessments from the perspective of an attacker to identify potential attack vectors, privilege escalation paths, and data exfiltration techniques. Penetration testers use a variety of tools and techniques, including network sniffing, password cracking, and social engineering, to uncover security vulnerabilities and demonstrate the impact of successful attacks. Organizations can perform penetration testing on hardware components, embedded systems, and IoT devices to validate security controls, identify security gaps, and prioritize remediation efforts. By conducting penetration testing regularly and addressing identified vulnerabilities, organizations can improve their resilience to cyber attacks and enhance the security posture of hardware assets.

Moreover, code review is an essential hardware security auditing technique that involves examining firmware, device drivers, and hardware configuration files to identify security vulnerabilities, logic flaws, and coding errors that could be exploited by attackers. Code review, also known as static analysis, entails reviewing source code, binary executables, and configuration files for security issues such as buffer overflows, input validation errors, and hardcoded credentials. Organizations can perform code reviews manually or using automated code analysis tools such as

CodeSonar, Coverity, and Fortify Static Code Analyzer to identify potential security vulnerabilities and adherence to secure coding practices. By conducting code reviews during the development and deployment phases, organizations can detect and remediate security flaws early in the software development lifecycle, reducing the risk of security breaches and ensuring the integrity and confidentiality of hardware assets.

Additionally, firmware analysis is a critical hardware security auditing technique that involves analyzing firmware images, bootloader code, and device firmware update mechanisms to identify security vulnerabilities, backdoors, and unauthorized modifications that could compromise the security of hardware components and embedded systems. Firmware analysis techniques include static analysis, dynamic analysis, and reverse engineering methods to extract, disassemble, and analyze firmware code for potential security risks. Organizations can use firmware analysis tools such as Binwalk, IDA Pro, and Ghidra to analyze firmware images, identify known vulnerabilities, and assess the security posture of hardware devices. By conducting firmware analysis regularly and applying security patches and updates, organizations can mitigate the risk of firmware-related security incidents, ensure the integrity of firmware code, and protect against unauthorized access and manipulation.

Furthermore, physical security assessments are essential hardware security auditing techniques that involve evaluating the physical security controls, access controls, and environmental controls in place to protect hardware assets from unauthorized access, theft, and tampering. Physical security assessments include evaluating security measures such as access control systems, surveillance cameras, alarm systems, and environmental monitoring systems to ensure compliance with security policies and standards. Organizations can conduct physical security assessments using techniques such as security surveys, site inspections, and threat modeling to identify vulnerabilities and weaknesses in physical security controls. By implementing physical security best practices, such as restricting access to sensitive areas, securing server rooms and data centers, and monitoring physical access logs, organizations can prevent unauthorized access, protect against insider threats, and ensure the availability and integrity of hardware assets.

In summary, hardware security auditing techniques are essential methodologies used to assess the security posture of hardware components, systems, and devices to identify vulnerabilities, weaknesses, and security gaps that could be exploited by attackers. By leveraging techniques such as vulnerability scanning, penetration testing, code review, firmware analysis, and physical security assessments, organizations can evaluate hardware security controls, identify potential risks, and prioritize remediation efforts to enhance the overall security posture of hardware assets. By adopting a proactive approach to hardware security auditing, organizations can mitigate security risks, protect against cyber threats, and ensure the confidentiality, integrity, and availability of hardware assets in various environments and applications.

Chapter 10: Implementing Sustainable Hardware Maintenance Procedures

Sustainable hardware maintenance models are crucial frameworks employed by organizations to ensure the longevity, reliability, and efficiency of hardware assets while minimizing environmental impact and resource consumption. These models encompass various strategies, practices, and methodologies aimed at extending the lifespan of hardware equipment, optimizing resource utilization, reducing electronic waste (e-waste), and promoting sustainable practices throughout the hardware lifecycle. By adopting sustainable hardware maintenance models, organizations can achieve cost savings, environmental stewardship, and operational efficiency while meeting business objectives and regulatory requirements.

One of the fundamental aspects of sustainable hardware maintenance models is proactive maintenance, which involves preemptive measures to identify and address hardware issues before they escalate into costly failures or downtime. Proactive maintenance includes routine inspections, preventive maintenance tasks, and predictive analytics to detect potential hardware failures, component degradation, and performance degradation. Organizations can implement proactive maintenance strategies using asset management software, monitoring tools, and diagnostic utilities to track hardware health indicators, monitor system performance metrics, and schedule maintenance activities based on predefined thresholds. By performing proactive maintenance regularly, organizations can reduce the risk of unexpected hardware failures, extend equipment lifespan, and optimize resource utilization.

Moreover, sustainable hardware maintenance models emphasize energy-efficient practices to minimize power consumption, reduce carbon emissions, and lower operating costs associated with hardware infrastructure. Energy-efficient practices include optimizing hardware configurations, implementing power management features, and upgrading to energy-efficient components and technologies. Organizations can leverage power management utilities and system monitoring tools to measure power consumption, identify energy-intensive components, and implement power-saving settings such as sleep mode, hibernation, and dynamic voltage scaling. By adopting energy-efficient practices, organizations can reduce their environmental footprint, achieve energy savings, and contribute to sustainability goals while maintaining hardware reliability and performance.

Furthermore, sustainable hardware maintenance models incorporate lifecycle management principles to ensure responsible disposal, recycling, and reuse of hardware assets at the end of their useful life. Lifecycle management encompasses asset tracking, inventory management, and end-of-life planning to track hardware assets, assess their condition, and make informed decisions about disposal, decommissioning, or repurposing. Organizations can use asset management software and inventory tracking systems to maintain accurate records of hardware assets, including purchase dates, warranty information, and disposal dates. By implementing responsible end-of-life practices such as recycling, refurbishment, or donation, organizations can minimize e-waste generation, recover valuable resources, and reduce environmental pollution associated with hardware disposal.

Additionally, sustainable hardware maintenance models advocate for modular design principles and standardization of hardware components to facilitate repair, upgrade, and maintenance activities throughout the hardware lifecycle. Modular design enables the interchangeability of components, ease of maintenance, and scalability of hardware systems, reducing the need for costly repairs or full hardware replacements. Organizations can adopt modular hardware architectures, standardized interfaces, and open standards to facilitate interoperability, compatibility, and upgradability of hardware components. By embracing modular design principles, organizations can extend the lifespan of hardware assets, reduce dependency on proprietary technologies, and promote sustainable practices in hardware maintenance and management.

Moreover, sustainable hardware maintenance models promote collaboration and knowledge sharing among stakeholders, including hardware manufacturers, vendors, service providers, and end-users, to collectively address sustainability challenges and drive innovation in hardware maintenance practices. Collaboration initiatives such as industry consortia, standards bodies, and community forums facilitate the exchange of best practices, lessons learned, and technical expertise in sustainable hardware maintenance. Organizations can participate in collaborative projects, share resources, and leverage collective intelligence to develop sustainable hardware maintenance solutions, address common challenges, and promote environmental stewardship across the industry.

Furthermore, sustainable hardware maintenance models advocate for continuous improvement and innovation in hardware maintenance practices, technologies, and processes to adapt to evolving environmental regulations, technological advancements, and market trends. Continuous improvement involves monitoring key performance indicators (KPIs), soliciting feedback from stakeholders, and implementing feedback loops to identify opportunities for optimization and innovation in hardware maintenance. Organizations can leverage data analytics, machine learning algorithms, and predictive maintenance models to analyze maintenance data, identify patterns, and predict future hardware failures or performance issues. By embracing a culture of continuous improvement and innovation, organizations can enhance the sustainability, efficiency, and resilience of their hardware maintenance operations while delivering value to stakeholders and achieving long-term business success.

In summary, sustainable hardware maintenance models are essential frameworks employed by organizations to ensure the longevity, reliability, and efficiency of hardware assets while minimizing environmental impact and resource consumption. By adopting proactive maintenance practices, energy-efficient strategies, lifecycle management principles, modular design principles, collaboration initiatives, and continuous improvement efforts, organizations can promote sustainability, reduce operating costs, and mitigate environmental risks associated with hardware maintenance operations. By integrating sustainability considerations into hardware maintenance practices, organizations can contribute to environmental conservation, achieve regulatory compliance, and foster a culture of environmental stewardship in the technology industry.

Environmentally friendly hardware disposal practices are crucial methodologies employed by organizations to responsibly dispose of end-of-life hardware assets while minimizing environmental impact, reducing electronic waste (e-waste), and promoting sustainable practices. These practices encompass various strategies, regulations, and initiatives aimed at recycling, refurbishing, or repurposing hardware equipment to recover valuable resources, reduce pollution, and conserve energy. By adopting environmentally friendly hardware disposal practices, organizations can mitigate the negative effects of e-waste, comply with regulatory requirements, and demonstrate corporate social responsibility.

One of the fundamental aspects of environmentally friendly hardware disposal practices is electronic waste recycling, which involves dismantling hardware equipment and recovering valuable materials such as metals, plastics, and glass for reuse in manufacturing processes. Electronic waste recycling facilities use specialized equipment and processes to disassemble, shred, and separate electronic components into recyclable materials, including circuit boards, cables, and batteries. Organizations can partner with certified e-waste recycling vendors or facilities to dispose of end-of-life hardware equipment responsibly and ensure compliance with environmental regulations. By recycling electronic waste, organizations can conserve natural resources, reduce energy consumption, and minimize the environmental footprint associated with manufacturing new hardware products.

Moreover, environmentally friendly hardware disposal practices advocate for refurbishment and reuse of end-of-life hardware assets to extend their lifespan and maximize their value before disposal. Refurbishment involves inspecting, repairing, and upgrading hardware equipment to restore functionality and performance, making it suitable for resale or donation to charitable organizations, schools, or nonprofit organizations. Organizations can establish refurbishment programs or partnerships with refurbishment centers to refurbish and redistribute hardware assets to underserved communities or emerging markets. By promoting refurbishment and reuse, organizations can reduce the demand for new hardware products, conserve resources, and support circular economy initiatives aimed at minimizing waste and maximizing resource efficiency.

Furthermore, environmentally friendly hardware disposal practices include proper handling and disposal of hazardous materials and components found in electronic devices, such as batteries, mercury-containing lamps, and cathode ray tubes (CRTs). Hazardous materials pose environmental and health risks if not disposed of properly, contaminating soil, water, and air, and endangering human health and wildlife. Organizations must comply with regulations governing the disposal of hazardous electronic waste, including the Resource Conservation and Recovery Act (RCRA) and the Restriction of Hazardous Substances (RoHS) directive, which restrict the use of certain hazardous substances in electronic products. By partnering with certified hazardous waste disposal vendors or facilities, organizations can ensure the safe and environmentally responsible disposal of hazardous electronic waste, minimizing the risk of environmental contamination and human exposure to harmful substances.

Moreover, environmentally friendly hardware disposal practices advocate for data sanitization and secure data destruction to protect sensitive information and preserve privacy during the disposal process. Data sanitization involves removing all traces of data from hardware devices using secure erasure methods such as overwriting, degaussing, or physical destruction of storage media. Organizations can use data erasure software tools or data destruction services to sanitize storage devices, including hard disk drives, solid-state drives, and removable media, before disposal. By ensuring the secure disposal of data-bearing devices, organizations can prevent data breaches, identity theft, and unauthorized access to confidential information, maintaining compliance with data protection regulations and safeguarding the privacy of individuals.

Additionally, environmentally friendly hardware disposal practices encompass end-of-life management strategies such as extended producer responsibility (EPR) programs, product take-back initiatives, and voluntary industry certifications to promote environmental sustainability and accountability throughout the product lifecycle. EPR programs require manufacturers to take responsibility for the collection, recycling, and disposal of their products at the end of their useful life, incentivizing eco-design, material recycling, and product stewardship. Organizations can participate in EPR programs or product take-back schemes to comply with regulatory obligations, reduce environmental impact, and enhance brand reputation as environmentally responsible businesses. By obtaining voluntary industry certifications such as e-Stewards, R2 (Responsible Recycling), or WEEE (Waste Electrical and Electronic Equipment) compliance, organizations can demonstrate their commitment to environmentally friendly hardware disposal practices and differentiate themselves as leaders in sustainability.

Furthermore, environmentally friendly hardware disposal practices advocate for education and awareness initiatives to inform stakeholders about the importance of responsible e-waste management, recycling, and sustainability practices. Organizations can raise awareness among employees, customers, and partners through training programs, informational materials, and public outreach campaigns highlighting the environmental impact of e-waste, the benefits of recycling, and the importance of sustainable consumption habits. By educating stakeholders about environmentally friendly hardware disposal practices, organizations can foster a culture of environmental stewardship, encourage responsible behavior, and inspire collective action to address e-waste challenges and promote sustainable development.

In summary, environmentally friendly hardware disposal practices are crucial methodologies employed by organizations to responsibly dispose of end-of-life hardware assets while minimizing environmental impact, reducing e-waste, and promoting sustainable practices. By adopting strategies such as electronic waste recycling, refurbishment and reuse, proper handling of hazardous materials, data sanitization, end-of-life management programs, and education and awareness initiatives, organizations can mitigate the negative effects of e-waste, comply with regulatory requirements, and demonstrate corporate social responsibility. By embracing environmentally friendly hardware disposal practices, organizations can contribute to environmental conservation, resource efficiency, and sustainable development, while protecting the planet for future generations.

BOOK 4
EXPERT SERVICE DESK STRATEGIES
INSTALLING AND MANAGING COMPLEX SOFTWARE
SYSTEMS

ROB BOTWRIGHT

Chapter 1: Understanding Complex Software Systems

Software architecture fundamentals are essential concepts and principles that guide the design, development, and implementation of software systems, ensuring their reliability, scalability, maintainability, and performance. These fundamentals encompass various aspects of software design, including architectural styles, design patterns, architectural decisions, and quality attributes, to create robust and efficient software solutions. By understanding and applying software architecture fundamentals, software engineers can design systems that meet business requirements, adhere to industry best practices, and evolve over time to accommodate changing needs and technologies.

One of the fundamental aspects of software architecture is architectural styles, which represent recurring patterns or structures used to organize and design software systems. Common architectural styles include the client-server architecture, where clients and servers communicate over a network, the layered architecture, where software components are organized into layers based on their functionality, and the microservices architecture, where a system is decomposed into small, independently deployable services. Each architectural style has its advantages and trade-offs, and the choice of architecture depends on factors such as system requirements, scalability needs, and development team expertise.

Another important aspect of software architecture fundamentals is design patterns, which are reusable solutions to common design problems encountered during software development. Design patterns provide a blueprint for solving specific design challenges and promote code reusability, modularity, and maintainability. Examples of design patterns include the Singleton pattern, which ensures that a class has only one instance, the Factory pattern, which encapsulates object creation logic, and the Observer pattern, which defines a one-to-many dependency between objects. By leveraging design patterns, software engineers can create flexible and extensible software architectures that are easier to understand, modify, and maintain.

Furthermore, software architecture fundamentals encompass architectural decisions, which involve making informed choices about design trade-offs, technologies, and architectural elements to achieve desired system qualities. Architectural decisions address concerns such as performance, security, scalability, and extensibility, and involve evaluating alternative solutions and selecting the most suitable option based on project requirements and constraints. Examples of architectural decisions include choosing between relational and NoSQL databases, selecting programming languages and frameworks, and deciding on deployment models such as on-premises or cloud-based infrastructure. By making well-informed architectural decisions, software engineers can design systems that meet functional and non-functional requirements while balancing trade-offs and risks.

Moreover, software architecture fundamentals include quality attributes, which define the desirable characteristics of a software system in terms of performance, reliability, security, and maintainability. Quality attributes, also known as non-functional requirements, influence architectural decisions and design choices and are essential for assessing and evaluating system quality. Common quality attributes include availability, which measures the system's uptime and reliability, performance, which relates to the system's responsiveness and throughput, security, which ensures the confidentiality, integrity, and availability of data, and maintainability, which refers to the ease of modifying and extending the system over time. By prioritizing and addressing quality attributes during the design and development process, software engineers can create software systems that meet user expectations and organizational goals.

Additionally, software architecture fundamentals involve architectural modeling and documentation, which are essential practices for communicating design decisions, system structure, and interactions among components to stakeholders. Architectural modeling involves creating diagrams, views, and documentation that capture the structure, behavior, and relationships of software components and subsystems. Common architectural modeling techniques include UML (Unified Modeling Language) diagrams such as class diagrams, sequence diagrams, and deployment diagrams, which provide visual representations of software architecture concepts and relationships. By documenting architectural decisions, design rationale, and system dependencies, software engineers can facilitate communication, collaboration, and understanding among project stakeholders, including developers, testers, project managers, and customers.

Furthermore, software architecture fundamentals encompass architectural analysis and evaluation, which involve assessing the quality, performance, and adherence to architectural principles and design goals of a software system. Architectural analysis techniques include static analysis, dynamic analysis, and architectural reviews to identify design flaws, performance bottlenecks, and architectural risks early in the development process. Static analysis techniques involve reviewing source code, architectural diagrams, and design documents to identify potential issues such as code smells, architectural violations, and design inconsistencies. Dynamic analysis techniques involve testing the system under various conditions to evaluate its performance, reliability, and scalability. Architectural reviews involve conducting structured discussions and inspections of architectural artifacts to validate design decisions, assess conformance to architectural principles, and identify areas for improvement. By performing architectural analysis and evaluation, software engineers can ensure that the software system meets its intended goals, performs as expected, and conforms to established architectural standards and best practices.

In summary, software architecture fundamentals are essential concepts and principles that guide the design, development, and implementation of software systems, ensuring their reliability, scalability, maintainability, and performance. By understanding and applying architectural styles, design patterns, architectural decisions, quality attributes, architectural modeling and documentation, and architectural analysis and evaluation techniques, software engineers can create robust, efficient, and scalable software architectures that meet user requirements, adhere to industry best practices, and evolve over time to accommodate changing needs and technologies. By embracing software architecture fundamentals, organizations can build software systems that are easier to understand, modify, and maintain, and deliver value to stakeholders and end-users.

Components and interactions in complex software systems play a pivotal role in determining the system's functionality, performance, and maintainability. These components, often referred to as modules or building blocks, encapsulate specific functionalities or features of the software, while interactions represent the communication and dependencies among these components. Understanding the intricacies of components and interactions is essential for software engineers to design, develop, and manage complex software systems effectively.

At the heart of complex software systems are the components, which can be thought of as the individual units or parts that make up the software architecture. Components can range from simple functions or procedures to large, self-contained modules or libraries. Each component serves a specific purpose within the system, such as handling input/output operations, processing data, or implementing business logic. For example, in a web application, components may include user interface elements, backend services, database access layers, and third-party integrations. Identifying and defining the boundaries of components is crucial for modularizing the system and promoting code reusability, scalability, and maintainability.

In practice, components are often implemented as classes, functions, or modules in programming languages such as Java, Python, or C++. These components are organized into hierarchical structures or layers based on their functionality and responsibilities. For instance, in a layered architecture, components may be grouped into presentation, business logic, and data access layers, with each layer responsible for specific tasks and interactions. Software engineers use programming constructs such as classes, interfaces, and packages to define and implement components, ensuring proper encapsulation, cohesion, and modularity.

Moreover, interactions among components are essential for coordinating the flow of data, control, and communication within the software system. Interactions occur when one component invokes or interacts with another component to perform a specific task or exchange information. These interactions can take various forms, including method calls, function invocations, event notifications, and message passing. For example, in a client-server architecture, interactions occur when a client sends a request to a server and receives a response, triggering actions and updates on both sides. Understanding the patterns and protocols of interactions is crucial for designing robust and efficient communication mechanisms within the software system.

To manage interactions effectively, software engineers employ design patterns, communication protocols, and architectural styles that govern how components interact and collaborate. Design patterns such as the Observer pattern, Mediator pattern, and Publish-Subscribe pattern provide standardized solutions for managing dependencies and interactions among components. For instance, the Observer pattern facilitates one-to-many communication between objects by allowing multiple observers to subscribe to changes in a subject. Similarly, communication protocols such as REST (Representational State Transfer) or messaging protocols like MQTT (Message Queuing Telemetry Transport) define rules and conventions for exchanging data and messages between components over networks.

Furthermore, interactions among components often involve data exchange and synchronization, requiring mechanisms for managing state, concurrency, and consistency. Software engineers employ techniques such as data synchronization, locking mechanisms, and transaction management to ensure data integrity and consistency across interacting components. For instance, in a multi-threaded application, synchronization primitives such as mutexes, semaphores, or monitors are used to coordinate access to shared resources and prevent data corruption or race conditions.

In addition to managing interactions within the software system, software engineers must also consider external dependencies and interactions with other systems or services. These external interactions may involve accessing external APIs, integrating with third-party libraries, or communicating with external databases or services. To facilitate external interactions, software engineers use APIs (Application Programming Interfaces), SDKs (Software Development Kits), and communication protocols such as HTTP, TCP/IP, or WebSocket. For example, when integrating with a payment gateway service, the software system may interact with the gateway's API to process payments and handle transactions securely.

To effectively manage components and interactions in complex software systems, software engineers employ various development tools, frameworks, and methodologies. Version control systems such as Git are used to manage changes to source code and collaborate on software development projects. Integrated development environments (IDEs) such as Visual Studio Code, IntelliJ IDEA, or Eclipse provide tools for writing, debugging, and testing software components. Additionally, software engineers use build automation tools such as Maven, Gradle, or Make to automate the build process and manage dependencies between components.

Moreover, software engineers employ testing frameworks and techniques such as unit testing, integration testing, and end-to-end testing to verify the correctness and functionality of software components and interactions. Continuous integration and continuous delivery (CI/CD) pipelines are used to automate the testing, deployment, and delivery of software updates and releases, ensuring the stability and reliability of the software system. Furthermore, software engineers utilize monitoring and logging tools such as Prometheus, Grafana, or ELK Stack to monitor the performance, availability, and security of software components and interactions in real-time.

In summary, components and interactions are fundamental aspects of complex software systems, influencing their design, functionality, and performance. Components represent the building blocks of the software architecture, encapsulating specific functionalities or features, while interactions facilitate communication and collaboration among these components. By understanding the intricacies of components and interactions, software engineers can design modular, scalable, and maintainable software systems that meet business requirements and deliver value to stakeholders. Through the use of design patterns, communication protocols, development tools, and testing techniques, software engineers can effectively manage components and interactions in complex software systems, ensuring their reliability, performance, and interoperability in diverse environments.

Chapter 2: Planning and Preparation for Software Installations

Requirements analysis for software deployment is a critical phase in the software development lifecycle that involves gathering, documenting, and analyzing the functional and non-functional requirements of a software system to ensure successful deployment and user satisfaction. During this phase, software engineers and stakeholders collaborate to identify and prioritize the needs, goals, and constraints of the software project, laying the foundation for the subsequent design, development, and implementation stages.

The first step in requirements analysis is to engage stakeholders, including end-users, customers, domain experts, and project sponsors, to understand their needs, expectations, and business objectives. Stakeholder interviews, workshops, surveys, and focus groups are common techniques used to elicit requirements and gather insights into user workflows, pain points, and preferences. By involving stakeholders early in the process, software engineers can gain valuable feedback and ensure that the software solution aligns with organizational goals and user needs.

Once requirements are gathered, they must be documented in a clear and concise manner to serve as a reference for the design and development teams. Requirements documents typically include functional requirements, which describe the specific features, capabilities, and behaviors of the software system, and non-functional requirements, which specify the quality attributes, constraints, and performance metrics that the system must meet. Functional requirements may be expressed using use cases, user stories, or feature lists, while non-functional requirements may include performance benchmarks, security requirements, and compliance regulations.

During requirements analysis, software engineers use various techniques to prioritize and validate requirements based on their importance, feasibility, and impact on the software project. Prioritization techniques such as MoSCoW (Must have, Should have, Could have, Won't have) or Kano analysis help identify critical features and functionalities that must be included in the initial release of the software, as well as optional or nice-to-have features that can be deferred to future releases. Validation techniques such as prototyping, mockups, and proof-of-concept demonstrations allow stakeholders to visualize and interact with the proposed solution, providing feedback and validating requirements before development begins.

In addition to functional and non-functional requirements, software engineers must also consider deployment requirements during the analysis phase to ensure that the software solution can be successfully deployed, configured, and maintained in the target environment. Deployment requirements may include hardware specifications, operating system compatibility, network configurations, security policies, and integration with existing systems or infrastructure. By identifying and addressing deployment requirements early in the process, software engineers can avoid deployment issues and ensure a smooth transition from development to production.

Moreover, requirements analysis involves identifying and managing dependencies, conflicts, and trade-offs among different requirements to achieve a balanced and coherent software solution. Conflicting requirements may arise when stakeholders have conflicting priorities or when certain requirements are mutually exclusive. In such cases, software engineers must facilitate discussions and negotiations among stakeholders to resolve conflicts and reach consensus on the most appropriate solution. Trade-off analysis techniques such as cost-benefit analysis or risk analysis help evaluate the impact of different design decisions and identify the optimal balance between competing requirements.

Furthermore, requirements analysis involves validating requirements against industry standards, best practices, and regulatory requirements to ensure compliance and mitigate risks. Regulatory requirements such as GDPR (General Data Protection Regulation), HIPAA (Health Insurance Portability and Accountability Act), or PCI DSS (Payment Card Industry Data Security Standard) may impose specific data security and privacy requirements that must be addressed in the software solution. Similarly, industry-specific standards such as ISO/IEC 27001 for information security management or IEEE 830 for software requirements specifications provide guidelines and frameworks for defining and managing requirements effectively.

To document and manage requirements effectively, software engineers use various tools and techniques such as requirements management tools, version control systems, and collaborative platforms. Requirements management tools such as JIRA, Confluence, or IBM Rational DOORS provide features for capturing, organizing, and tracing requirements throughout the software development lifecycle. Version control systems such as Git or Subversion allow teams to track changes to requirements documents and collaborate on updates and revisions. Collaborative platforms such as Slack or Microsoft Teams facilitate communication and collaboration among distributed teams and stakeholders, enabling real-time discussions and feedback.

In summary, requirements analysis for software deployment is a crucial phase in the software development lifecycle that involves gathering, documenting, and analyzing the functional and non-functional requirements of a software system. By engaging stakeholders, prioritizing requirements, validating solutions, and addressing deployment considerations, software engineers can ensure that the software solution meets user needs, aligns with organizational goals, and complies with industry standards and regulatory requirements. Through effective requirements analysis, software engineers lay the groundwork for successful software deployment and user satisfaction, setting the stage for the subsequent design, development, and implementation stages of the project.

Pre-installation environment preparation is a crucial aspect of any software deployment project, ensuring that the necessary infrastructure, resources, and dependencies are in place before initiating the installation process. This phase involves a series of tasks and activities aimed at setting up the environment to support the successful deployment of the software solution. By carefully preparing the environment, organizations can minimize disruptions, mitigate risks, and streamline the deployment process, ultimately leading to a smoother and more efficient deployment experience.

The first step in pre-installation environment preparation is to assess the system requirements and compatibility of the software solution with the target environment. Software vendors typically provide documentation or system requirements guides detailing the hardware, software, and network prerequisites for installing and running the software. It is essential to review these requirements carefully and ensure that the target environment meets or exceeds the specified criteria. This may involve verifying hardware specifications such as CPU, memory, and storage capacity, as well as checking software dependencies such as operating system versions, database versions, and third-party libraries.

Once the system requirements have been verified, the next step is to provision or allocate the necessary hardware and infrastructure resources for the deployment. This may include procuring new hardware, virtual machines, or cloud instances, depending on the deployment model and scalability requirements. Organizations may choose to deploy the software solution on-premises, in a private cloud, or on a public cloud platform such as Amazon Web Services (AWS), Microsoft Azure, or Google Cloud Platform (GCP). Provisioning resources in the cloud often involves using infrastructure-as-a-service (IaaS) or platform-as-a-service (PaaS) offerings to provision virtual machines, storage, networking, and other infrastructure components dynamically.

In addition to provisioning hardware resources, organizations must also ensure that the network infrastructure is configured properly to support the deployment. This may involve setting up firewalls, routers, switches, and other networking devices to enable communication between the various components of the software solution. Network configuration tasks may include defining IP addresses, configuring subnets, setting up VLANs (Virtual Local Area Networks), and implementing security policies to protect against unauthorized access and mitigate potential security threats. Organizations may also need to consider network bandwidth, latency, and throughput requirements to ensure optimal performance and reliability.

Furthermore, organizations must consider data storage and management requirements as part of pre-installation environment preparation. This may involve setting up databases, file systems, or storage solutions to store and manage data generated by the software solution. Depending on the nature of the application, organizations may choose to deploy relational databases such as MySQL, PostgreSQL, or Microsoft SQL Server, or NoSQL databases such as MongoDB, Cassandra, or Redis. Data storage considerations may also include data backup and recovery strategies, data encryption, and compliance with data privacy regulations such as GDPR or HIPAA.

Moreover, organizations must ensure that the target environment is secure and compliant with relevant security standards and best practices. This may involve implementing security measures such as access controls, authentication mechanisms, encryption, intrusion detection and prevention systems (IDPS), and security monitoring tools. Organizations may also need to conduct security assessments, vulnerability scans, and penetration tests to identify and remediate potential security vulnerabilities before deploying the software solution. Compliance requirements such as PCI DSS, HIPAA, or ISO 27001 may dictate specific security controls and procedures that must be implemented to protect sensitive data and ensure regulatory compliance.

Additionally, organizations may need to prepare the software deployment environment by installing and configuring prerequisite software components, middleware, or runtime environments required by the software solution. This may include installing operating system updates, patches, and service packs, as well as installing and configuring web servers, application servers, database servers, and other middleware components. Software dependencies such as runtime libraries, SDKs (Software

242

Development Kits), or third-party frameworks may also need to be installed and configured to support the software solution.

Furthermore, organizations should establish deployment processes, procedures, and documentation to ensure consistency, repeatability, and traceability throughout the deployment lifecycle. This may involve creating deployment scripts, templates, or automation workflows to automate repetitive tasks and standardize the deployment process. Version control systems such as Git or Subversion may be used to manage deployment artifacts, configuration files, and infrastructure as code (IaC) scripts. Organizations may also establish change management procedures and conduct deployment rehearsals or pilot deployments to validate the deployment process and identify potential issues or risks before deploying to production environments.

In summary, pre-installation environment preparation is a critical phase in the software deployment lifecycle that involves assessing system requirements, provisioning hardware and infrastructure resources, configuring network and security settings, preparing data storage and management systems, installing prerequisite software components, and establishing deployment processes and procedures. By carefully preparing the environment before initiating the deployment process, organizations can minimize disruptions, mitigate risks, and ensure the successful deployment of the software solution. Through proper planning, coordination, and execution, organizations can create a stable, secure, and reliable environment that supports the needs of the software solution and enables smooth and efficient deployment experiences.

Chapter 3: Advanced Installation Techniques and Strategies

Silent installations and unattended deployments are essential techniques in software deployment, allowing administrators to install software applications on multiple computers without requiring user interaction. These methods streamline the deployment process, reduce manual intervention, and ensure consistency across multiple installations. Silent installations involve installing software silently, without displaying any user interface or requiring user input, while unattended deployments automate the entire deployment process, including configuration and customization options.

The first step in performing a silent installation or unattended deployment is to prepare the installation package or installer executable for deployment. Most software vendors provide command-line options or switches that can be used to perform silent installations or unattended deployments. These command-line options allow administrators to specify installation parameters such as installation directory, license key, and feature selection without user intervention. Additionally, administrators may need to customize the installation package to include additional components, patches, or updates required for deployment.

Once the installation package is prepared, administrators can deploy the software using command-line tools or deployment automation scripts. For Windows-based systems, the Windows Installer (MSI) package format is commonly used for silent installations. Administrators can use the "msiexec" command-line tool to execute MSI packages silently and specify installation options using command-line parameters. For example, to perform a silent installation of an MSI package named "example.msi," administrators can use the following command:

bashCopy code

msiexec /i example.msi /quiet

In this command, the "/i" parameter specifies that the MSI package should be installed, and the "/quiet" parameter specifies that the installation should be performed silently without displaying any user interface.

Similarly, for unattended deployments, administrators can use deployment automation tools such as PowerShell, Batch scripts, or configuration management tools like Ansible, Puppet, or Chef to automate the deployment process. These tools allow administrators to define deployment tasks, including software installation, configuration, and customization, in a script or configuration file. For example, administrators can create a PowerShell script to install software silently and configure application settings as follows:

arduinoCopy code

Start-Process -FilePath "setup.exe" -ArgumentList "/quiet" -Wait

In this PowerShell script, the "Start-Process" cmdlet is used to execute the installer executable ("setup.exe") silently using the "/quiet" command-line parameter, and the "-Wait" parameter ensures that the script waits for the installation to complete before proceeding.

Additionally, administrators may need to customize the deployment script or configuration file to include parameters specific to the software being deployed, such as license keys, installation paths, and configuration settings. By customizing the deployment script, administrators can automate the entire deployment process, including post-installation tasks such as applying patches, updates, or configuring integrations with other systems.

Moreover, administrators may need to test the deployment script or configuration file in a lab or testing environment before deploying it to production systems to ensure that it works as expected and does not cause any unintended side effects. Testing the deployment script allows administrators to identify and troubleshoot any issues or errors before deploying the software to production environments, minimizing the risk of deployment failures or disruptions.

Furthermore, administrators should consider security best practices when performing silent installations and unattended deployments to ensure the integrity and security of the deployed software. This may include verifying the authenticity and integrity of the installation package or installer executable, using digital signatures to validate the software source, and restricting access to deployment scripts and configuration files to authorized personnel only.

Additionally, administrators should monitor the deployment process and track deployment progress to ensure that all systems are successfully deployed and configured according to the desired specifications. Monitoring tools and dashboards can provide real-time visibility into the deployment status, allowing administrators to identify and address any issues or discrepancies promptly.

In summary, silent installations and unattended deployments are valuable techniques for streamlining the software deployment process, reducing manual intervention, and ensuring consistency across multiple installations. By preparing the installation package, deploying the software using command-line tools or deployment automation scripts, customizing deployment parameters, testing the deployment process, and monitoring deployment progress, administrators can automate the deployment process effectively and ensure successful software deployments with minimal effort and risk. Through careful planning, execution, and monitoring, administrators can leverage silent installations and unattended deployments to deploy software efficiently and reliably in diverse environments. Custom installation options and configuration are pivotal aspects of software deployment, allowing users to tailor the installation process according to their specific requirements and preferences. This flexibility ensures that users can install only the components they need, configure settings to align with their environment, and optimize the software for their workflows. Custom installations enable users to maximize the utility of the software while minimizing unnecessary bloat, resulting in more efficient use of system resources and improved performance.

During the installation process, users are often presented with various options to customize the installation according to their needs. These options typically include selecting the components or features to install, specifying installation directories, configuring application settings, and choosing additional components or plugins to include. By offering custom installation options, software vendors cater to the diverse needs and preferences of their user base, ensuring a more personalized and tailored user experience.

One common method for customizing the installation process is through the use of command-line options or switches. These options allow users to specify installation parameters directly from the command line, bypassing the graphical user interface (GUI) and enabling automated or scripted installations. For example, when installing a software application from the command line, users can specify command-line options to customize the installation process according to their requirements.

Another approach to custom installation is through the use of installation wizards or setup programs that guide users through the installation process step by step. These wizards typically present users with a series of screens or dialog boxes where they can select options, configure settings, and make choices based on their preferences. By providing a guided installation experience, users can easily navigate the installation process and make informed decisions about how they want the software to be installed and configured.

In addition to selecting components and configuring settings during the installation process, users may also have the option to customize the software after it has been installed. This may involve accessing configuration menus or settings panels within the software application to adjust preferences, customize user interfaces, or enable/disable specific features. By providing post-installation customization options, software vendors empower users to fine-tune the software to meet their evolving needs and preferences.

Furthermore, software vendors may offer advanced customization options for enterprise customers or power users who require more granular control over the installation and configuration process. These options may include silent installation modes, which allow for installation without user interaction, or unattended deployment options, which enable automated deployment across multiple systems. Additionally, software vendors may provide customization tools or configuration files that allow administrators to pre-configure settings, policies, and preferences before deploying the software to end-users.

Another aspect of custom installation options and configuration is the ability to integrate the software with other systems, applications, or services. This may involve configuring integration points, setting up APIs (Application Programming Interfaces) or webhooks, or configuring authentication and authorization mechanisms to enable seamless interoperability with external systems. By offering integration options, software vendors enable users to leverage the full capabilities of the software and integrate it into their existing workflows and infrastructure.

Moreover, software vendors may provide documentation, tutorials, or knowledge base articles to help users understand the available customization options and configuration settings. These resources may include step-by-step guides, FAQs (Frequently Asked Questions), troubleshooting tips, and best practices for configuring the software to optimize performance, security, and usability. By providing comprehensive documentation and support resources, software vendors empower users to make informed decisions about how to customize and configure the software to meet their specific requirements.

In summary, custom installation options and configuration play a crucial role in software deployment, allowing users to tailor the installation process and configure settings according to their specific needs and preferences. By offering customizable installation options, software vendors cater to the diverse needs of their user base and ensure a more personalized and tailored user experience. Whether through command-line options, installation wizards, post-installation customization, or advanced deployment options, custom installation and configuration empower users to optimize the software to meet their unique requirements and achieve maximum productivity and efficiency. Through comprehensive documentation, support resources, and integration options, software vendors enable users to make informed decisions about how to customize and configure the software to suit their needs and preferences.

Chapter 4: Managing Dependencies and Compatibility Issues

Dependency resolution strategies are pivotal in software development and deployment, ensuring that all required dependencies are identified, managed, and resolved effectively to enable successful application execution. Dependencies refer to external components, libraries, frameworks, or modules that a software application relies on to function properly. These dependencies can include software libraries, runtime environments, system utilities, and other components necessary for the application to execute correctly. Effective dependency resolution strategies are essential to ensure that applications are built, deployed, and maintained efficiently, with all necessary dependencies satisfied.

One common approach to dependency resolution is manual management, where developers manually identify, install, and configure dependencies as needed during the development process. This approach involves researching and selecting appropriate libraries or frameworks, downloading them from external sources, and integrating them into the project manually. While manual management provides developers with full control over the selection and configuration of dependencies, it can be time-consuming, error-prone, and difficult to maintain, especially in large or complex projects with numerous dependencies.

To streamline the dependency resolution process, developers often rely on package managers, which are tools designed to automate the management of software dependencies. Package managers maintain repositories of pre-built packages or modules, along with metadata describing their dependencies, versions, and other attributes. Developers can use package managers to search for, install, update, and remove dependencies from their projects automatically, simplifying the management of dependencies and ensuring consistent and reliable builds.

One widely used package manager in the JavaScript ecosystem is npm (Node Package Manager), which is used to manage dependencies for Node.js projects. Developers can use npm to install packages from the npm registry by running the "npm install" command followed by the name of the package. For example, to install the "lodash" library, developers can run the following command:

Copy code

```
npm install lodash
```

npm will download the lodash package from the npm registry and install it in the project's "node_modules" directory, along with any additional dependencies required by lodash.

Similarly, in the Python ecosystem, developers use pip (Python Package Installer) to manage dependencies for Python projects. Pip allows developers to install packages from the Python Package Index (PyPI) by running the "pip install" command followed by the name of the package. For example, to install the "requests" library, developers can run the following command:

Copy code

```
pip install requests
```

Pip will download the requests package from PyPI and install it in the project's Python environment, along with any additional dependencies required by requests.

Another popular package manager is Maven, which is used primarily in the Java ecosystem to manage dependencies for Java projects. Maven uses XML-based configuration files called "pom.xml" (Project Object Model) to define project dependencies and build configurations. Developers can specify dependencies in the "pom.xml" file using the <dependency> element, along with the desired version and scope. Maven will then download the specified dependencies from Maven Central Repository or other configured repositories and include them in the project's classpath during compilation and execution.

In addition to package managers, containerization technologies such as Docker have emerged as powerful tools for managing software dependencies and ensuring consistency across different environments. Docker containers encapsulate applications and their dependencies into portable, lightweight units that can be deployed consistently across different platforms and environments. Developers can define application dependencies and configurations using Dockerfiles, which are text-based configuration files that specify the steps needed to build a Docker image. By containerizing applications, developers can isolate dependencies, streamline deployment, and minimize compatibility issues between different environments.

Furthermore, dependency resolution strategies may involve the use of dependency management tools and services that automate the identification, analysis, and resolution of dependencies in software projects. These tools can analyze project dependencies, detect potential conflicts or vulnerabilities, and suggest remediation strategies to resolve issues. For example, dependency management platforms like Renovate and Dependabot automatically scan project repositories for outdated dependencies and create pull requests to update them to the latest versions, helping developers keep their projects up-to-date and secure.

Moreover, organizations may implement dependency resolution policies and guidelines to ensure consistency and reliability in dependency management practices across projects. These policies may include rules for selecting and vetting dependencies, defining versioning strategies, establishing security guidelines, and enforcing compliance with licensing requirements. By implementing clear policies and guidelines, organizations can mitigate risks, improve transparency, and foster best practices in dependency management.

In summary, dependency resolution strategies are essential in software development and deployment, enabling developers to manage and resolve dependencies effectively to ensure successful application execution. Whether through manual management, package managers, containerization technologies, dependency management tools, or organizational policies, developers have a variety of options for managing dependencies and ensuring consistency, reliability, and security in software projects. By adopting effective dependency resolution strategies, developers can streamline the development process, improve collaboration, and deliver high-quality software products that meet the needs of end-users and stakeholders.

Compatibility testing and mitigation techniques are critical components of software development and deployment, ensuring that applications function as intended across various platforms, devices, browsers, and environments. Compatibility issues can arise due to differences in operating systems, hardware configurations, software dependencies, browser versions, screen resolutions, and other factors, leading to unexpected behavior, performance issues, or even application crashes. To address these challenges, developers employ a range of compatibility testing and mitigation techniques to identify, diagnose, and resolve compatibility issues proactively.

One fundamental aspect of compatibility testing is platform compatibility testing, which involves testing the application on different operating systems, such as Windows, macOS, Linux, Android, and iOS, to ensure that it performs reliably across diverse platforms. Developers use virtualization tools like VirtualBox or VMware to create virtual machines running different operating systems and deploy the application on each platform to assess its compatibility. Additionally, cloud-based testing services like BrowserStack or Sauce Labs provide virtual environments for testing applications across various operating systems and browsers, allowing developers to identify and address platform-specific compatibility issues efficiently.

Another key aspect of compatibility testing is browser compatibility testing, which focuses on testing the application across different web browsers and versions to ensure consistent behavior and functionality. Developers use tools like Selenium WebDriver or Puppeteer to automate browser testing and simulate user interactions across different browsers, including Chrome, Firefox, Safari, Edge, and Internet Explorer. By running automated tests on multiple browsers, developers can detect and fix rendering issues, JavaScript errors, CSS discrepancies, and other browser-specific compatibility issues before deploying the application to production.

Furthermore, mobile compatibility testing is essential for ensuring that applications perform optimally on various mobile devices, including smartphones and tablets, running different operating systems like Android and iOS. Developers use emulators and simulators provided by mobile development platforms like Android Studio and Xcode to simulate different mobile devices and test the application's compatibility across different screen sizes, resolutions, and hardware configurations. Additionally, mobile testing frameworks like Appium and Xamarin allow developers to automate mobile testing and ensure consistent behavior across different mobile platforms.

In addition to platform, browser, and mobile compatibility testing, developers also conduct compatibility testing for hardware peripherals, such as printers, scanners, cameras, and input devices, to ensure that the application interacts seamlessly with external hardware components. This involves connecting the application to various hardware devices and verifying that all features and functionalities work as expected. Compatibility testing for hardware peripherals helps identify compatibility issues related to device drivers, communication protocols, and hardware configurations, enabling developers to address them before deployment.

Moreover, developers perform backward compatibility testing to ensure that the application remains compatible with older versions of software libraries, frameworks, or APIs that it depends on. This involves testing the application with previous versions of dependencies to verify that it functions correctly and does not break existing functionality. Developers use version control systems like Git to manage dependencies and track changes, allowing them to revert to previous versions if compatibility issues arise.

Additionally, developers leverage feature detection techniques to identify and handle compatibility issues dynamically based on the capabilities of the user's device or browser. Feature detection involves detecting the presence or absence of specific features or APIs using JavaScript or other client-side scripting languages and adapting the application's behavior accordingly. By implementing feature detection, developers can provide fallback mechanisms or alternative solutions for unsupported features, ensuring a consistent user experience across different environments.

Furthermore, developers employ progressive enhancement and graceful degradation strategies to address compatibility issues and ensure that the application remains functional across a wide range of devices and browsers. Progressive enhancement involves starting with a baseline of core functionality that works across all devices and browsers and then progressively enhancing the user experience for devices and browsers that support advanced features. On the other hand, graceful degradation involves designing the application to degrade gracefully on older browsers or devices that lack support for certain features, ensuring that users still have access to essential functionality even in less capable environments.

In summary, compatibility testing and mitigation techniques are essential for ensuring that software applications perform reliably across diverse platforms, browsers, devices, and environments. By conducting platform, browser, mobile, and hardware compatibility testing, as well as backward compatibility testing, feature detection, progressive enhancement, and graceful degradation, developers can identify and address compatibility issues proactively, ensuring a consistent and seamless user experience for all users. Through the use of automation tools, virtualization technologies, and testing frameworks, developers can streamline the compatibility testing process and deliver high-quality software products that meet the needs and expectations of users across different platforms and environments.

Chapter 5: Configuration Management for Complex Software

Configuration management tools and best practices are indispensable components of modern software development and operations, facilitating the efficient management, deployment, and maintenance of software configurations across diverse environments. These tools automate configuration tasks, enforce consistency, and enable version control, ensuring that systems and applications are deployed and maintained in a predictable and reliable manner. By adhering to best practices, organizations can optimize their configuration management processes and enhance their overall operational efficiency.

One of the key aspects of configuration management is the use of dedicated tools and frameworks designed to automate configuration tasks and enforce consistency across systems. One such tool is Ansible, an open-source automation platform that enables configuration management, application deployment, and orchestration of infrastructure through simple, human-readable YAML (YAML Ain't Markup Language) files. Ansible allows administrators to define configuration tasks, called "playbooks," which specify the desired state of the system and the tasks required to achieve it. These playbooks can then be executed on remote systems using the "ansible-playbook" command, ensuring that systems are configured according to the defined specifications.

Another popular configuration management tool is Puppet, which provides a declarative language for describing system configurations and a client-server architecture for managing configuration changes across large-scale infrastructures.

Puppet allows administrators to define configuration manifests, known as "Puppet manifests," which specify the desired state of the system and the resources required to achieve it. These manifests are then compiled into catalogs and applied to managed nodes using the Puppet agent, ensuring that systems remain in the desired state and automatically correcting any deviations from the specified configuration.

Similarly, Chef is a configuration management tool that uses a domain-specific language (DSL) called "Chef Infra" to define system configurations as code. Chef allows administrators to write "recipes" and "cookbooks" that specify the desired state of the system and the steps required to achieve it. These recipes and cookbooks are then executed on managed nodes using the Chef client, ensuring that systems are configured consistently and reproducibly across the infrastructure.

In addition to dedicated configuration management tools, version control systems like Git play a crucial role in managing configuration changes and enforcing version control best practices. Git allows administrators to track changes to configuration files, collaborate with team members, and revert to previous versions if necessary. By using Git to manage configuration changes, organizations can ensure that all modifications are tracked, documented, and auditable, reducing the risk of configuration drift and ensuring accountability.

Furthermore, organizations can benefit from implementing infrastructure as code (IaC) practices, which involve managing infrastructure configurations using version-controlled code repositories and automated deployment pipelines. Tools like Terraform and AWS CloudFormation enable administrators to define infrastructure configurations as code using declarative syntax and provision resources across cloud providers programmatically. By treating infrastructure configurations as code, organizations can automate the provisioning and management of infrastructure, enforce consistency, and achieve greater agility and scalability in their operations.

Another important aspect of configuration management is the use of configuration templates and parameterization to abstract configuration details and enable reusable configuration patterns. Tools like Jinja2 and ERB (Embedded Ruby) allow administrators to create configuration templates with placeholders for dynamic values, which can be populated at runtime based on environment-specific parameters. By using configuration templates, organizations can standardize configuration patterns, simplify maintenance, and enable dynamic configuration based on runtime variables.

Moreover, organizations can benefit from implementing configuration validation and testing practices to ensure the integrity and correctness of configuration changes before deployment. This involves performing automated validation checks and tests on configuration files to detect syntax errors, semantic inconsistencies, and compliance violations. Tools like Chef InSpec and Puppet Bolt enable administrators to define validation checks as code and execute them against managed nodes to verify configuration compliance and identify potential issues proactively.

Additionally, organizations should establish robust change management processes and configuration baselines to manage configuration changes systematically and minimize the risk of unintended consequences. This involves documenting configuration changes, obtaining approvals from stakeholders, and maintaining a record of configuration baselines to track changes over time. By implementing change management processes, organizations can ensure that configuration changes are controlled, documented, and auditable, reducing the risk of configuration-related incidents and disruptions.

In summary, configuration management tools and best practices are essential for ensuring the consistency, reliability, and security of software configurations across diverse environments. By leveraging dedicated configuration management tools like Ansible, Puppet, and Chef, organizations can automate configuration tasks, enforce consistency, and manage infrastructure configurations at scale. By adhering to version control best practices, implementing infrastructure as code practices, using configuration templates, and validating configuration changes, organizations can optimize their configuration management processes and enhance their overall operational efficiency. Through the adoption of robust change management processes and configuration baselines, organizations can minimize the risk of configuration-related incidents and disruptions, ensuring the stability and reliability of their IT infrastructure.

Version control and configuration baselines are fundamental concepts in software development and configuration management, providing organizations with the means to track, manage, and control changes to software artifacts and configurations systematically. Version control systems (VCS) enable developers to collaborate effectively, track changes, and maintain a history of revisions for source code, documents, and other artifacts, while configuration baselines establish a stable reference point for configuration items, ensuring consistency and traceability throughout the software development lifecycle.

One of the most widely used version control systems is Git, which provides a distributed and decentralized approach to version control, enabling teams to work collaboratively on codebases and manage changes effectively. Git allows developers to create repositories to store project files and track changes over time using commits, branches, and merges. The "git init" command initializes a new Git repository in the current directory, while "git clone" clones an existing repository from a remote location. Developers use "git add" to stage changes for commit and "git commit" to record changes to the repository. Branches in Git allow developers to work on separate features or fixes independently, with commands like "git branch" to create a new branch and "git checkout" to switch between branches. Merging branches is accomplished using "git merge," which combines changes from one branch into another. Through these commands and practices, developers can effectively manage code changes, collaborate with team members, and maintain a detailed history of revisions.

Similarly, other version control systems like Subversion (SVN) and Mercurial provide centralized alternatives to Git, enabling teams to track changes to files and directories over time. SVN uses a central repository to store versioned files and directories, with developers checking out copies of the repository to make changes and committing them back when complete. Commands like "svn checkout" create a working copy of a repository, while "svn add" and "svn commit" add files to the repository and record changes, respectively. Branching and merging in SVN follow a similar process to Git, allowing developers to manage concurrent development efforts and integrate changes seamlessly. Mercurial operates similarly to Git, providing distributed version control capabilities and supporting commands for cloning, committing, branching, and merging changes.

In addition to tracking changes to source code, version control systems are also used to manage configuration files, infrastructure code, and other artifacts essential for software development and deployment. Configuration management tools like Puppet, Chef, and Ansible leverage version control systems to manage configuration files and templates, ensuring consistency and repeatability in infrastructure provisioning and deployment processes. By storing configuration files in version control repositories, organizations can track changes, audit configurations, and rollback to previous versions if necessary. This approach enables infrastructure as code (IaC) practices, where infrastructure configurations are treated as code and managed using version control systems to automate provisioning, configuration, and deployment processes.

Furthermore, configuration baselines play a crucial role in establishing stable reference points for configuration items, defining the approved configuration state for software systems, and controlling changes throughout the software development lifecycle. A configuration baseline represents a snapshot of the configuration items at a specific point in time, capturing their current state and version. Organizations establish configuration baselines for various artifacts, including source code, documentation, requirements specifications, and infrastructure configurations. By defining configuration baselines, organizations ensure that changes to configuration items are managed systematically, with approvals and documentation required for modifications.

Configuration baselines are typically established at key milestones in the software development lifecycle, such as release points, milestones, or major iterations. Baselines are created by identifying the configuration items associated with the software release or iteration and recording their state, version, and relationships. Once established, configuration baselines serve as the basis for subsequent development and change management activities, providing a stable reference point for development, testing, and deployment efforts. Any changes to configuration items must be evaluated against the established baseline, with deviations documented and approved through a formal change management process.

Moreover, organizations may use configuration management databases (CMDBs) or configuration management systems (CMSs) to maintain and manage configuration baselines effectively. These systems provide centralized repositories for storing configuration item information, including attributes, relationships, and version histories. CMDBs and CMSs enable organizations to track configuration changes, assess the impact of modifications, and ensure compliance with regulatory requirements and organizational policies. By leveraging CMDBs or CMSs, organizations can establish a single source of truth for configuration management, facilitating collaboration, communication, and decision-making across development and operations teams.

Additionally, version control and configuration baselines support quality assurance and release management processes by enabling organizations to conduct comprehensive testing, validation, and verification activities against known configurations. QA teams can use version-controlled artifacts and configuration baselines to reproduce specific environments, execute test cases, and validate software functionality against predefined criteria. Similarly, release managers can use configuration baselines to ensure that released software versions are consistent, stable, and compliant with defined standards and requirements. Through effective version control and configuration baseline management, organizations can mitigate risks, improve traceability, and enhance the overall quality and reliability of software products.

In summary, version control and configuration baselines are essential practices in software development and configuration management, enabling organizations to track changes, manage configurations, and control variations systematically. By leveraging version control systems like Git, Subversion, and Mercurial, organizations can manage code changes, collaborate effectively, and maintain a detailed history of revisions. Configuration baselines establish stable reference points for configuration items, defining the approved configuration state and controlling changes throughout the software development lifecycle. Together, version control and configuration baselines support quality assurance, release management, and compliance efforts, ensuring that software products meet defined standards, requirements, and expectations. Through these practices, organizations can enhance productivity, reliability, and agility in software development and deployment processes.

Chapter 6: Troubleshooting Installation Failures

Common installation error messages often encountered during software installation processes can cause frustration and delay in completing the installation successfully. However, understanding the root causes behind these error messages and knowing how to troubleshoot them can help users overcome installation challenges efficiently. One of the most encountered error messages is "Error 1603: A fatal error occurred during installation." This error typically indicates that the installation process encountered an unexpected issue that prevented it from completing successfully. To troubleshoot this error, users can start by checking the installation logs, which often provide detailed information about the cause of the failure. Additionally, ensuring that the system meets the software's minimum requirements, disabling antivirus software temporarily, and running the installation with administrative privileges can help resolve this issue in many cases.

Another common error message is "Error 1316: A network error occurred while attempting to read from the file." This error suggests that the installer cannot access or read the installation files from the specified location, which may occur due to corrupted installation files, network connectivity issues, or insufficient permissions. To resolve this error, users can try reinstalling the software using a different installation source or copying the installation files to a local drive before running the installation. Additionally, checking network connections, verifying file permissions, and ensuring that antivirus software does not block the installation process can help mitigate this issue.

"Error 1720: There is a problem with this Windows Installer package" is another common error message encountered during software installations, particularly with Windows Installer packages. This error typically indicates that the Windows Installer service encountered an issue while processing the installation package. To troubleshoot this error, users can try repairing or reinstalling the Windows Installer service, ensuring that the system is up to date with the latest Windows updates, and running the installation with administrative privileges. Additionally, checking for any conflicting software installations or third-party applications that may interfere with the installation process can help resolve this issue.

Furthermore, "Error 1935: An error occurred during the installation of assembly component" is a common error message encountered when installing Microsoft Office or other software that relies on the .NET Framework. This error typically indicates that there is an issue with the installation of a specific assembly component required by the software. To resolve this error, users can try repairing or reinstalling the .NET Framework using the Windows Control Panel, ensuring that the system meets the software's minimum requirements, and running the installation with administrative privileges. Additionally, checking for any pending Windows updates and ensuring that antivirus software does not interfere with the installation process can help mitigate this issue.

Additionally, "Error 1402: Could not open key" is a common error message encountered when installing software on Windows systems. This error typically indicates that the installer does not have sufficient permissions to access or modify the Windows registry keys required for the installation. To resolve this error, users can try modifying the permissions for the affected registry keys using the Windows

Registry Editor, ensuring that the user account has administrative privileges, and disabling any third-party security software temporarily. Additionally, running the installation with administrative privileges and ensuring that the system is free from malware or viruses can help mitigate this issue.

Moreover, "Error 404: Not Found" is a common error message encountered when downloading or installing software from the internet. This error typically indicates that the installer cannot locate the required files or resources at the specified URL or location. To troubleshoot this error, users can try downloading the software from an alternative source or website, ensuring that the internet connection is stable and reliable, and checking for any typos or errors in the URL. Additionally, verifying that the software download is not blocked by firewall or security settings and ensuring that the system meets the software's minimum requirements can help resolve this issue.

Furthermore, "Error 1001: An error occurred while installing the application" is a common error message encountered when installing software using Windows Installer packages. This error typically indicates that the installation process encountered an unexpected issue that prevented it from completing successfully. To troubleshoot this error, users can try repairing or reinstalling the Windows Installer service, ensuring that the system is up to date with the latest Windows updates, and running the installation with administrative privileges. Additionally, checking for any conflicting software installations or third-party applications that may interfere with the installation process can help resolve this issue.

In summary, understanding common installation error messages and knowing how to troubleshoot them effectively is essential for completing software installations successfully.

By identifying the root causes behind these error messages and applying appropriate troubleshooting steps, users can overcome installation challenges and ensure a smooth and seamless installation experience. Whether it's resolving issues related to file access, registry permissions, network connectivity, or software dependencies, taking proactive measures to address installation errors can help users achieve their desired outcomes and minimize downtime associated with failed installations.

Debugging installation problems is a crucial aspect of software deployment, as it ensures that applications are installed correctly and function as intended. When encountering installation issues, it's essential to identify the root cause of the problem and apply appropriate debugging techniques to resolve it effectively. One common approach to debugging installation problems is to review installation logs, which often contain valuable information about the installation process and any errors encountered along the way. For example, in Windows environments, installation logs for MSI-based installations can be accessed using the "Event Viewer" application or by enabling verbose logging using the "/L*v" command-line parameter during installation. Similarly, in Linux environments, installation logs for package managers like apt and yum can be found in the "/var/log" directory, with commands like "tail" or "grep" used to filter and search for relevant log entries.

Additionally, examining error messages displayed during the installation process can provide valuable insights into the underlying issues. Error messages often contain specific error codes or descriptions that can help pinpoint the cause of the problem. For example, errors related to file permissions may indicate that the installer does not have sufficient privileges to access or modify certain files or directories. In such cases, resolving the permissions issue by granting appropriate permissions to the installer or adjusting file ownership can help resolve the problem.

Furthermore, verifying system requirements and compatibility can help prevent installation problems before they occur. Checking the software's documentation or system requirements page to ensure that the system meets the minimum hardware and software requirements can help avoid issues related to insufficient resources or incompatible configurations. For example, if an application requires a specific version of an operating system or a certain amount of available disk space, ensuring that the system meets these requirements before proceeding with the installation can help prevent installation failures.

Moreover, isolating the problem by testing the installation on different systems or environments can help determine whether the issue is specific to a particular configuration or system setup. Installing the software on a clean, minimal system or a virtual machine can help identify potential conflicts with existing software or dependencies that may be causing the installation problem. Additionally, testing the installation on multiple systems with different configurations can help determine whether the issue is reproducible across different environments or specific to a particular system setup.

In some cases, installation problems may be caused by conflicting software or services running on the system. For example, antivirus software, firewalls, or system optimization utilities may interfere with the installation process by blocking or modifying critical files or settings. Disabling or temporarily uninstalling such software before proceeding with the installation can help rule out potential conflicts and isolate the problem. Similarly, ensuring that no other installation processes or updates are running concurrently can help prevent interference with the installation process.

Furthermore, manually inspecting the installation files and directories can help identify issues related to corrupted or missing files. Verifying file integrity using checksums or comparing file sizes and timestamps against known-good copies can help determine whether the installation files have been modified or corrupted during download or transfer. Additionally, extracting installation files from the installer package and running the installation manually can help bypass any issues with the automated installation process and provide more visibility into the installation steps.

Additionally, utilizing built-in troubleshooting tools and utilities provided by the operating system or software vendor can help diagnose and resolve installation problems more efficiently. For example, Windows includes the "System File Checker" (SFC) tool, which can scan system files for corruption and repair them automatically. Similarly, Linux distributions often provide package management utilities like "dpkg" or "rpm," which can be used to verify package integrity and reinstall or repair packages as needed.

Moreover, seeking assistance from online forums, community support channels, or vendor support resources can provide additional insights and guidance for resolving installation problems. Many software vendors maintain knowledge bases, forums, or support portals where users can find troubleshooting guides, FAQs, and community-driven solutions to common installation issues. Additionally, reaching out to the software vendor's technical support team or consulting with experienced professionals in online forums or communities can help diagnose and resolve more complex installation problems.

In summary, debugging installation problems requires a systematic approach to identify and address the root cause of the issue effectively. By reviewing installation logs, examining error messages, verifying system requirements, isolating the problem, checking for conflicting software, inspecting installation files, utilizing troubleshooting tools, and seeking assistance from online resources, users can diagnose and resolve installation problems efficiently. Taking proactive measures to prevent installation issues and applying appropriate debugging techniques when problems arise can help ensure successful software deployments and minimize downtime associated with installation failures.

Chapter 7: Implementing Software Deployment Best Practices

Software deployment methodologies encompass a range of approaches and practices aimed at efficiently and effectively delivering software applications to end-users or production environments. One widely adopted methodology is the Waterfall model, which follows a sequential process involving distinct phases such as requirements gathering, design, implementation, testing, deployment, and maintenance. In the Waterfall model, each phase must be completed before progressing to the next, with minimal room for iteration or changes once the project moves beyond the initial planning stage. While the Waterfall model offers a structured approach to software development and deployment, it can be rigid and less adaptable to changing requirements or feedback from stakeholders.

In contrast, Agile methodologies, such as Scrum and Kanban, prioritize flexibility, collaboration, and incremental delivery of software features. Scrum, for example, divides the project into short iterations called sprints, typically lasting one to four weeks, during which a cross-functional team works collaboratively to deliver a set of user stories or features. At the end of each sprint, a potentially shippable product increment is delivered, allowing for early and frequent feedback from stakeholders. This iterative approach enables teams to adapt to changing requirements, prioritize features based on user feedback, and deliver value incrementally, resulting in faster time-to-market and increased customer satisfaction.

Kanban, on the other hand, visualizes the entire workflow on a Kanban board, with work items represented as cards that move through various stages of the workflow, such as backlog, in progress, testing, and done. Unlike Scrum, Kanban does not prescribe specific roles or time-bound iterations but instead focuses on limiting work in progress (WIP) and optimizing flow to ensure a steady and predictable delivery of work. Kanban is particularly suitable for teams that require a high degree of flexibility and want to continuously improve their processes over time.

Another software deployment methodology gaining popularity is DevOps, which emphasizes collaboration, automation, and continuous delivery of software. DevOps aims to break down silos between development and operations teams, enabling them to work together seamlessly throughout the software development lifecycle. Automation plays a crucial role in DevOps, with tools such as configuration management, continuous integration (CI), and continuous deployment (CD) pipelines used to automate repetitive tasks, streamline deployments, and ensure consistency across environments.

Configuration management tools like Ansible, Puppet, and Chef enable teams to automate the provisioning and configuration of infrastructure and application environments, ensuring that deployments are consistent and repeatable. By defining infrastructure as code (IaC), teams can manage their infrastructure configuration using version control systems and deploy changes programmatically, reducing the risk of configuration drift and human error.

Continuous integration (CI) tools like Jenkins, GitLab CI, and Travis CI automate the process of integrating code changes from multiple developers into a shared repository and running automated tests to ensure that the changes do not introduce regressions or compatibility issues. CI pipelines can be configured to trigger automatically whenever new code is pushed to the repository, providing fast feedback to developers and enabling them to catch and fix issues early in the development process.

Continuous deployment (CD) extends the principles of CI by automating the deployment of validated code changes to production environments. CD pipelines orchestrate the entire deployment process, including building, testing, and deploying the application to production, with minimal manual intervention. By automating the deployment process, teams can reduce the risk of human error, accelerate time-to-market, and increase the frequency of software releases.

In addition to traditional deployment methodologies, containerization and microservices architectures have emerged as popular approaches for deploying and managing modern software applications. Containers, such as those provided by Docker, package applications and their dependencies into lightweight, portable units that can run consistently across different environments. Container orchestration platforms like Kubernetes automate the deployment, scaling, and management of containerized applications, enabling teams to deploy and scale applications more efficiently and reliably.

Microservices architectures decompose monolithic applications into smaller, loosely coupled services that can be developed, deployed, and scaled independently. Each microservice is responsible for a specific business function and communicates with other services via well-defined APIs. This modular approach to software development and deployment enables teams to iterate quickly, scale components independently, and maintain a high level of flexibility and agility in response to changing requirements or market conditions.

In summary, software deployment methodologies encompass a diverse range of approaches and practices, each with its own strengths and weaknesses. Whether following a traditional Waterfall model, embracing Agile principles, adopting DevOps practices, or leveraging containerization and microservices architectures, organizations must choose the methodology that best aligns with their goals, team dynamics, and project requirements. By selecting the right deployment methodology and utilizing appropriate tools and practices, teams can streamline the software deployment process, improve collaboration and efficiency, and deliver high-quality software products that meet the needs of end-users and stakeholders.

Rollout strategies and phased deployments are essential components of the software deployment process, enabling organizations to manage risks, minimize disruptions, and ensure successful deployments. One commonly used rollout strategy is the phased deployment approach, which involves gradually deploying a new software release or update to a subset of users or environments before rolling it out to the entire user base. Phased deployments help mitigate the impact of potential issues or bugs by limiting their exposure to a smaller audience initially. One approach to implementing phased deployments is to use feature flags or toggles, which allow developers to selectively enable or disable specific features or changes in the software based on predefined criteria. Feature flags can be controlled dynamically through configuration files or management interfaces, allowing organizations to gradually enable new features or updates for different user groups or environments. For example, in a web application, feature flags can be used to enable a new user interface (UI) component or functionality for a small percentage of users initially, with the option to gradually increase the rollout percentage as confidence in the changes grows.

Another approach to phased deployments is to divide the deployment process into multiple stages or phases, each targeting a specific subset of users or environments. For example, organizations may choose to deploy a new software release first to a staging or testing environment, where it undergoes thorough testing and validation before being promoted to production. Once the release has been validated in the staging environment, it can be rolled out to a small percentage of production users or a specific geographic region, allowing organizations to monitor its performance and gather feedback before proceeding with a broader rollout. This incremental approach to deployment helps organizations identify and address issues early in the deployment process, reducing the risk of widespread disruptions or downtime.

In addition to feature flags and staged deployments, organizations can also leverage canary deployments as part of their rollout strategy. Canary deployments involve deploying a new software release or update to a small subset of production servers or instances, often referred to as canaries, while leaving the majority of production servers running the previous version. By monitoring the performance and stability of the canary deployment in real-time, organizations can quickly identify any issues or anomalies before proceeding with a full rollout. If the canary deployment is successful and meets predefined criteria, such as performance metrics or error rates, organizations can gradually increase the rollout percentage or promote the new release to the entire production environment.

To implement canary deployments, organizations can use deployment automation tools like Kubernetes, which provides built-in support for canary deployments through features such as rolling updates and traffic splitting. For example, Kubernetes allows organizations to define multiple versions of a deployment, with traffic automatically routed to the canary deployment based on predefined rules or weights. By gradually increasing the traffic to the canary deployment and monitoring its performance, organizations can gain confidence in the new release before promoting it to the entire production environment. Similarly, cloud providers like AWS and Google Cloud Platform offer managed services for canary deployments, allowing organizations to implement canary deployments with minimal setup and configuration.

Another rollout strategy that organizations may consider is the blue-green deployment approach, which involves maintaining two identical production environments, referred to as blue and green. While one environment, known as the blue environment, serves live production traffic, the other environment, the green environment, remains inactive. When a new software release or update is ready to be deployed, organizations can deploy it to the inactive green environment and perform thorough testing and validation before switching traffic from the blue to the green environment. This approach ensures zero downtime during the deployment process, as organizations can switch back to the blue environment immediately if any issues are detected in the green environment. To facilitate blue-green deployments, organizations can use deployment automation tools like AWS CodeDeploy or Jenkins, which provide built-in support for blue-green deployments and automate the process of switching traffic between environments.

In summary, rollout strategies and phased deployments are critical components of the software deployment process, enabling organizations to manage risks, minimize disruptions, and ensure successful deployments. Whether using feature flags, staged deployments, canary deployments, or blue-green deployments, organizations must carefully plan and execute their rollout strategy to minimize the impact on users and maintain the stability and reliability of their systems. By adopting a phased approach to deployment and leveraging automation tools and techniques, organizations can confidently deploy new software releases and updates while maintaining a high level of control and visibility throughout the deployment process.

Chapter 8: Patch Management for Complex Software Environments

Patch management frameworks and procedures are integral components of maintaining the security and stability of software systems and infrastructure. These frameworks establish systematic approaches to identify, assess, prioritize, deploy, and monitor software patches across an organization's IT environment. One widely adopted patch management framework is the Microsoft Windows Server Update Services (WSUS), which provides centralized management for deploying and managing updates to Microsoft products within a Windows environment. WSUS enables administrators to download updates from Microsoft Update servers and distribute them to computers on the network, ensuring that systems remain up-to-date with the latest security patches and bug fixes. Administrators can configure WSUS to automatically approve and deploy updates based on predefined criteria, such as severity levels or update classifications, or manually review and approve updates before deployment.

Similarly, Linux-based systems often utilize package management tools like apt (Advanced Package Tool) or yum (Yellowdog Updater Modified) to manage software updates and patches. These tools allow administrators to Install, update, and remove software packages from the system's package repositories, ensuring that the system's software stack remains current and secure. For example, administrators can use the apt-get update and apt-get upgrade commands on Debian-based systems to synchronize package indexes and install available updates, respectively. Similarly, on Red Hat-based systems, administrators can use the yum update command to update installed packages to their latest versions.

In addition to operating system updates, organizations must also manage updates for third-party software applications and dependencies. Patch management solutions like Ivanti Patch for Endpoints and ManageEngine Patch Manager Plus provide centralized management for deploying updates to a wide range of third-party applications, including web browsers, productivity suites, and multimedia players. These solutions automate the patch management process by scanning endpoints for missing patches, downloading updates from vendor websites or repositories, and deploying them to endpoints based on predefined schedules or criteria. Administrators can customize patch deployment policies, configure deployment targets, and monitor patch compliance and status through centralized dashboards and reporting tools.

To establish effective patch management procedures, organizations should adhere to industry best practices and guidelines, such as those outlined by the Center for Internet Security (CIS) and the National Institute of Standards and Technology (NIST). These guidelines provide recommendations for prioritizing patches based on severity levels, mitigating risks associated with unpatched vulnerabilities, and establishing processes for testing and deploying patches in production environments. For example, organizations may adopt a risk-based approach to patch prioritization, focusing on addressing critical vulnerabilities that pose the greatest security risks to the organization's assets and data. Additionally, organizations should establish change management processes to assess the potential impact of patches on system stability and performance before deploying them to production environments.

Automating patch management processes can significantly reduce the burden on IT teams and improve the efficiency and effectiveness of patch deployment efforts. Configuration management tools like Ansible, Puppet, and Chef enable organizations to automate the deployment of patches and updates across heterogeneous IT environments, including servers, workstations, and cloud instances. These tools allow administrators to define patching policies and configurations as code, ensuring consistency and repeatability across deployments. For example, administrators can use Ansible playbooks to define tasks for updating packages on Linux systems, ensuring that all managed systems receive the necessary updates in a consistent and controlled manner.

Furthermore, organizations should implement mechanisms for monitoring and reporting on patch compliance and status to ensure that systems remain adequately protected against known vulnerabilities. Patch management solutions typically provide dashboards and reports that display the current patch status of endpoints, including the number of missing patches, patch deployment success rates, and compliance levels. Administrators can use this information to identify endpoints that are out of compliance, troubleshoot deployment issues, and take corrective actions as needed. Additionally, organizations should conduct regular vulnerability assessments and penetration tests to identify new vulnerabilities and prioritize patches accordingly.

In summary, patch management frameworks and procedures play a critical role in maintaining the security and stability of IT environments by ensuring that systems are kept up-to-date with the latest software patches and updates. By adopting industry best practices, automating patch deployment processes, and implementing robust monitoring and reporting mechanisms, organizations can effectively mitigate security risks associated with unpatched vulnerabilities and maintain a strong security posture across their infrastructure.

Testing and validation of software patches are crucial processes in ensuring the reliability, functionality, and security of IT systems. When a software patch is released, whether it's for an operating system, application, or firmware, it must undergo rigorous testing to verify that it functions as intended and does not introduce any unintended side effects or vulnerabilities. One common approach to testing patches is to set up a test environment that mirrors the production environment, allowing IT teams to evaluate the patch's impact on various system configurations and scenarios before deploying it in a live environment. This test environment typically includes representative hardware, software, and network configurations to simulate real-world conditions accurately.

Once the test environment is prepared, IT teams can begin the testing process by applying the patch to a subset of systems or virtual machines and performing functional testing to ensure that the patched software behaves as expected. Functional testing involves executing test cases that validate the patch's intended changes, such as fixing specific bugs or adding new features, and verifying that existing functionality remains intact. Automated testing tools like Selenium and Apache JMeter can help automate the execution of test cases and generate reports on test results, allowing IT teams to efficiently validate patches across different platforms and configurations.

In addition to functional testing, IT teams should also conduct regression testing to identify any unintended changes or regressions introduced by the patch. Regression testing involves re-executing existing test cases to verify that previously working functionality has not been affected by the patch. This is especially important in complex software systems where changes in one area of the codebase can inadvertently impact other areas. By systematically retesting critical functionality after applying the patch, IT teams can detect and address any regressions before deploying the patch to production.

Another aspect of patch testing is compatibility testing, which involves verifying that the patch is compatible with other software and hardware components in the IT environment. This includes testing the patch's compatibility with different operating systems, application versions, databases, and third-party integrations. Compatibility testing helps ensure that the patch does not disrupt existing workflows or dependencies and minimizes the risk of compatibility issues arising after deployment. Tools like Docker and virtualization platforms enable IT teams to create isolated test environments with specific configurations for compatibility testing, allowing them to validate patches across a wide range of environments efficiently.

Security testing is also an essential component of patch validation, particularly for patches that address security vulnerabilities. Security testing involves assessing the patch's effectiveness in addressing the identified vulnerability and evaluating its impact on the overall security posture of the system. This may include vulnerability scanning, penetration testing, and code analysis to identify potential security weaknesses or vulnerabilities introduced by the patch. Security testing helps ensure that the patch adequately mitigates the identified risk and does not introduce new security vulnerabilities that could be exploited by attackers.

Once testing is complete, IT teams should thoroughly document the testing process and results, including details of test cases executed, test environments used, and any issues or findings encountered during testing. This documentation provides valuable insights into the patch's quality and readiness for deployment and serves as a reference for future patch testing efforts. Additionally, IT teams should establish formal change management processes to review and approve patches before deployment, ensuring that only validated patches are promoted to production environments.

In summary, testing and validation of software patches are critical steps in maintaining the stability, functionality, and security of IT systems. By systematically testing patches in representative environments and evaluating their impact on system performance, functionality, compatibility, and security, organizations can minimize the risk of disruptions and vulnerabilities introduced by patch deployment. Through a comprehensive testing and validation process, IT teams can confidently deploy patches that address known issues and vulnerabilities while minimizing the risk of unintended consequences or disruptions to business operations.

Chapter 9: Monitoring and Performance Tuning of Software Systems

Performance monitoring metrics and tools are indispensable components of modern IT operations, providing valuable insights into the health, efficiency, and stability of computer systems, networks, applications, and infrastructure. These metrics and tools enable organizations to proactively identify performance bottlenecks, diagnose issues, optimize resource utilization, and ensure optimal user experiences. One of the fundamental performance monitoring metrics is CPU utilization, which measures the percentage of time the CPU spends executing non-idle tasks. Monitoring CPU utilization helps administrators assess system load and identify processes or applications that consume excessive CPU resources, impacting overall system performance. The 'top' command in Linux and Unix-based systems and the 'Task Manager' in Windows environments are commonly used tools to view CPU utilization in real-time.

Memory utilization is another critical performance metric that measures the amount of physical or virtual memory used by processes and applications. Monitoring memory utilization helps administrators identify memory leaks, inefficient memory usage, and potential out-of-memory conditions that could lead to system instability or performance degradation. Tools like 'free' and 'vmstat' in Linux and Unix-based systems and the 'Resource Monitor' in Windows provide insights into memory usage and allocation, allowing administrators to optimize memory configurations and allocate resources efficiently.

Disk I/O (Input/Output) performance metrics measure the speed and efficiency of data read and write operations on storage devices, including hard disk drives (HDDs), solid-state drives (SSDs), and network-attached storage (NAS) devices. Monitoring disk I/O metrics helps administrators identify storage bottlenecks, disk saturation, and latency issues that can impact application performance and responsiveness. Tools like 'iostat' and 'iotop' in Linux and Unix-based systems and the 'Performance Monitor' in Windows enable administrators to monitor disk I/O activity, identify high-traffic disks, and optimize storage configurations to improve performance.

Network throughput and latency metrics assess the performance and efficiency of network communication between systems, devices, and applications. Monitoring network throughput helps administrators identify network congestion, bandwidth limitations, and packet loss that can degrade network performance and impact application responsiveness. Latency metrics measure the time it takes for data packets to travel between source and destination endpoints, providing insights into network latency, round-trip times, and network performance bottlenecks. Tools like 'iftop' and 'netstat' in Linux and Unix-based systems and the 'Performance Monitor' in Windows enable administrators to monitor network throughput, analyze network traffic patterns, and troubleshoot network performance issues.

Application-specific metrics provide insights into the performance and behavior of individual applications and services running on IT infrastructure. These metrics include response times, throughput, error rates, and resource utilization metrics specific to the application or service being monitored. For example, web servers may track metrics like HTTP request latency, response codes, and server error rates, while databases may monitor metrics like query execution times, transaction throughput, and connection pool utilization. Application performance monitoring (APM) tools like New Relic, Datadog, and AppDynamics provide comprehensive insights into application performance, user experience, and business transactions, enabling organizations to optimize application performance and ensure high availability.

Infrastructure monitoring tools aggregate and visualize performance metrics from various sources, providing administrators with a centralized view of system health and performance. These tools collect, store, and analyze performance data from servers, network devices, storage systems, and applications, enabling administrators to identify trends, anomalies, and performance degradation issues. Popular infrastructure monitoring tools include Nagios, Zabbix, Prometheus, and Grafana, which offer customizable dashboards, alerting mechanisms, and reporting capabilities to help administrators monitor and manage IT infrastructure effectively.

Cloud-based performance monitoring services offer scalable and cost-effective solutions for monitoring performance metrics in cloud environments. These services provide native integrations with cloud platforms like AWS, Azure, and Google Cloud Platform, enabling administrators to monitor resource utilization, performance, and availability of cloud-based services and applications. Cloud monitoring services like AWS CloudWatch, Azure Monitor, and Google Cloud

Monitoring offer a wide range of performance metrics, automated scaling capabilities, and advanced analytics to help organizations optimize cloud resources and ensure high-performance cloud-based applications.

In summary, performance monitoring metrics and tools play a critical role in maintaining the stability, reliability, and efficiency of IT systems and infrastructure. By monitoring key performance indicators like CPU utilization, memory usage, disk I/O, network throughput, and application-specific metrics, organizations can identify performance bottlenecks, diagnose issues, and optimize resource utilization to ensure optimal system performance and user experience. With a comprehensive set of performance monitoring tools and metrics, administrators can proactively manage IT infrastructure, troubleshoot performance issues, and make informed decisions to improve overall system performance and reliability.

Optimization strategies for software performance are essential for ensuring that applications deliver the best possible user experience while efficiently utilizing system resources. These strategies encompass various techniques and methodologies aimed at improving application responsiveness, throughput, and resource utilization. One fundamental optimization strategy is code optimization, which involves enhancing the efficiency and speed of software algorithms, data structures, and logic to reduce execution time and resource consumption. Profiling tools such as 'gprof' for C/C++ programs and 'cProfile' for Python applications can help identify performance bottlenecks in the code, allowing developers to focus their optimization efforts on critical sections of the codebase.

Another optimization strategy is memory management optimization, which involves minimizing memory usage and optimizing memory access patterns to improve application performance. Techniques such as object pooling, memory caching, and memory reuse can help reduce memory allocation overhead and mitigate the impact of memory fragmentation. Memory profiling tools like Valgrind and Memcheck can identify memory leaks, excessive memory usage, and inefficient memory access patterns, enabling developers to optimize memory usage and improve application performance.

Concurrency optimization is another critical aspect of software performance optimization, particularly in multi-threaded and parallel applications. By leveraging concurrency techniques such as thread pooling, task parallelism, and asynchronous programming, developers can improve application scalability, responsiveness, and throughput. However, concurrent programming introduces challenges such as race conditions, deadlocks, and thread contention, which must be carefully managed to avoid performance bottlenecks and synchronization overhead. Profiling tools like 'perf' and 'ThreadSanitizer' can help identify concurrency issues and bottlenecks, allowing developers to optimize thread utilization and synchronization mechanisms.

I/O optimization is another optimization strategy focused on improving the efficiency and performance of input/output operations in software applications. Techniques such as batching, buffering, and asynchronous I/O can help minimize I/O latency and maximize throughput, particularly in applications with high I/O requirements, such as databases, file servers, and web servers. File system tuning, disk caching, and I/O scheduling algorithms can also improve disk I/O performance and reduce disk access latency. Tools like 'iostat' and 'iotop' can monitor I/O performance metrics and identify bottlenecks in I/O-bound applications, enabling developers to optimize I/O operations and improve overall application performance.

Network optimization is essential for applications that rely on network communication to deliver data and services to users. Techniques such as connection pooling, pipelining, and protocol optimization can help reduce network latency, minimize overhead, and maximize network throughput. Load balancing, content delivery networks (CDNs), and caching mechanisms can also improve network performance and scalability by distributing network traffic and caching frequently accessed content closer to users. Network profiling tools like Wireshark and tcpdump can capture and analyze network traffic patterns, helping developers identify network bottlenecks and optimize network communication for better performance.

Database optimization is crucial for applications that interact with databases to store, retrieve, and manipulate data. Techniques such as indexing, query optimization, and database caching can improve database performance and reduce query execution time. Database schema design, normalization, and denormalization strategies can also impact database performance and scalability. Database profiling tools like MySQL's Performance Schema and PostgreSQL's pg_stat_statements can analyze database performance metrics and query execution plans, enabling developers to optimize database queries and improve overall application performance.

In summary, optimization strategies for software performance are essential for ensuring that applications meet performance requirements and deliver a responsive and efficient user experience. By applying techniques such as code optimization, memory management optimization, concurrency optimization, I/O optimization, network optimization, and database optimization, developers can improve application performance, scalability, and resource utilization. Profiling and monitoring tools play a crucial role in identifying performance bottlenecks, analyzing performance metrics, and guiding optimization efforts. By continuously optimizing software performance, organizations can enhance the competitiveness, reliability, and efficiency of their applications in today's fast-paced digital landscape.

Chapter 10: Disaster Recovery and Backup Strategies for Software Systems

Disaster recovery planning for software environments is a critical aspect of ensuring business continuity and mitigating the impact of unforeseen events or disasters on software systems and applications. It involves the development and implementation of strategies, processes, and procedures to recover software systems and data in the event of a natural disaster, cyberattack, hardware failure, or other disruptive incidents. One essential component of disaster recovery planning is risk assessment, which involves identifying potential threats and vulnerabilities that could affect software environments, such as data breaches, malware infections, server failures, and network outages. Risk assessment helps organizations prioritize resources and investments to address the most significant risks and vulnerabilities to their software systems and applications.

Another crucial aspect of disaster recovery planning is defining recovery objectives and strategies based on the organization's tolerance for downtime, data loss, and service disruption. Recovery time objectives (RTOs) and recovery point objectives (RPOs) are key metrics used to determine the acceptable downtime and data loss tolerances for different software systems and applications. Organizations must establish appropriate RTOs and RPOs based on business requirements, regulatory compliance, and service level agreements (SLAs) to ensure timely recovery and minimal data loss in the event of a disaster.

Backup and data protection are essential components of disaster recovery planning, allowing organizations to restore software systems and data from backups in the event of data loss or corruption. Regularly scheduled backups, both onsite and offsite, help ensure that critical data and system configurations are safely preserved and can be restored in the event of a disaster. Backup strategies may include full backups, incremental backups, and differential backups, depending on the organization's data retention requirements and recovery objectives. Backup validation and testing are also critical to ensure the integrity and reliability of backup data and recovery processes.

High availability and redundancy are key principles of disaster recovery planning, enabling organizations to maintain continuous access to software systems and applications even in the event of hardware failures or infrastructure disruptions. Redundant systems, failover mechanisms, and load balancing techniques help minimize single points of failure and ensure uninterrupted service availability. Virtualization technologies, such as server clustering and virtual machine replication, can also enhance the resilience and availability of software environments by enabling rapid failover and recovery in the event of hardware or software failures.

Disaster recovery testing and rehearsal are essential aspects of disaster recovery planning, allowing organizations to validate their recovery procedures, assess their readiness for emergencies, and identify any gaps or deficiencies in their disaster recovery plans. Regularly scheduled disaster recovery drills and tabletop exercises simulate various disaster scenarios and enable IT teams to practice their response procedures, communication protocols, and recovery workflows. By conducting regular disaster recovery testing, organizations can ensure that their software environments are adequately protected and prepared to withstand potential disasters effectively.

Cybersecurity is a critical consideration in disaster recovery planning, as cyberattacks and data breaches can have devastating consequences for software systems and applications. Implementing robust cybersecurity measures, such as intrusion detection systems, firewalls, antivirus software, and data encryption, helps prevent unauthorized access, data theft, and system compromise. Additionally, organizations should develop incident response plans and procedures to quickly detect, contain, and mitigate cybersecurity incidents, minimizing the impact on software environments and data assets.

Documentation and documentation management are essential aspects of disaster recovery planning, enabling organizations to maintain comprehensive records of their software configurations, recovery procedures, and incident response protocols. Detailed documentation helps ensure that IT staff have access to critical information and instructions during a disaster recovery event, facilitating a prompt and effective response. Documenting changes to software environments, infrastructure configurations, and recovery processes also helps organizations maintain compliance with regulatory requirements and industry best practices.

Continuous monitoring and review are essential for ensuring the effectiveness and relevance of disaster recovery plans and procedures over time. Regularly reviewing and updating disaster recovery plans based on changes in software environments, business requirements, and emerging threats helps organizations adapt to evolving risks and ensure the resilience of their software systems and applications. Continuous monitoring of software performance, security vulnerabilities, and environmental conditions enables organizations to detect and address potential issues proactively, reducing the likelihood of disruptive incidents and minimizing the impact of disasters on software environments.

In summary, disaster recovery planning for software environments is a multifaceted process that involves risk assessment, recovery objective definition, backup and data protection, high availability and redundancy, disaster recovery testing, cybersecurity, documentation, and continuous monitoring and review. By implementing comprehensive disaster recovery plans and procedures, organizations can minimize the impact of disasters on their software systems and applications, maintain business continuity, and protect critical data and assets from loss or compromise.

Backup strategies for data and configuration recovery are fundamental components of information technology (IT) infrastructure management, safeguarding against data loss, system failures, and disasters. These strategies encompass a range of techniques and methodologies aimed at ensuring the availability, integrity, and recoverability of critical data and system configurations. One common backup strategy is to perform regular, scheduled backups of data and system configurations using dedicated backup software or utilities. This involves creating backup copies of files, databases, and configuration settings and storing them in secure, offsite locations to protect against data loss caused by hardware failures, human error, or malicious attacks.

In Unix-like operating systems, the 'tar' command is commonly used to create compressed archive files containing directories and files for backup purposes. For example, to create a backup of the '/home/user' directory and compress it into a tarball named 'backup.tar.gz', the following command can be used:

bashCopy code

```
tar -czvf backup.tar.gz /home/user
```

Similarly, in Windows environments, the 'robocopy' command can be used to copy files and directories while preserving their attributes and permissions. For example, to copy the contents of the 'C:\Data' directory to a backup destination named 'D:\Backup', the following command can be used:

cmdCopy code

```
robocopy C:\Data D:\Backup /E /COPYALL /R:3 /W:1
```

Backup strategies often involve implementing a combination of full backups, incremental backups, and differential backups to optimize storage space and minimize backup time. Full backups involve copying all data and system configurations in their entirety, providing a comprehensive snapshot of the entire system at a specific point in time. Incremental backups, on the other hand, only copy data that has changed since the last backup, significantly reducing backup time and storage requirements. Differential backups copy all data that has changed since the last full backup, offering a balance between backup time and data recovery speed.

In addition to regular backups, organizations often implement disk imaging or snapshotting techniques to create point-in-time copies of entire disk volumes or system partitions. Disk imaging tools such as 'Clonezilla' or 'Acronis True Image' can create exact replicas of disk partitions or volumes, enabling quick and easy restoration of entire systems in the event of hardware failures or system crashes. Disk snapshots provided by virtualization platforms such as VMware vSphere or Microsoft Hyper-V allow administrators to capture the current state of virtual machines, providing a reliable recovery point for virtualized environments.

Offsite backups are essential for protecting data against catastrophic events such as fires, floods, or earthquakes that could destroy both the primary data center and its backups.

Offsite backup strategies involve replicating backup data to geographically dispersed locations, ensuring redundancy and disaster recovery capability. Cloud storage services such as Amazon S3, Microsoft Azure Blob Storage, or Google Cloud Storage provide reliable and scalable offsite backup solutions, allowing organizations to store backup data securely in remote data centers.

Encryption is a critical aspect of backup strategies, ensuring that backup data remains confidential and secure, even if it is intercepted or stolen. Backup encryption techniques such as AES encryption can be applied to backup files or volumes to protect sensitive data from unauthorized access. Backup software often includes built-in encryption capabilities, allowing administrators to encrypt backup data using strong encryption algorithms and secure encryption keys.

Testing and validation are essential components of backup strategies, ensuring that backup processes are reliable and effective. Regularly testing backup procedures and restoring data from backups allows organizations to verify the integrity and recoverability of backup data and identify any issues or errors that may arise during the recovery process. Backup validation techniques such as integrity checks, data consistency checks, and disaster recovery drills help ensure that backup strategies meet the organization's recovery objectives and compliance requirements.

Versioning and retention policies are essential considerations in backup strategies, determining how long backup data should be retained and how many backup versions should be preserved. Versioning allows organizations to maintain multiple copies of backup data, enabling them to recover data from different points in time and recover from data corruption or deletion. Retention policies define the duration for which backup data should be retained, ensuring compliance with regulatory requirements and minimizing storage costs associated with long-term data retention.

In summary, backup strategies for data and configuration recovery are essential for protecting against data loss, system failures, and disasters. By implementing a combination of regular backups, disk imaging, offsite backups, encryption, testing, and versioning, organizations can ensure the availability, integrity, and recoverability of critical data and system configurations, safeguarding against unforeseen events and ensuring business continuity.

Conclusion

In summary, the "Service Desk Analyst Bootcamp: Maintaining, Configuring, and Installing Hardware and Software" bundle offers a comprehensive and structured approach to equipping service desk analysts with the essential skills and knowledge needed to excel in their roles. Throughout the four books included in this bundle, readers are guided through a journey from the fundamentals of hardware and software basics to mastering troubleshooting techniques, advanced hardware maintenance, and optimizing complex software systems.

Book 1, "Service Desk Essentials: A Beginner's Guide to Hardware and Software Basics," lays the foundation by providing beginners with a solid understanding of hardware and software fundamentals. It covers essential topics such as hardware components, operating systems, software installation, and basic troubleshooting techniques, setting the stage for further learning and development.

Building upon the foundational knowledge gained in Book 1, Book 2, "Mastering Service Desk Troubleshooting: Configuring Software for Efficiency," delves deeper into troubleshooting techniques specifically focused on software configuration. Readers learn how to identify and resolve common software issues, optimize software performance, and troubleshoot application compatibility problems, empowering them to efficiently resolve software-related issues encountered by end-users.

Book 3, "Advanced Service Desk Techniques: Hardware Maintenance and Optimization," takes a comprehensive look at hardware maintenance and optimization strategies. From hardware diagnostics and troubleshooting to preventive maintenance and performance optimization, readers gain the expertise needed to ensure the reliability, availability, and performance of hardware systems.

Finally, Book 4, "Expert Service Desk Strategies: Installing and Managing Complex Software Systems," addresses the complexities of installing and managing complex software systems. Readers learn advanced techniques for deploying, configuring, and managing enterprise-level software applications, including strategies for software deployment automation, configuration management, and patch management.

Collectively, these four books provide a holistic and practical approach to service desk management, empowering service desk analysts with the skills, techniques, and strategies needed to effectively maintain, configure, and install hardware and software systems. Whether you are a beginner seeking to establish a strong foundation or an experienced professional looking to expand your expertise, the "Service Desk Analyst Bootcamp" bundle offers valuable insights and practical guidance to help you succeed in your role.